MAJOR EUROPEAN AUTHORS

BOILEAU
AND THE NATURE OF NEO-CLASSICISM

Odette de Mourgues: *Racine, or The Triumph of Relevance*
Ronald Gray: *Goethe: A Critical Introduction*
C. B. Morris: *A Generation of Spanish Poets 1920–1936*
R. F. Christian: *Tolstoy: A Critical Introduction*
Richard Peace: *Dostoyevsky: An Examination of the Major Novels*
John Bayley: *Pushkin: A Comparative Commentary*
Dorothy Gabe Coleman: *Rabelais: A Critical Study in Prose Fiction*
W. E. Yates: *Grillparzer: A Critical Introduction*
Ronald Gray: *Franz Kafka*
John Northam: *Ibsen: A Critical Study*
Geoffrey Strickland: *Stendhal: The Education of a Novelist*
Ronald Gray: *Brecht the Dramatist*
Henry Gifford: *Pasternak: A Critical Study*
Beverly Hahn: *Chekhov: A study of the Major Stories and Plays*
Odette de Mourgues:
Two French Moralists: La Rochefoucauld and La Bruyère
J. P. Stern: *A Study of Nietzsche*
C. A. Hackett: *Rimbaud: A Critical Introduction*

OTHER VOLUMES IN PREPARATION

BOILEAU
AND THE NATURE OF
NEO-CLASSICISM

GORDON POCOCK

CAMBRIDGE UNIVERSITY PRESS

CAMBRIDGE

LONDON   NEW YORK   NEW ROCHELLE
MELBOURNE   SYDNEY

CAMBRIDGE UNIVERSITY PRESS
Cambridge, New York, Melbourne, Madrid, Cape Town, Singapore,
São Paulo, Delhi, Dubai, Tokyo

Cambridge University Press
The Edinburgh Building, Cambridge CB2 8RU, UK

Published in the United States of America by Cambridge University Press, New York

www.cambridge.org
Information on this title: www.cambridge.org/9780521136754

First published 1980
This digitally printed version 2010

A catalogue record for this publication is available from the British Library

Library of Congress Cataloguing in Publication data
Pocock, Gordon.
Boileau and the nature of neo-classicism.
(Major European authors)
Bibliography: p.
Includes index.
1. Boileau-Despréaux, Nicolas, 1636–1711.
2. Neoclassicism (Literature) 3. Authors, French –
17th century – Biography. I. Title.
PQ1723.P6   841'.4   79–50885

ISBN 978-0-521-22772-8 Hardback
ISBN 978-0-521-13675-4 Paperback

GENERAL PREFACE TO THE SERIES

The Major European Authors series, as the name implies, considers the most important writers of the European literatures, most often giving a volume to each author, but occasionally treating a group or a genre. The basic assumption is that the general reader and the student will be able to find information on biography and literary history fairly easily elsewhere. What he will look for in this series is a single volume which gives a critical survey of the entire œuvre or the most important works. Authors of books in the series are asked to keep this general objective in mind: to write critical introductions which will help the reader to order his impressions of the works of art themselves; to assume little prior knowledge, and so far as possible either to quote in English or to translate quotations.

It is hoped that the series will help to keep the classics of European literature alive and active in the minds of present-day readers: both those reading for a formal literary examination, and those who in the original languages and in translation wish to keep in touch with the culture of Europe.

FOR AUDREY

CONTENTS

Neo-classicism and Boileau

I

Boileau's reputation has two aspects, and this book is concerned with both. First, there is Boileau's standing as an individual critic and poet: a seventeenth-century writer of Satires and Epistles on moral and literary subjects, and of a verse *Art Poétique* and prose works of criticism. This reputation has varied extravagantly. To many of his contemporaries a writer of low lampoons and clumsy panegyrics, to others and to the eighteenth century a model of poetic elegance and critical perception, to the nineteenth century an example of stilted unreality, Boileau had dwindled by the mid-twentieth century to the status of an interesting but minor poet.[1]

The second aspect of Boileau's reputation has reflected his standing as a representative rather than an individual. To the eighteenth and nineteenth centuries, he was pre-eminently the theorist, polemist and spokesman of French neo-classicism. To those who admired neo-classicism, he could seem the legislator of Parnassus, the critic who had shown how all good writing depended on the discipline of Reason and Good Sense, the master and model of poets, the wise and severe friend who had guided La Fontaine, Racine and Molière towards their highest achievements. To those who reacted against the values of neo-classicism, he could seem the pedant who had cramped and shackled French poetry in the interests of rationalism, the prosaic and pompous versifier, the critic who had denigrated Corneille, underestimated Molière, and further narrowed the already narrow taste of Racine.

Recent criticism has moved in different directions in evaluating these two aspects of Boileau's reputation. There has been a considerable reappraisal of Boileau the critic and poet. This has taken place in several stages, and with differences of emphasis between French scholars on the one hand and North American and English scholars on the other. Starting with Révillout at the end of the nineteenth century, renewed study by French scholars of Boileau's life and historical context has encouraged a fresh appreciation of the relevance to seventeenth-century events of Boileau's works.[2] Although historical rather than literary, these studies have brought into relief his realism and verve, his taste for the bizarre, the passion and moral commitment underlying his poems, the pungent flavour of the temperament they express.

English and American approaches have been critical rather than historical. Brody has emphasised the seriousness and depth of Boileau's preoccupation with the ideas of the second-century Greek rhetorician Longinus, and what it reveals about his attitude to literature: in particular, his stress on the intuitive nature of critical perception, and on the way in which for Boileau this intuition is linked with 'knowledge' in the widest sense – not so much factual knowledge as experience, wisdom and mental vigour.[3] More recently there has been a new interest in Boileau's literary techniques. Orr has demonstrated some of the astonishing punning virtuosity in *L'Art Poétique*.[4] Others – notably France and Edelman – have brought out the extent to which his poems make their effect by taking as their subject the manipulation of their ostensible subject-matter and purpose. A poem praising Louis XIV may become a sophisticated and ambiguous game playing with the possibility of praising him.[5] *L'Art Poétique* is, in part at least, a poem which explores the possibilities of writing poetry on the subject of writing poetry.[6]

At the same time, Boileau has come to seem less important as a representative of neo-classical doctrine. In part, as will be discussed later in this chapter, this is because neo-classical doctrine itself has come to seem less important. Even if we concede its importance, however, it is clear that the neo-classical principles enunciated by Boileau were worked out long before him, mainly by the critics and commentators of sixteenth-century Italy; that they were adopted in France under the influence of critics active in the 1630s – notably one of the butts of his satire, Jean Chapelain; that the use Boileau made of them often appears inconsequential; and, finally, that his influence on his peers was negligible, coming as he did too late to form the taste of La Fontaine, Molière, or even Racine.

It is difficult not to feel a sense of liberation in recent critical approaches, which have moved the emphasis from study of Boileau as a literary influence to enjoyment of his poetry as poetry. Equally, it is hard not to agree that modern scholarship has exploded many of the old generalisations about neo-classicism and Boileau's role as law-giver. Nevertheless, I think that both these scholarly and critical approaches have gained their successes at the cost of fragmenting our view of him. The individual and representative aspects of his reputation are linked. In my view, the difficulty of reaching a unified picture of Boileau stems from the difficulty of bringing these two aspects into focus simultaneously. I propose to attempt to do so from a starting-point which is now unfashionable: that is, by tackling the significance of that complex of literary ideas which are grouped together under the heading of neo-classicism. I would argue that both Boileau's importance, and the value of his poetry, are bound up with questions about what part the doctrines of neo-classicism play in his poems, and, to some extent, what functions neo-classicism fulfilled in the society in which he moved.

2

These issues arise only because of one fact about French seventeenth-century literature which must sooner or later strike the reader. In their critical comments, the authors of the period commonly claim (or assume) that there is a doctrine relating to poetry. (And in the seventeenth century, 'poetry' usually means 'imaginative literature', though I shall use it in its more restricted modern sense.) They suppose that poetry has a function which critics can formulate; that there are techniques which can help poets to ensure their works fulfil this function, and critics to judge whether the poets have succeeded; and that there are therefore rules which are binding on poets and poetry.

Over the last three centuries, the nature and importance of this doctrine have been very variously assessed. To many students, the apparent existence of the doctrine is a stumbling-block: how can intelligent people have spent so much energy on questions which seem always pedantic, often trivial, and sometimes patently nonsensical? To others – and this is an attractive view – the whole question of doctrine is largely irrelevant, and we can concentrate on the power and beauty of the individual poems. Nevertheless, the doctrine, in some sense at least, did exist. It has been described in detail in a famous and much-criticised book, René Bray's *La Formation de la Doctrine Classique en France*, but I will attempt an outline of it here.[7]

To take the most superficial aspect first, neo-classical doctrine included a body of rules, in the sense of more or less technical prescriptions for poetry. The basis of the more detailed of these was that each work of literature had to fit into one of a set of definite kinds of poem: *les genres*. These *genres* were ranked in a more-or-less agreed order of merit. At the top came the great Classical *genres* of Epic and Tragedy, though opinions might differ as to which was the more 'noble'. Comedy came next, with a distinction between elegant literary comedy and 'low' comedy or farce, which condescended to amuse the lower classes. Pastoral poetry and the more elevated forms of lyric came somewhere in the middle. Satire was usually less elevated, because of its 'low' content. Minor forms of lyric and such miscellaneous forms as epigram came at the bottom. New prose *genres* such as the novel might be slotted in somewhere, the novel sometimes being regarded as a form of epic. Mixed forms such as tragi-comedy were usually frowned on by the stricter critics, though tragi-comedy might be considered as lying between tragedy and comedy.

The individual *genres* had their own rules, sometimes extremely detailed, and quarrels about them fill the pages of the theorists. Everyone agreed that an epic should be noble in tone and language, that it should deal with heroic actions and stimulate people to admire them, that it should be a unity, and that it should be further elevated by using machines – that is, by introducing supernatural beings who take part in the action. But did the treatment of heroic actions require that the poem should end happily? (Having chosen Joan of Arc as the heroine of his epic *La Pucelle*, Chapelain had to explain that her death at the stake was happy, because a martyrdom.) Did unity demand that an epic should observe a unity of time? (The favourite period was a year.) Should the supernatural machines be pagan (which would be incredible) or Christian (which might be blasphemous)?

The theatre was especially well provided with rules, which have been exhaustively analysed by Scherer. Tragedies must be elevated in tone and subject, and admit no comic or low elements, though they need not end unhappily. By the 1640s, it was generally agreed that a tragedy must keep strictly to the three unities. Of these, the unity of action was the most important, though the most difficult to define. For most writers, it meant that the plot should be unified, but not that it should be simple. The unity of time meant that the imagined duration of the action should not be more than twenty-four hours, or perhaps twelve, or perhaps even the length of the performance itself. (Corneille, while agreeing that the last was best, was willing to stretch the limit to thirty hours if need be.) In the 1620s, unity of place meant that the action should take place within one town and its surroundings. By the middle of the century, it usually meant that the action must take place in a single spot, though there are occasional exceptions. A proper tragedy must have five acts. Within each act, the scenes must follow each other in such a way that the stage is never empty. Exits (and, if possible, entrances) must be plausibly motivated. Comedy must be amusing instead of serious, but ideally such rules as the three unities apply to comedies as much as to tragedies. In practice, they are followed much more loosely in comedies, and also in such novel *genres* as the spectacular 'machine play' and opera, in which scenic effects and music are the main attractions.

It would be tedious to enumerate the rules proposed for all the minor *genres*. Although a considerable part of Boileau's *Art Poétique* deals with rules for the minor *genres*, the critics never in fact succeeded in achieving a comprehensive set of rules for them.

But neo-classicism was by no means concerned only with rules at this technical level. The technical rules rested on two requirements which were from one aspect aesthetic but in a more fundamental way moral. First, poetry must treat of what is natural and probable; and, second, in doing so it must be decent. In seventeenth-century terms, it must be *vraisemblable* and respect *les bienséances*. Both these requirements proved difficult to define in the abstract, and there were considerable differences of opinion among the critics and creative writers. Poetry certainly had to concern itself with what in some senses was striking and unusual:

le merveilleux, in seventeenth-century language. *Vraisemblance* did not mean realistic representation of everyday happenings, although (and this is a significant point) some critics came close to implying it should. Nor did it mean that the happenings depicted should be literally true: though Corneille was inclined to appeal to factual truth, *le vrai*, as a means of justifying departures from the banality of *vraisemblance*. *Le vraisemblable* usually meant a generalised, idealised probability. As such, it had philosophical and even religious overtones. The concept was derived from respectable Classical precedent. Aristotle had said that poetry was more philosophical than history because it imitated not what had happened but what was likely to happen: universals, not particulars. The expression of his thought is not entirely clear, and in the seventeenth century it was nearly always interpreted as meaning that poetry imitated what ought to happen. More prosaically, but more intelligibly, Horace had recommended playwrights to express human character in terms of what was known or traditionally thought about named individuals (Medea: fierce; Orestes: sorrowful), or in terms of what was appropriate to the character's age, sex and situation. These two strands of the concept, *vraisemblance* as idealised truth and *vraisemblance* as what we normally expect, run through neo-classical criticism. At times, critical debate is concerned with high principles of morality and truth; at another, critics are arguing whether it is probable that a man can fight two duels and a battle within twenty-four hours.

There is a similar quality about the purpose of observing *la vraisemblance*. To judge from some seventeenth-century pronouncements, the purpose is an expression of that aspiration of Classical art towards the permanent and universally valid, disdaining the ephemeral and freakish. But in many seventeenth-century critics, it is motivated by what seems to us an excessive timidity about the imaginative capacity of the audience or reader. Following Horace's celebrated maxim: 'I dislike it if I don't believe it', critics insisted that events which strained an audience's belief would disturb their aesthetic response. Modern critics have tended to defend rules like the three unities as means of achieving a concentrated and hence powerful aesthetic effect. Seventeenth-century critics usually defended them on the grounds that they were necessary for *vraisemblance*, and in the narrowest sense: the spectator would be confused and upset if a single stage which he watched for two hours had to be taken as several places distant from each other, accommodating events taking place over a long period.

Vraisemblance is closely connected with *les bienséances*, and the requirements imposed on the author in observing them are often hard to distinguish. In both cases, there is a mixture of what we should be inclined to regard as moral and aesthetic factors at work, expressed in arguments on points which sometimes seem to us serious but more often trivial. The root idea is that *les bienséances* represent what is seemly or fitting: the high Renaissance concept of Decorum. At its lowest, it is often a footling concern with the minutiae of social convention. It is not in accordance with etiquette that in *Andromaque* a king (Pyrrhus) should seek out an ambassador (Oreste). The idea of *vraisemblance* is also present here: because behaviour of this sort is not conventional, it is unlikely and hence *invraisemblable*. But *les bienséances* are also linked with decency in a moral sense. In French seventeenth-century literature, no heterodox ideas or behaviour must be represented, except in very muted form and in contexts which clearly show they are not to be admired. Anything which smacks of political or religious subversion is banned. Sexual passion is, of course, prominent in literature, and adultery, incest, and even homosexuality are occasionally portrayed. But their expression is always extremely discreet. Neither the language nor the physical actions described or acted are sexually explicit. Again, *vraisemblance* and *les bienséances* work together. In a comic verse tale, relatively 'low' characters may do relatively 'low' things. In a noble *genre* like Tragedy, it is neither probable nor seemly that kings and queens should behave in an unbuttoned fashion.

At their highest interpretation, however, observance of the rules of *les bienséances* and *vraisemblance* work in a deeply moral and philosophical way. An example comes from the most famous of all seventeenth-century critical debates, that over Corneille's *Le Cid*. The crucial point was whether the subject was well chosen, in that it required the heroine, Chimène, to marry the hero, Rodrigue, even though he had killed her father. Modern disdain for this controversy seems to me misplaced. That Chimène should marry her father's murderer is a breach of *vraisemblance* and *les bienséances*, in the sense that it is indeed unconventional, and might be regarded as a breach of good manners. But if we take her dilemma seriously, it is more than that. For a woman we like and admire to do such a thing should be a shock to our sensibilities, a blow to assumptions on which civilised behaviour rests, an affront to our conceptions of how people do and should behave. Familiarity lessens the shock to us, just as we miss the sense of outrage in Chapelain's criticism of Chimène as 'dénaturée' – a violation of the order of Nature, a betrayal of normal human decency, a monstrous contradiction of natural impulses. When Corneille's contemporaries made this criticism they may have been influenced by many factors, but the criticism itself is not nonsense. To them, Chimène's behaviour 'feels wrong', in the sense both that this is not how people behave, and that if it were it would still be morally wrong.

This duality of moral and aesthetic arguments comes out most strongly at the most fundamental level of neo-classical theory, which deals with the purpose of poetry. The question had occupied Aristotle, and his answers seem to modern scholars reasonably clear. The purpose of poetry is pleasure. Other statements expand or refine this fundamental assumption: poetry expresses a fundamental urge in human nature to make rhythmical imitations; poetry satisfies the natural pleasure in learning; each type of poetry must give its proper pleasure; serious poetry (or perhaps only Tragedy) is 'more philosophic' than history; and Tragedy performs the famous act of catharsis (which, even if interpreted in the modern physiological or psychological sense of removing excessive passions, seems to have some moral implications).

Horace is pithier. In a famous line, he emphasises that a poet who combined the pleasant and useful has won every suffrage: 'Omnia tulit punctum qui miscuit utile dulci.'[8] By its neatness and brevity, the dictum invites quotation. Familiarity, and the connotations since acquired by its key words, may hinder us from appreciating its depth. 'Dulcis' has English echoes, in 'dulcet', of 'soft' and 'sweet'. 'Utilis', with its English echo of 'utilitarian', suggests something very humdrum, and the moral aim implicit in the epigram does not make it any more enticing. It is only when we consider the greatest Latin poetry, as written by Horace and his contemporaries, that we begin to suspect the power and complexity of the effects which the formula attempts to cover. Whatever we get from the *Aeneid*, it is rarely dulcet, or didactic in the sense of giving useful advice. And I think the same is true of Horace's own *Odes*, though here the moral element is more explicit. What we get from the *Aeneid* and the *Odes* is rather that eliciting of an effort of emotional and intellectual imagination which great literature achieves.

There is a similar difficulty with the corresponding formula in French neo-classicism, which is that poetry should 'plaire' and 'instruire'. The meaning of 'plaire' has weakened since the seventeenth century, but even so these little words do not at first convey the effects achieved by the works of the great writers. The word 'pleasure' can certainly embrace the delight afforded by word-play, smooth cadences and striking turns of phrase, which is perhaps what 'plaire' at first sight implies. But it also means the excitement and disturbance induced by such works as *Phèdre*, the effect of which can be compared with that of any Greek or Shakespearean tragedy. 'Instruction' can take such simple forms as the moral maxims abundantly found in tragedies of the period; but what we value in French seventeenth-century literature is rather its insights into the dilemmas of moral behaviour, which work on us through our imaginations, as literature always must. It is hard, on reflection, to identify any effect of great literature which cannot be brought under the heading of either 'pleasure' or 'instruction', if interpreted in any other than the most literal way. And the formula, like that of Horace, links the 'useful' and the 'pleasant'. This, again, corresponds to our experience. Characteristically, the pleasure and instruction are fused, and we should be hard put to it to distinguish the two elements. The formula is apparently simple, but full of complexity: in itself it is one more effort to capture the effect on us of poetry, which can be so powerful, but is so difficult to define.

This interpretation of the formula in terms of the effect which the poems themselves have on us seems to me important, in view of the fact that those who wrote and first responded to the poems were apparently content to think of their experience in these terms. But, if we turn to the works of the theorists of neo-classicism, matters appear in a different light. There is no doubt of the slant which neo-classical critics – including often the poets themselves when speaking as critics – give to the pronouncements of Aristotle and Horace, or to the formula that poetry should please and instruct. The emphasis so far as critical theory is concerned is strongly placed on instruction. As Bray has shown, the over-whelming consensus is that art has a moral function; and this moral function is conceived of in an extremely literal way. There are, of course, exceptions. The Italian critic Castelvetro had insisted that pleasure was the aim, and many of the great seven-teenth-century French poets – Corneille, Molière, La Fontaine, Racine – emphasise that poetry must give pleasure and stir the emotions. But, with very rare exceptions, even the most heterodox acknowledge that moral instruction is, or should be, one of its aims.[9] The main weight of opinion is on the side of moral instruc-tion, with pleasure as the means or a secondary purpose. Aristotle's theories are interpreted in a moralistic fashion. The function of Tragedy is not psychological catharsis, but the demonstration of poetic justice, which rewards the good and punishes evil. Morality is the centre of neo-classicism, and its gravitational force governs the greater and lesser rules. *Vraisemblance* is important because it alone provides the basis for persuasive teaching. In Bray's words, 'la fonction moralisatrice de la poésie est la base la plus sure que puisse trouver Chapelain pour établir l'omnipotence du vraisem-blable'.[10] Observance of *les bienséances* ensures moral conformity, as well as reinforcing *vraisemblance*. And the technical rules, in the eyes of seventeenth-century critics, are derived from these fundamental principles.

3

This outline has not explicitly included three points which are often said to be cardinal: imitation of Nature, imitation of the Ancients, and the importance of Reason. Of these, imitation of Nature can be quickly dismissed. The 'Nature' to be imitated does not consist of trees and mountains but is contained in the concepts of *vraisemblance* and *les bienséances*, and of the moral function of art. It is a general, idealised Nature (what usually is, or what ought to be), and the objects to be depicted are human activities, which are the stuff of moral dilemmas.

Imitation of the Ancients seems to me less important in neo-classicism than is sometimes claimed. First, it is not a special characteristic of neo-classicism. Poets of many schools have imitated, or claimed to imitate, the poets of Greece and Rome. If we were to look for a school who carried out the principle most vigorously, it would probably be poets of the French Renaissance, who are hardly neo-classicists in the usual sense. Second, although many of the greatest writers of the seventeenth century had a deep love and admiration of the Ancients, it is clear that French neo-classical poetry is very different in feeling from that of the Greeks or Romans. This is so even if we take a *genre* like Tragedy, and a poet like Racine who had an undoubted feeling for Greek poetry. Romantic polemists had no difficulty in showing the gulf between Greek Tragedy – outdoor, public, spectacular, lyrical, religious, hardly treating of sexual love, expressing its themes through an indeterminate number of scenes – and French Tragedy – played indoors for a relatively restricted audience, eschewing spectacle and lyricism, secular, dwelling on sexual relationships, presented through a tightly marshalled plot in a fixed scheme of five acts. Third, if the Ancients were to be imitated, it was because they had produced poems which still worked, rather than because they were Ancients. Chapelain refers to the practice of the 'good' Ancients, but also of the successful poets among the modern Italians, Spanish and French.[11] The Ancient to whom he appeals constantly is Aristotle, because of his authority as a critic. Among the imaginative writers, he includes the Ancients of whom he approves, as one group of successful practitioners: but only one group among others.

Finally, we come to the cult of Reason. The word occurs constantly in neo-classical criticism. Like Nature, the Reason invoked is usually an impersonal, idealised version of what commonly exists, or ought to exist, or is generally thought normal. As such, it is closely linked to the concepts of *vraisemblance* and *les bienséances*, and is virtually included in them. But there is also a kind of rationalism implicit in the existence of the doctrine: a belief that reasoning is the instrument by which critics can establish the importance of these basic concepts, and so lay down rules for poetry. What Reason does not mean is the willingness to follow a logical argument wherever it leads. The reasoning used to justify the unity of time, say, is often surprisingly feeble. The rational process in neo-classical argument is a system-building activity. It is rationalisation rather than rationalism.

4

This survey has set out some of the main features of the doctrine as established by people other than Boileau. Scholars and critics used traditionally to emphasise the importance of this doctrine for literature from the second quarter of the seventeenth century until the end of the eighteenth and beyond. But, though critics might take up positions for or against the doctrine, until the mid-twentieth century few doubted its existence as a coherent body of thought, or its importance for neo-classical literature. The modifications proposed by modern scholarship to this traditional view are now very considerable. They may conveniently be classified under three heads.

First, the doctrine was not as complete or monolithic or binding as was often supposed. It is clear enough from Bray's work that the rules concentrated on a few major issues, and that even on these there were irreconcilable views. My brief survey has given some indication of this. Corneille's preference for *le vrai* is perhaps the most significant example of a break in the consensus, but differences of emphasis on the relative importance of pleasure and utility reveal a fundamental difficulty. As Bray says, it is difficult to find rules for the minor *genres*.[12] In practice, authors and public went their own way, with or without lip-service to what the theorists said. The rules hardly apply to the works of La Rochefoucauld, or Madame de la Fayette, or La Bruyère. They do not seem to weigh heavily on Molière's *Dom Juan*, say, or La Fontaine's *Fables*. Even in Tragedy, strict observance of the neo-classical doctrine is rarer than might appear. The public continued to enjoy spectacle, complication and surprise. Racine's tragedies are not typical of contemporary theatre as a whole.

Second, the theory itself and the utterance of the major writers lay much more emphasis than used to be recognised on matters having little to do with rules, morality or rationalism. In various guises, such as the *je ne sais quoi* or the *sublime*, the crucial element in poetry is seen to be the intuitive, irrational, indefinable.

Even the strictest writers insist that 'La principale règle est de plaire et de toucher.'[18] These ideas are very strong in Boileau, in whom Brody and others have rightly stressed the importance of his conception of *le sublime*, with all its implications.

The third class of modifications is sociological and historical. Detailed study of the history of French society and literature in the seventeenth century has shown how great the range of variation was, and how literary theory and practice responded to changes in the social climate. From the vogue for baroque and romanesque effects to that for ingenuity and wit, and then to the stress in certain circles on nobility of style and moral seriousness, literature responded to the taste of influential groups in the upper levels of society. The rules themselves were in part founded on observation of what pleased contemporary audiences, rather than on the moral and rational grounds that were asserted. Quarrels over the rules were often a reflection of clashes of personalities and taste, in which the critical commonplaces were merely ammunition.

While giving full weight to these modifications, however, I do not think they justify the modern reluctance to accept that neo-classical doctrine addressed itself to matters of real importance, or even that it seemed important to those who held it. It is, of course, true that what matters to us now is the direct response of the reader or spectator to the poem or play, not whether it conforms to this or that neo-classical rule. This is pure gain, and no-one would now wish to argue that Corneille's *Rodogune* is a better play than *Le Cid* because it observes the three unities more strictly. One may also welcome the illumination shed on neo-classicism by new information about its historical and social context. One may concede that the acceptance of the rules for some *genres* was fostered by the fashion for Italian literature, or that partly for political reasons the influence of Chapelain on literary patronage became important. It is easy to see that poets and critics might take up the new critical ideas for polemical purposes and without much regard for the principles behind them. Equally, in the few *genres* for which detailed rules were laid down, playwrights might find that the practical limitations of the stage and a regard for the tastes of powerful sections of their audience would favour observance of the unities and the *liaison des scènes*. Epic poets might find observance of the critics' precepts a prop for endeavours beyond their unaided powers, or a means of impressing their patrons and salon audiences with the seriousness of their efforts. On a more general plane, it is perhaps possible to see an affinity between the characteristics of neo-classicism and the tastes of a society striving towards *honnêteté* and away from braggadocio, or between the legislating tendency in neo-classicism and the authoritarianism of the Counter-Reformation Church and State.

Nevertheless, these modern views seem to me seriously inadequate, on three main counts. First, they do not explain why the neo-classical doctrines became so uniquely powerful. The most remarkable thing about Bray's book is that it could be written at all. No-one could write a book on 'The Formation of the Elizabethan Doctrine in England'. It would be quite possible to construct a thesis on 'The Formation of Classical Doctrine in Greece', but the differences from Bray's book would be instructive. The account would no doubt run from Plato to Longinus: Homer, the tragic poets, Pindar and Sappho would figure in it mainly as historical figures, raw material for later critics. It is certainly possible to write books about the doctrines of Parnassianism or Symbolism; they have been written, and often include the critical thinking of the poets themselves: but in each case they deal with one short-lived doctrine competing with others equally ephemeral. Neo-classicism is unique in its combination of three features: that it precedes and accompanies the works written in accordance with its doctrines; that the great writers themselves subscribed to and influenced these doctrines; and that it was long-lasting and widely accepted.

The second point is that the explanations offered seem too local for a doctrine which flourished in such different social and intellectual contexts, beginning in France in the years when Richelieu was coming to power, consolidating itself in the 1630s, and enduring through the Frondes, the absolutism of Louis XIV, into the Regency, and well into the second half of the eighteenth century. These are years of profound social and intellectual change: of civil wars; of the establishment and partial failure of absolutism; of recession followed by eighteenth-century prosperity; of the Counter-Reformation and Enlightenment. It surely requires some explanation that the same critical themes and doctrines should occupy such diverse minds as Chapelain, Boileau and Voltaire.

French political and cultural prestige no doubt helped to foster neo-classicism in other countries, but this does not explain why it flourished in them. Despite important differences, the work of the great English writers from Dryden to Johnson deserves to be called neo-classical. Clearly, the work of Dryden, Pope and Johnson draws largely on French criticism, and reflects some similar attitudes. Neo-classicism at least seems to have been able to perform for Protestant, commercial, oligarchic England something of the same function as it performed for Catholic, aristocratic, absolutist France. The continuity is the more striking in that it bridges the great divide of early modern history: from the Counter-Reformation to the Enlightenment, from Renaissance magic to modern science, from the so-called General Crisis of the 1640s and 1650s (if it existed) to Europe's take-off into the industrial revolution and colonial expansion. It is a truism that the intellectual revolution of the seventeenth century brought profound changes which were to transform not only material civilisation but also mankind's wider culture. Many have seen these changes as causing the decline of poetry. Rationalism and science, it is said, weakened the poetic spirit. Whether this is true or not, the importance of neo-classical doctrine during this crucial period must at least attract our curiosity.

There is a third reason why the modern attempt to devalue neo-classical doctrine, and say that it had no real importance even to writers of the time, seems inadequate as an explanation of the historical facts. This is harder to demonstrate, but may be the most important reason of all. Perhaps the writers of the time thought the doctrine irrelevant, or the result of social and political pressures, or a codification of literary techniques which worked in practice: but this is not the impression they give.

Perhaps the clearest example is from Chapelain, who is usually regarded as the decisive figure for the development and acceptance of the doctrine in France. Towards the end of his life, probably in 1672, having completed the last twelve books of his epic, *La Pucelle*, he composed a Preface to them. Remembering the equivocal reception of the first twelve books in 1656, and the ridicule heaped on him by younger men such as Boileau, perhaps he felt his cause was lost. Neither these last twelve books nor his Preface were printed until 1882. Indeed, the Preface was not printed in an authoritative text until 1936. It is a remarkable and touching document, and highly revealing of how neo-classical doctrine was regarded by its main proponent. Chapelain does not dare ask readers to admire his poem, but he does think it reasonable to ask them to familiarise themselves with poetic doctrine. And here his awkward prose stumbles into life, with an effect that only quotation can convey:

Ce n'est pas une règle ployable comme la lesbienne, mais une règle inflexible, qui sert également à connaître ce qui est droit et ce qui ne l'est pas. C'est le résultat et la quintessence de mille remarques diverses qui ont produit des préceptes invariables, des dogmes d'éternelle vérité, qui convainquent l'esprit, qui lui épargnent des recherches douteuses, et qui l'informent en un moment de ce qu'un homme n'aurait pu découvrir tout seul qu'en plusieurs centaines d'années...Je me promets, qu'étant guidés par ce flambeau, ils [poets and critics] sentiront le plaisir qu'il y a d'édifier sûrement et sans craindre d'être obligés à détruire, de prononcer sur le bien et le mal des poèmes sans appréhender qu'on appelle de leur sentence comme d'abus; et il me semble déjà voir naître de cette précieuse semence mille nouvelles productions qui, ne le cédant point aux anciennes, rendront encore en cela notre siècle égal aux siècles passés...[14]

There is nothing provisional or irrelevant about the rules here. They are 'unchanging precepts, dogmas of eternal truth', the 'torch' and 'precious seed' which make masterpieces possible. Towards the end of the long reign of neo-classicism, La Harpe was to describe the doctrine as set out in Boileau's *Art Poétique* in similar terms:

une législation parfaite dont l'application se trouve juste dans tous les cas, un code imprescriptible dont les décisions serviront à jamais à savoir ce qui doit être condamné, ce qui doit être applaudi.[15]

This is not the hysterical exaggeration of an obstinate defender of a dying tradition. It is an expression of an attitude commonly held, and present in neo-classicism from the beginning.

All this points up a number of questions which are hard to avoid when reading Boileau. What is it that makes the rules so important? What is the relationship between the neo-classical doctrine and the works of the great neo-classical writers? Much of Boileau's poetry is ostensibly about the doctrine. It is possible, perhaps, that he is not much interested in neo-classical theory: but if so, why does he so constantly take it as his subject?

5

In what follows, I shall look briefly at Boileau's life and personality, and then examine his poetry, concentrating on his treatment of neo-classical doctrine. I shall not be concerned so much with his explicitly critical writings (notably his translation of Longinus and his *Réflexions* on Longinus) as with how his poems work, and with the attitudes to the functions and nature of poetry that emerge from them. This will, I hope, also throw light on the wider significance of neo-classicism. We shall see as we go the conclusions to which this study leads. Nevertheless, it may be as well to indicate at this stage the general direction in which it points. The conclusions reached during this work have caused me to modify the views on Boileau I have expressed elsewhere.[16] The views expressed in the present book take account of recent criticism. Their novelty is that they reassert the importance of matters on which earlier critics concentrated. I have been led back to something like the view of Boileau that has long been out of favour: that his neo-classicism embodies a firmly worked-out position on the function and nature of poetry which is of lasting validity; that he is largely concerned to impose and defend this position; and that his poetry successfully exemplifies it.

2

Life and early works

On the face of it, Boileau had a fairly uneventful life. He was born in Paris in 1636, the fifteenth child of his father, a legal official, and the fifth child of his mother, his father's second wife. During his lifetime he was usually referred to as Despréaux, to distinguish him from his numerous relatives. Although his mother died when he was eighteen months old and his father was neglectful, his social environment all his life was prosperous. He was able to abandon a career at the Bar when he found it uncongenial, and to devote himself to writing. His health was poor, but in his early manhood this did not prevent him from acquiring a reputation for wildness. He did not marry, and continued to live in Paris, mainly in the houses of relatives near the Law Courts.

In the early 1660s, the audaciousness of his *Satires* may have put him in some danger of reprisals from his victims or from the Government. Towards the end of the decade, he moved closer to the establishment. It is customary to lay stress on his association with the literary circle round a high magistrate in the Paris Parlement, the Premier Président de Lamoignon. Lamoignon's emphasis on moral and literary seriousness may have influenced the *Épîtres* which Boileau began to write from the late 1660s onwards. At the same time, Boileau was high in favour with the influential Mortemart family: the Duc de Vivonne, Madame de Thiange and the King's mistress, Madame de Montespan. They were enthusiastic and discerning patrons of literature, and their closeness to the King gave them great social influence, but their life-style was a good deal more raffish than Lamoignon's. Another patron was Condé, the King's cousin and First Prince of the Blood, whose social position enabled him to favour independent thinkers and whose heterodox manners and opinions were notorious.

In 1677 came the great peripety of Boileau's life. He supported

Racine when *Phèdre* was attacked, and was suspected with Racine of composing the scandalous sonnet satirising the Duc de Nevers and the Duchesse de Bouillon. For a moment, it looked as though there would be serious repercussions. Thanks to Condé's protection, Boileau survived, and later in the year his social position was transformed. The Mortemarts persuaded the King to appoint him and Racine historiographers royal. Boileau was now a public functionary of some importance, with the right of close attendance on the King and a large pension (though this was later reduced when war made economies necessary). In order to devote himself to his task, Boileau was expected to give up writing poetry, though he and Racine were called in from time to time to contribute to Court entertainments. Boileau seems to have found writing history uncongenial. As his troubles with his health increased he appeared less and less at Court, and he accepted the reduction of his pension happily. He turned back to poetry, and the three *Satires* and three *Épîtres* he wrote during the last years of his life reflect the religious and literary polemics of the day, in which he championed the Ancients against the Moderns and attacked what he considered the relaxed morality of the Jesuits.

In his last years, he perhaps turned more in on himself. From the records left by his admirers Le Verrier and Brossette, who were close to him at this period, he seems to have been preoccupied with constructing his own version of his influence on the glorious literary achievements of 1660–77. At the very end of his life, his estrangement from the régime was shown by his failure to get permission to publish his last *Satire*, because the King's Jesuit confessor objected to it. Discouragement at this set-back perhaps hastened his death in 1711, but he was old and had been ill for some time.

Boileau frequently appears in his own poems, but his poetry rarely seems confessional. Most of his appearances are in his authorial persona rather than his own person: in the structure of his poems, he is object, not subject. When he does present himself biographically (in terms of his physical appearance, character, pursuits, background) he does so for polemical purposes: there is no sense of Romantic confession. This combination of reticence and self-advertisement does perhaps suggest one link between his poetry and his biography. The function of his poetry never seems to be to display his inner life, even unconsciously: what it does display is his temperament. Boileau's biography suggests a tension between emotional ebullience and restraint, perhaps due in part to crippling experiences in childhood and adolescence.

In later years, Boileau often referred to the miseries of his child-hood.[1] He was early attacked by the stone, and one of the crucial experiences of his life must have been the operation he underwent when he was about twelve.[2] Apart from the physical agony, the psychological trauma must have been severe. The operation left him with 'une difficulté particulière', presumably some genital injury. His enemies were later to sneer at his sexual incapacity.

Most of our first-hand evidence of Boileau's temperament comes from his letters towards the end of his life, and they present a striking picture. On the one hand, he appears as egocentric and obsessive, untidy,[3] embarrassingly eager to repay debts,[4] prudish,[5] and hypochondriacal.[6] At the same time, he displays an extra-ordinary sensitivity, swinging from gloom to exaltation,[7] on occasion bursting with emotional excitement,[8] and capable of passionate friendship.[9]

One complex of emotions which must interest us, in view of his later rôle as law-giver, is Boileau's attitude to authority. This shows a marked ambivalence. In his youth, he was notorious for his lack of respect for the régime: we have only to think of his attacks on Colbert and on the poets who flattered the King. In middle life, he became more respectable, even an establishment figure, but his iconoclasm continued to show. He compared the Academy to monkeys admiring themselves,[10] and in his letters to Brossette is critical of Government policy.[11] His letters to Racine refer to Louis XIV with more than a touch of irony,[12] and we can understand that in his youth he was accused of satirising the King. This is a topic we will often have to touch on in discussing his poems.

If Boileau was accused by his contemporaries of *lèse-majesté*, Voltaire was to make the opposite accusation: *flatteur de Louis*. More recently, Adam has emphasised Boileau's independence, and his courage at the end of his life in representing the sincere and patriotic Christianity of the bourgeoisie against 'un roi de plus en plus aveugle et tyrannique'.[13]

Boileau's successive attitudes as critic and flatterer of the régime raise questions about his social status. In a hierarchical society like seventeenth-century France, such questions are obviously important. There is no doubt that Boileau and his family were Parisian bourgeois, and Clarac in particular (like Lanson before him) has seen Boileau as a representative of middle-class qualities.[14] Yet Boileau himself was touchy on the subject. He claimed noble birth, quite falsely, and the social and moral implications of *noblesse* are a recurring theme in his work.

This brings us to the question of Boileau's philosophical and religious attitudes. In his youth he consorted with *libertins*, and Cotin was able to accuse him of atheism. *Satire IV* and *Satire VIII* show an interest in scepticism (though this need imply no disbelief in Christianity: scepticism was used as a tool of Christian apologetics).[15] In middle life he became more *bien pensant*. There is some doubt how far he can be said to have been a Jansenist in the strict sense – that is, of subscribing to the views of Jansen on divine grace, with their implied emphasis on predestination as opposed to free-will. He always claimed to be orthodox. But there is no doubt that he was attracted by the seriousness and moral rigour of Jansen's supporters, and sympathised with them as a persecuted minority. His sympathy with Jansenism grew as he aged, and his late poems show a deep concern with Port-Royal, its morality and its doctrines. Goldmann has argued that there were sociological reasons why Jansenism appealed to many members of the traditional office-holding middle classes. Having been the accepted supports and instruments of the royal power, they felt dispossessed and devalued by the growth of a modernising absolutism which worked instead through agents appointed directly by the King and holding office at his pleasure. The gloomy world-view of the Jansenists, and their sense of being a beleaguered minority of the elect, appealed to this mood of disillusionment.[16] Whether or not this view has substance, it would fit well enough with Boileau's bourgeois origin and unease about it.

Many of the men of Port-Royal were followers of the rationalism of Descartes.[17] Boileau may have been attracted to Cartesianism in his youth, and his *Arrêt Burlesque* of 1671 pokes fun at the Aristotelianism of the University, but in later life he is said to have complained that the philosophy of Descartes had been the ruination of poetry.[18] Perhaps because he was temperamentally inclined to doubt the possibility of progress, he was as scornful of scientific advance as of literary innovations. *Épître V* and *Satire X* show his ignorance and dislike of science. We see here again the gap that divides him from the eighteenth century. Order, reason and rationalism seem to fit together so well, and to link Boileau with the Augustans in England and the *philosophes* in France. But it is clear that the economic, religious and intellectual climate of the middle years of Louis XIV's reign is very different from that of the eighteenth century. If Boileau's neo-classical ideals in literature attracted men's minds in the eighteenth century, they did so in a radically changing environment. I shall come back to this problem of neo-classicism in considering *L'Art Poétique*. It does seem to me of fundamental importance in considering Boileau, and indeed in much wider contexts. But first there is the earlier Boileau to consider, long before he seems to have any designs on laying down rules for poetry.

2

The remains of Boileau's juvenilia are unimportant, except perhaps when they throw light on facets of the later Boileau that are often ignored.[19] One of his earliest pieces is a riddle on a flea. The most substantial piece is his *Ode sur un bruit qui courut en 1656 que Cromwel et les Anglais allaient faire la guerre à la France*. It is not very good, but it shows a liking for grandiloquence and conceits which appears in his later works. He thought highly enough of this ode to revise and publish it in 1701, immediately in front of his *Ode sur la Prise de Namur* of 1691, which has been criticised for just these qualities.

His first work of substance is a *Satire contre les Mœurs de la Ville de Paris*, which appeared in the pirated Rouen 'édition monstrueuse' of 1666. The satires Boileau wrote up to 1668 pose special problems for the critic. This is partly because their chronology is doubtful: they were certainly not written in the order of their present numbering. Some of them were also revised over a long period. The satire in the Rouen edition was eventually transformed into *Satire I*. Boudhors accordingly dates *Satire I* 1657–64, and the poem went through many revisions between these dates. Some of the variants have been traced by Adam, but there may well have been others which have disappeared. According to Boileau's notes on Le Verrier's draft commentary (which date from the early 1700s), *Satire VI* originally formed part of *Satire I*. This combined poem would have made up a long diatribe on the corruption and inconveniences of the capital, somewhat on the lines of Juvenal's *Third Satire*, with Paris replacing Rome. Boileau's memory was not always accurate, and these two early satires seem very different in tone and theme, but they can reasonably be assumed to date from the same period. I will return briefly to *Satire VI* at the end of this section.

Both in its earliest published and in its final versions, *Satire I* consists of a long tirade against social abuses, placed in the mouth of an author leaving Paris. The flavour of the poem (more pungent in the Rouen edition than in the final version) can best be conveyed by quotation:

> Mais moi vivre à Paris, hé qui voudrait le faire?
> En l'âge où je me vois je ne sais pas mentir,
> Et quand je le pourrais je n'y puis consentir.
> Je ne sais pas placer au dessus de la lune
> Celui dont l'impudence a causé la fortune;
> Louer un mauvais livre avec déguisement,
> Le demander à lire avec empressement;
> Perdre près d'un faquin une journée entière;
> Je suis rustique et fier, et j'ai l'âme grossière;
> Je ne puis rien nommer si ce n'est par son nom.
> J'appelle un chat un chat, et Rollet un fripon.
>   (Rouen version, ll. 42–52)[20]

Although the tone occasionally recalls Juvenal, the poem is very different in the vices it attacks. Boileau is not composing an 'imitation' in the manner of Pope or Johnson, in which the poet gives a classically trained audience the pleasure of seeing a favourite Latin poem in modern dress. His classicism seems, rather, to consist in the assumption that the procedures by which Juvenal lashed vice in ancient Rome can be applied by a modern poet to Paris. On the surface, it seems as though his aim coincides with the requirements of neo-classical orthodoxy in the simplest way: he is reproving vice and preaching virtue. But one or two features – especially in the Rouen version – induce a faint doubt. The choice of targets is strange. The main target of his invective is the financiers, whose natural territory is the corrupted town

(l. 34 of the Rouen version). They are accused not simply of meanness (ll. 66–8), arrogance (ll. 95, 169), or ostentation (ll. 87–92, ll. 169–72), but of real crimes. 'Le chemin d'être riche est celui de la Grève' (l. 86): the financier is willing to employ not only homicide (l. 78), perjury (l. 97) and theft (l. 79) but also incest (l. 78) and adultery (l. 79); and he laughs at Heaven's anger (l. 104). But financiers are not the only target. Shafts are directed at the Law (ll. 147–60), at those who have bad taste in literature (ll. 47–8, ll. 125–6), and at those authors who have more talent for pushing their careers than for writing (ll. 121–4). The climax of the Rouen version is an attack on Italian influence, and especially on homosexuality (ll. 195– 202), which is practised by atheists (ll. 203–9).

Some of these points perhaps reveal Boileau's personal pre-occupations. But there is a note of exaggeration which recurs constantly in Boileau, and reminds us of the frequent contemporary comments on his intemperate energy (*fougue*) and his love of snapping at anyone and anything. It is hard to see the homosexuality then flaunted in some aristocratic circles, or the preference given to bad poets, as abuses of quite the same type as financial malpractice; and incest, homicide and adultery seem different again.

The second feature which raises some doubts about Boileau's moral aim is again one which points to something which runs through his work. The 'author' who is used as a mouthpiece in the poem seems to be a composite figure. At times, he may well represent Boileau's own feelings, as when he denounces the favour shown to authors interested mainly in pushing their careers (including, in one unpublished variant, the young Racine). At other times, the persona chosen is clearly unsuitable for Boileau: 'Je suis rustique et fier, et j'ai l'âme grossière' (l. 50) does not fit a life-long Parisian who prided himself (falsely) on his noble birth. No doubt some of the statements made by the persona are ironical, and some of the contradictions are partly due to changes made during the long period over which the poem was written and revised. But the peroration, with its insistence on Boileau's (or his mouthpiece's) naïve religious faith, suggests another line of explanation. Whatever Boileau's religious views at this stage, he was known in his youth as a friend of free-thinkers and loose-livers.

We know that he enjoyed reciting his poems to his friends in taverns. Many years later, in very different circumstances, he was to describe to Racine how he read *Épître XII* to Père de la Chaise, the King's confessor. His description brings out sharply his delight in his audience's reactions and in his own performance: 'Vous voyez donc, Monsieur, que si je ne suis bon poète il faut que je sois bon récitateur', he wrote proudly to Racine.[21] In the Rouen and authorised versions of *Satire I*, the assertion of faith by the 'je' of the poem sounds solemn enough, until we imagine Boileau reciting it to his ribald friends around 1660.

Although the version avowed by Boileau is considerably changed from the Rouen version, this dramatic quality is retained. The main changes seem to be directed towards disciplining the poem into a more straightforwardly moral discourse. Boileau has not become more timid. One of the couplets now added (ll. 131–2) has a reference to 'le Vice orgueilleux...la mitre en tête et la crosse à la main' which is as explicit and dangerous as anything in the first version, in that it is a direct attack on the Archbishop of Paris. What we have, rather, is the taking up of a moral and aesthetic position. The revised text lacks the *burlesque audace* of the Rouen version. The more picturesque elements, the gestures towards neo-classical dignity, the references to Juvenal, are all trimmed, so that the poem is restricted to a middle ground between classicism and burlesque. It has become more consistent in its strategy and aim: a plain attack on some contemporary abuses.

Satire VI (*Les Embarras de Paris*) confirms this conclusion from a different angle. *Satire I* is moral and political, with incidental literary references. *Satire VI* has been described as realistic genre-painting, because it pictures the discomforts of life in seventeenth-century Paris. This strikes me as highly dubious as a characterisation of the poem. A better starting-point seems to be the complaints of Boileau's contemporaries, who constantly attacked him for exaggeration, for bizarre turns of phrase, and for using language both too low and too exalted for satire. *Satire VI* is an exuberant farce, and the medium Boileau uses to convey it is a rich and highly flavoured blending of styles. The opening sets the tone – or, rather, the mixture of tones:

> Qui frappe l'air, bon Dieu! de ces lugubres cris?
> Est-ce donc pour veiller qu'on se couche à Paris?
> Et quel fâcheux démon, durant les nuits entières,
> Rassemble ici les chats de toutes les gouttières?
> J'ai beau sauter du lit, plein de trouble et d'effroi,
> Je pense qu'avec eux tout l'enfer est chez moi:
> L'un miaule en grondant comme un tigre en furie,
> L'autre roule sa voix comme un enfant qui crie.
> Ce n'est pas tout encor, les souris et les rats
> Semblent, pour m'éveiller, s'entendre avec les chats.
>
> (ll. 1–10)

The language is undoubtedly (by seventeenth-century standards) 'low', and Boileau emphasises this at the outset, with his 'bon Dieu!', 'chats', 'gouttières', 'miaule', 'souris' and 'rats'. But the language also includes plenty of expressions appropriate to the *style noble*: 'démon', 'l'enfer', 'un tigre en furie', and soon (l. 17) 'le ciel en courroux'. And later, at the climax of the poem, Boileau makes use of the richness of the high style in a full-blown epic reference:

> Car le feu, dont la flamme en ondes se déploie,
> Fait de notre quartier une seconde Troie,
> Où maint Grec affamé, maint avide Argien,
> Au travers des charbons va piller le Troyen.
>
> (ll. 107–10)

The tone is not of realism but of comic exaggeration:

> Vingt carrosses bientôt arrivant à la file,
> Y sont en moins de rien suivis de plus de mille.
>
> (ll. 51–2)

Like all the best farce, *Satire VI* brings out the absurd side of the most serious subjects, in this case death. Murder is a joke in lines 94–103, and in lines 35–6 funeral pomp appears ridiculously between the poet losing his hat and the lackeys quarrelling:

> Là, d'un enterrement la funèbre ordonnance,
> D'un pas lugubre et lent vers l'église s'avance.

At the centre of the farce is the 'je' of the poem. At the very end, 'je' appears to be the penniless outcast of *Satire I*, but in the body of the poem he is a farcical put-upon figure, scurrying with demented urgency from catastrophe to catastrophe:

> J'ai beau sauter du lit, plein de trouble et d'effroi
>
> (l. 5)

L'un me heurte d'un ais dont je suis tout froissé;
Je vois d'un autre coup mon chapeau renversé
(ll. 33–4)

Je saute vingt ruisseaux, j'esquive, je me pousse;
Guénaud sur son cheval en passant m'éclabousse
(ll. 67–8)

J'y passe en trébuchant; mais, malgré l'embarras,
La frayeur de la nuit précipite mes pas
(ll. 81–2)

Mais en ma chambre à peine ai-je éteint la lumière,
Qu'il ne m'est plus permis de fermer la paupière.
Des filous éffrontés, d'un coup de pistolet,
Ébranlent ma fenêtre, et percent mon volet.
(ll. 99–102)

His flight through the poem is what gives it its shape.

In all this, we are as far from an attempt at documentary realism as from the apparently direct moral aim of *Satire I*. Boileau seems to be giving rein to his manic verve, and inducing his audience to share the exhilaration. *Satire VI* shows us an important element in Boileau: not realism or morality, but that billowing sense of absurdity which surges through much of his best work.

3

Satire VII is Boileau's first masterpiece, and still retains its freshness despite its apparently occasional nature. In form, it is an address by Boileau to his Muse, in which he says it would be better to take up praise of the régime in place of satire, but that he will continue as a satirist because that is where his talent lies. Whether or not provoked by the royal *gratifications* paid to official panegyrists like Chapelain, it is full of Boileau's *esprit frondeur*. It attacks the authors of boring eulogies and frigid panegyrics (l. 9). Chapelain is a target (l. 30), but most of the named victims are very obscure. (As was his habit, Boileau revised the list in later editions.) Criticism of the régime is implicit throughout, but in one place at least Boileau is sailing very near the wind. In lines 23–4, he implies that there is no hero in the world worthy of praise. Boudhors remarks that in the early 1660s Louis XIV had done little of note. This is doubtful: the King's

decision in 1661 to govern personally was a notable break with
tradition, and aroused the wonder of contemporaries. But even
if Boileau's statement were literally true, and if the poem had
been written in a neutral context, he was hardly likely to be
excused in the eyes of contemporaries for hinting that the King
was unworthy of praise. In the context of the royal government's
efforts to organise a chorus of praise from its poets, the lines are
unmistakably insolent; Boileau's enemies were not slow to make
the dangerous accusation of *lèse-majesté*.

It would be easy, then, to interpret *Satire VII* as having a
direct, moral relationship to contemporary society in the way that
the authorised version of *Satire I* apparently had. This impression
is heightened by the personal element in the poem. Boileau
depicts himself in the act of writing, shows how satire suits his
temperament, and asserts his desire to fulfil himself. In the words
of line 68 (final version),

> Riche, gueux, triste ou gai, je veux faire des vers.

As will appear later, I do not believe that Boileau's presentation
of himself here differs from that in *Satire II*. Here, he expresses in
famous lines the exhilaration of feeling inspiration come:

> Alors, certes, alors, je me connais poète.   (l. 34)

In *Satire II*, we shall find the same doctrine of inspiration.
As often in Boileau, this apparently personal element is explicitly
linked in *Satire VII* with a moral element, in which vice and
stupidity stand together in opposition to virtue and genius:

> Le mérite pourtant m'est toujours précieux;
> Mais tout fat me déplaît, et me blesse les yeux.
> > (ll. 55–6)

In part, this is perhaps the common satirist's pose, a polemical
device. But it seems to me to recur so often in Boileau, and in such
convincing tones, that I think it is an important clue to his
aesthetic. Up to a point it is valid to interpret *Satire VII* in moral
terms: poetry has a direct social function in attacking vice and
defending virtue. However, it is equally valid to read it in confessional terms: the poem is Boileau's assertion of his vocation.
The two views indeed reinforce each other: the poet's independence in fulfilling himself is the cause and result of his indepen-

dence in judging the régime and its poets. We cannot ignore either
of these aspects.

Nevertheless, there is another important element in the poem
which needs discussion. As this is expressed in the structure and
texture of the poem itself, it is hard to abstract and define in other
terms. I can only describe it as self-contradiction, or the division of
an attitude against itself. If this sounds obscure, it can perhaps be
clarified by an examination of some points in the text.

This element is introduced in the easy, conversational opening:

> Muse, changeons de style, et quittons la satire:
> C'est un méchant métier que celui de médire;
> A l'auteur qui l'embrasse il est toujours fatal:
> Le mal qu'on dit d'autrui ne produit que du mal.
> Maint poète, aveuglé d'une telle manie,
> En courant à l'honneur trouve l'ignominie;
> Et tel mot, pour avoir réjoui le lecteur
> A coûté bien souvent des larmes à l'auteur.
> (ll. 1–8)

The author begins by addressing his Muse, who apparently is part
of himself. The trade (*métier*) of satire is *méchant*, a bad business,
in the sense of doing the author no good: but *méchant* also has
overtones of 'evil'. The forceful antitheses of lines 6–8 (honour
brings shame; what gives pleasure to the reader brings pain to the
author) emphasise the double-edged nature of satire. This might
seem banal enough, but lines 13–20 go deeper. The author is in
danger not so much from those who are outraged by his attacks
as from those who admire and enjoy them. The author:

> Des ses propres rieurs se fait des ennemis.   (l. 16)

Boileau warns the poet (or the Muse) that there is a division
within each admirer:

> Et tel, en vous lisant, admire chaque trait,
> Qui dans le fond de l'âme et vous craint et vous hait.
> (ll. 19–20)

If the readers are divided against themselves, so in lines 25–36
is the poet: he wants to write eulogies, but instead writes satire,
and then his inspiration runs away with him. But inspiration does
not take over entirely: he remains divided against himself:

C'est en vain qu'au milieu de ma fureur extrême
Je me fais quelquefois des leçons à moi-même;
En vain je veux au moins faire grâce à quelqu'un:
Ma plume aurait regret d'en épargner aucun.

(ll. 49–52)

He asserts his delight in writing, whatever happens (ll. 63–8), and then the split in attitudes comes into the open. An imagined dialogue begins, in which an interlocutor reproaches him:

Pauvre esprit, dira-t-on, que je plains ta folie!
Modère ces bouillons de ta mélancolie;
Et garde qu'un de ceux que tu penses blâmer
N'éteigne dans ton sang cette ardeur de rimer.

(ll. 69–72)

Boileau protests that neither Horace nor Juvenal came to grief because of their satires. In any case, he goes on:

Personne ne connaît ni mon nom ni ma veine:
On ne voit point mes vers, à l'envi de Montreuil,
Grossir impunément les feuillets d'un recueil.
A peine quelquefois je me force à les lire,
Pour plaire à quelque ami que charme la satire,
Qui me flatte peut-être, et, d'un air imposteur,
Rit tout haut de l'ouvrage, et tout bas de l'auteur.
Enfin c'est mon plaisir; je veux me satisfaire.
Je ne puis bien parler, et ne saurais me taire;
Et, dès qu'un mot plaisant vient luire à mon esprit,
Je n'ai point de repos qu'il ne soit en écrit:
Je ne résiste point au torrent qui m'entraîne.

(ll. 82–93)

Even in this defence, however, the theme of internal division appears. Boileau's friend, perhaps, 'Rit tout haut de l'ouvrage, et tout bas de l'auteur' (l. 88). Boileau himself rushes on, however badly: 'Je ne puis bien parler, et ne saurais me taire' (l. 90). The poem ends with a contradiction of himself, expressed in the form of an address from himself to the Muse which is a personification of part of himself:

Finissons. Mais demain, Muse, à recommencer. (l. 96)

The prominence of this theme explains some curious features of the poem. Why does Boileau attack the harmless student of archives, Sauval, who seems to have been a friend of his? Is the Colletet of line 45 the father, whom *Satire I* seems to praise, or the son, and why does Boileau not say which? Why, in the first version, did line 44 attack Maucroix, another friend (or, if the reference is really to Mauroy, why did the poet not make the matter clearer)? Why does the reference to the friend of line 86 turn into an attack (and one which gave offence to its subject)? Why, in a poem that attacks Chapelain, does Boileau use in line 70 a phrase from *La Pucelle*? Is this chance, or does the fact that it is put in a speech by his imaginary interlocutor suggest that it is meant to discredit the speaker?

Commentators have laboured with more or less success to explain some of these points. But my view would be that the apparent inconsistencies point to an important element in Boileau's poetry which goes a long way to explaining its successes. There is a doubleness or self-contradictoriness in *Satire VII* which comes out not only in these details but in its general form. I would argue that it is by means of these very qualities that Boileau escapes from either direct didacticism or direct self-expression into the world of poetry, since poetry lives by producing such complex effects. *Satire VII* is full of easy, playful lines, of bursts of energy in which the verse carries us along, of powerful statements of position. But the quasi-dramatic form is not simply a device. It is an expression of something which is basic to the poem: its complex emotional structure. In later poems, Boileau carries the method further – in the case of *Satire IX*, taking up motifs from *Satire VII*. *Satire VII* is simpler than Boileau's later masterpieces, but it shows some of the complexities underlying his art.

4

Satire II (*La Rime et la Raison*) and the *Stances sur l'École des Femmes* are both addressed to Molière. The *Stances* are chiefly notable because they show Boileau's ability to recognise genius among his contemporaries. He is remarkable, if for no other reason, for his almost unerring intuitive power in recognising merit. Without exception, the contemporaries he attacked have proved to be minor at best, whereas, with only the rarest exceptions, those he singled out for the highest praise are still respected.

Apart from demonstrating this skill, however, the *Stances* have some interesting features. Anyone who cares to examine these lines, and Boileau's revisions of them, will find they contain conceits, bombast and padding in plenty. They also display attitudes that recur in Boileau's work. Molière is associated with Terence, and Terence is assimilated to Scipio the younger, conqueror of Numantia and Carthage. The use of the tradition that Scipio helped Terence write his plays might be taken as an insinuation that Molière also was helped by someone else. The insinuation is strange, unless it is intended to emphasise that support of Molière is worthy of the greatest in the land. There is also in the poem the implication that the battle is between poets who know what they are doing and those who do not. The emphasis is on the *savoir* of Molière and Terence/Scipio: 'Que tu badines savamment!'; 'Celui qui sut vaincre Numance...Sut-il mieux badiner que toi?'; 'Si tu savais un peu moins plaire....'. As Brody has shown, *savoir* for Boileau has overtones of 'reasoned taste', 'practised judgment', rather than 'knowledge'.[22] Nevertheless, in seventeenth-century criticism there is a frequent stress on *doctrine* and the knowledge of poetic theory possessed by *les doctes*, and the wider use of *savoir* as connected with 'knowledge' or 'learning' cannot be ignored. In this poem, Boileau compares Molière's jokes with a 'docte sermon' (learned sermon). Pleasure, utility, morality, taste, knowledge and skill are closely linked in these stanzas as the conditions and results of good poetry, and they will often appear together in Boileau's thought.

Satire II is a more substantial piece. It is cast in the form of an epistle from Boileau, who has trouble in finding rhymes which fit the sense, to Molière, who does not. A traditional comment, which derives from Boileau's own views in later life as reflected by Le Verrier, is that in fact Boileau is a more accomplished rhymer than Molière, so that there is an element of jokiness in Boileau's attitude in this poem. This comment is linked with the assumptions that in 1663 Boileau and Molière were close friends and regarded each other as equals, and that Boileau is at least in part assuming an unwonted modesty for the purposes of the poem: in Le Verrier's words, 'l'auteur donne ici à son ami une facilité de tourner un vers et de rimer que son ami n'avait pas, mais il est question de le louer et de lui faire plaisir'.

The assumption about the relationship between Boileau and Molière is open to doubt. Molière was fourteen years older than

Boileau, and a famous and successful author. Boileau was a
novice. The assumption about their rhyming skills is hardly more
solid. In view of Molière's incomparably greater literary output,
it is hard to deny him the greater facility which Boileau attributes
to him. Nor is it clear that his verse is more diffuse or negligent
than Boileau's. The requirements of dramatic verse are different
from those of satire, and Molière's verse is no doubt sometimes
slack in texture. But in general it is difficult to fault the verse of
Tartuffe or *Le Misanthrope* for its dramatic purpose; Molière's
verse is for the most part supple and economical. Boileau's, as
Hervier, Adam and many others have pointed out, is often
awkward, cliché-ridden and padded with redundant half-lines.
(We shall come to some examples in *Satire II*.)

Boileau's presentation of himself does not necessarily reflect
how difficult he found rhyming, but neither is it necessarily
modest. There are undertones in the poem which indicate a very
high opinion of himself. In much of the poem (e.g. ll. 11–14 and
57–64), he laments that he is a writer. When, towards the end, he
describes the truly great writer, it is not hard to connect the 'tel,
dont en tous lieux chacun vante l'esprit,/Voudrait, pour son
repos, n'avoir jamais écrit' with the Boileau of the earlier lines.
In the final four lines, there is a characteristic ambiguity:

> Toi donc, qui vois les maux où ma muse s'abîme,
> De grâce, enseigne-moi l'art de trouver la rime:
> Ou, puisque enfin tes soins y seraient superflus,
> Molière, enseigne-moi l'art de ne rimer plus.
>
> (ll. 97–100)

He begs Molière to teach him how to find rhymes, but says these
efforts would be 'superfluous'. 'Wasted', certainly, because
Boileau will still find it difficult; but is there an undertone of
'superfluous' also, because Boileau does in fact often find rhymes
easily, as lines 27–32 have asserted?

It is perhaps over-solemn to talk of the literary doctrines expressed in the poem, but Boileau's attitude to his ostensible critical
assumptions in it is different from what we might at first think.
Superficially, he is no doubt echoing critical commonplaces
(expressed, for instance, in his brother Gilles's *Avis à Ménage*,
which was certainly in his mind): difficulties in rhyming should
not be allowed to distort the sense; clichés and lazy imitations of

Malherbe should be avoided; the poet should write *poliment*
(in a correct and refined manner); the rules of art should be
followed. None of these points was novel or contentious, nor were
the attacks on such as Ménage or Scudéry. The interesting point
in this context is that Boileau himself fails by these criteria.
According to Le Verrier, Arnauld d'Andilly persuaded him to
change the Malherbian 'filés d'or et de soie' (spun of gold and
silk) because of the prohibition in lines 45–6. Boileau's revision of
the couplet is clumsy, and so are other lines:

> Pour qui tient Apollon tous ses trésors ouverts
>
> (l. 3)
>
> De rage quelquefois, ne pouvant la trouver.
>
> (l. 23)

Padding abounds:

> Mais moi, qu'un vain caprice, une bizarre humeur,
> Pour mes péchés, je crois, fit devenir rimeur
>
> (ll. 11–12)
>
> Mais depuis le moment que cette frénésie
> De ses noires vapeurs troubla ma fantaisie,
> Et qu'un démon jaloux de mon contentement
> M'inspira le dessein d'écrire poliment.
>
> (ll. 69–72)

The abuse of resounding numbers in 'mille serments' (l. 26)
and 'Malheureux mille fois' (l. 85) is obvious enough, as is the
facile rhyming of words such as 'affaire'/'faire' (ll. 61–2). As for
the rightness of thought, Boileau does not seem to be insistent
about matching what he says to the social facts he assumes his
audience will know. In the original version of lines 17–18, the
galant was Ménage, who had the reputation of being a ladies'
man; the later version has the Abbé de Pure, who did not. From
the purist's point of view, these are too many faults for a poem of
a hundred lines extolling the virtues of correctness.

As Brody has pointed out, the underlying position assumed in
the poem is quite different. Boileau (or Boileau as he presents
himself here) has to struggle with his rhymes, but when he has
ceased struggling inspiration comes (ll. 27–32). This does not
relieve him from the need for hard work, but it distinguishes him
from the insipid poets who take any rhyme which comes without
earning these moments of inspiration. Boileau admires Molière
because Molière is such a 'rare esprit' that his inspiration flows

easily, under the guidance of an informed good taste. Pelletier and Scudéry are despised (ll. 76 and 77–82) because they have the facility without the taste or inspiration.

We can perhaps take this thought a little further. Boileau sees himself and Molière as guided by inspiration and taste. In addition, there is a strong implication that they are 'right'. As Brody has remarked: 'As a creative and critical faculty *raison* had more to do with the expression *avoir raison* than with the verb *raisonner*.'[23] This quality of being right is linked with objective excellence in literature, with Virgil (l. 20) and with the rules of art (l. 86). Reason is chained to rhyme (l. 56), which is in part a way of putting the traditional complaint that the difficulty of rhyming can lead to a distortion of the sense. But it is also an assertion that the good poet stands out from the crowd of mediocrities because he decides to chain rhyme to Reason. The poem does not assert that poets should follow the prescriptions of Malherbe, and that Scudéry and Pelletier write badly because they fail to do so. If this were the intention, *Satire II* fails badly by its own criteria. Boileau is saying something quite different. On one side there are the elect, Molière and Boileau himself, who are guided by taste and inspiration, and possess the quality of being right, even when their verse breaks their own rules. On the other side are the mass of rhymesters, who do not have these sacred gifts of taste and inspiration, who are not 'right'; they are fools and are read by fools (ll. 82 and 87). Boileau's victims had reason to complain that he did not criticise them rationally, and to be outraged at his assumption of superiority. We may wonder whether Boileau's sympathy with Jansenism is not founded on an attitude evident in this poem: he and Molière are assumed to be the literary Elect. Yet even here we need to take care: *Satire II* may assert the primacy of inspiration, but it does not neglect hard work and 'the rules'. Taste and the doctrine are not incompatible.

5

Taking stock at this stage, we may find that a number of points can be deduced from these early and often tentative works. First, and most important, those critics have a point who see Boileau not as presenting a doctrine or fighting attitudes he disapproves of but as constructing poems: poems which depend largely on setting up two worlds in opposition (one usually represented by the poet or his persona) and then playing between them a dramatic game with a curiously lively to-and-fro movement. At the end of each poem the playful conflict does not resolve itself but just stops. It follows from this that the commentators are often wasting their time when they try to discern the historical person behind the target attacked in a poem, or to isolate Boileau's 'real' attitude in it. For the same reason, it is true, but not very important, to say that Boileau's values are not consistent, that he often misrepresents himself and others, and that he changes around the names of his targets without seeming to care, or attacks at random people of whom he has hardly heard. If we respond to his poems as poems, a consistency does emerge, but it is a consistency of characteristic attitudes and patterns of feeling, rather than of intellectual or moral principles.

On the other hand, I find it difficult to see this as the whole truth. Boileau does seem to see himself as attacking real abuses, whether social or literary – with some courage in *Satire I*, and with some consistency in *Satire VII* and *Satire II*, for all their lightness. There is, indeed, a seriousness in *Satire I* which comes frequently into his work, but which we have difficulty in accommodating into our modern picture of a poet: the seriousness of didacticism. Here at least, Boileau seems to be trying on rôles which have a simpler and more direct relationship to contemporary society than the rôle of writer of poems in the arcane sense which comes so easily within the terms of modern critical theory: trying on, in fact, the rôles of preacher and reformer. Similarly, he seems to be trying on in other parts of these early poems other rôles which we no longer usually look for in poetry: the rôles of painter of the contemporary scene or of society entertainer.

These considerations strongly suggest that in judging Boileau we cannot bypass the traditional account of him as moral legislator simply by concentrating on the analysis of his poems as poems. He is, after all, in some sense a neo-classical poet; and neo-classicism, however diverse the expression of its doctrines, was often preoccupied with the moral function of poetry in a way which our modern critical attitudes tend to reject. I do not think we can evade the difficulty by ignoring it: least of all in a poet like Boileau, whose work is so often explicitly concerned with neo-classical doctrine, and whose reputation was for so long bound up with his success in expressing and exemplifying that doctrine. I will return to these issues in the context of *L'Art Poétique*, where they are most acute. In the meantime, let us examine the development of Boileau's poetry in his middle *Satires* and in the early *Épîtres*.

3
The harvest of satire

It is wrong to be too solemn about Boileau. The most common element in his poems is enjoyment: the poet's enjoyment in writing, the enjoyment we can feel in the movement of his verse as his friends listen to his readings, our own enjoyment as we read his verse today. The nearest parallel in English literature seems to me the Byron of *Don Juan*. Despite the differences of form and tone, there is the same artful use of the poet's persona, a similar ability to move from the serious to the farcical, the same adroit passage from the high-falutin to the pratfall, the same joy in the manipulation of the reader's expectations. Clarac is no doubt right to lay stress on Boileau as the bourgeois bachelor, 'rancunier et vindicatif' (spiteful and vengeful).[1] But it is salutary, perhaps, to emphasise as well the similarities between Boileau and the exuberant and passionate Byron.

In part, Boileau's reputation in the early 1660s was simply that of a malicious and witty young man, reciting his lampoons to other young writers who shared his drinking sessions. But many of those he frequented were heterodox in more serious ways.

His friend Lignières was alleged to be an atheist. La Fontaine was certainly by temperament and conviction at this time opposed to Christian orthodoxy. Molière's religious position is harder to make out. Nineteenth-century writers tended to extract a moderate and worldly rationalism from pronouncements by some of the characters in his plays. Modern critics have rightly been wary of this procedure. Nevertheless, it is clear enough that the picture which emerges from his work as a whole is of a world-view totally at variance with that of Counter-Reformation Catholicism, and probably that of any type of Christianity. Certainly this was the view taken by the *dévots* of the time, for whom Molière was a *libertin* and a dangerous enemy of the Faith. And *libertinage* was literally a burning issue in the 1660s. Le Petit was mutilated and burned in Paris in 1662 for impiety. In 1664, the first *Tartuffe* was under attack by a cabal of *dévots*. In 1669, performance of the next version was forbidden.

Although Boileau was associating with dangerous men, they could perhaps be written off as impious or frivolous, rather than upholders of an alternative system. But he was also associated with representatives of the *libertinage érudit*: the *peu dévot*[2] Abbé La Mothe le Vayer, and also his father, who belonged to that prudent category of scholars who carried on the tradition of Renaissance humanism and nourished a discreet contempt for *les moines*.

Of more immediate scandal, perhaps, was the tenor of Boileau's politics. The early satires, especially in their first versions, had attacked men of power, including the King's brother and the Archbishop of Paris. He had also attacked the recipients of *gratifications*, and this impugned the policy of Colbert, and by implication the King. The surreptitious *Colbert Enragé* went much further, and accused the powerful Minister not only of malice and ingratitude but also of corruption and intended murder; it also called in question the attack on Foucquet, which had been decided on by the King himself as a corner-stone of his new policy. Boileau may not have collaborated on this poem, but the fact that contemporaries associated him with it shows the dangerous waters he was moving on.

Despite this, the satires of the early 1660s are fun. They show in the highest degree Boileau's *vis comica*, and are hard to read without laughing aloud. This chapter will examine the *Discours au Roi* and *Satires IV, V, III, IX* and *VIII*, in that order, which is more or less the order in which they were written.

2

At first sight, the *Discours au Roi* is a poem by a conformist poet trying to further his career. It celebrates the greatness of the young Louis XIV, laments that Boileau is inadequate to the task of praising him, and attacks in passing those bad poets who praise the King clumsily. The style is a mixture of the styles considered

appropriate by neo-classical theory: the *style pompeux* for panegyric, and the more familiar style for satire.

As usual with Boileau, however, first impressions are somewhat
misleading. The panegyric and the satire, the high style and the
low, become curiously blended.

The opening lines are in the usual direct address of formal
panegyric, as we find it in Malherbe, Chapelain and others:

> Jeune et vaillant héros, dont la haute sagesse
> N'est point le fruit tardif d'une lente vieillesse,
> Et qui seul, sans ministre, à l'exemple des dieux,
> Soutiens tout par toi-même, et vois tout par tes yeux,
> GRAND ROI. . .
>
> (ll. 1–5)

Though acceptable by the conventions of the day, this arouses
some faint doubts. Louis was young, but in his peaceful reign had
not yet shown valour or martial heroism. He prided himself on
having no *premier ministre*, and Boileau echoes the astonishment
and admiration of contemporaries. Or is he slightly exaggerating?
Louis had Ministers, if not a Prime Minister, and one was the
powerful Colbert. In Christianity, even God has his angels, who
are 'ministers'. Whether or not these doubts are justified, there is
something piquant about this praise from the irreverent Boileau.
But, of course, he does not say he has been silent because he is
hostile to the King's policy: he has kept silent because he is so
humble that he has hesitated to offer Louis incense so well
deserved.

In line 9, the tone changes: 'Mais je sais peu louer. . .'
Despite the gulf between the King and himself, Boileau in effect
buttonholes him and starts to chat. He points out the absurdity of
the official poets, whom Louis had notionally chosen, and certainly
paid: 'qui vont tous les jours, d'une importune voix,/T'ennuyer
du récit de tes propres exploits' (ll. 19–20). The *tutoiement* of the
formal opening here becomes the *tutoiement* of friendly conversation. With disarming effrontery, Boileau takes the King by the
arm, as it were, and invites him to agree – man to man – how
tiresome these panegyrists are. The examples are funny enough.
There is the writer of grandiloquent eclogues, and the laborious
poet who can find no more imaginative comparison for Louis

than the sun (ll. 21–8). No wonder 'leur veine méprisée/Fut toujours des neuf sœurs la fable et la risée' (ll. 29–30).

But again doubts intrude. Charpentier (Colbert's protégé, and the bad poet of lines 20–4) was no doubt wrong to use the *style pompeux* in an eclogue. But Boileau himself is writing satire, which is also a humble genre, and using grand language. As if to make the point, he passes almost immediately to a passage evoking 'Hélicon', the 'neuf sœurs', 'Calliope', 'Pégase', 'Parnasse', 'Apollon', and the spreading of Louis's fame 'du midi jusqu'à l'ourse' (from the South to the Great Bear). Chapelain's sonnet is absurd, despite its author's special status as organiser of official propaganda. But the comparison with the sun had a special significance. Astrology was not dead, and at Louis's birth Campanella, the Italian revolutionary and mystic – in a passage which Racine thought worth transcribing – had pointed out that the future king was born on the day of the sun, *ad solis instar*: 'in the likeness of the sun'. Louis XIV had consciously chosen the sun as his image. As recent scholarship has shown, in so doing he was carrying on a tradition deriving from the attempts of the last Valois in their Court festivals to attract favourable astrological influences on to the monarchy.[3] In asking Louis to mock, Boileau's friendliness has a sharp edge to it.

There is also at least the possibility of equivocation in his references to the incense to be offered to the King. In line 8, it is merited. When offered by inferior authors it is unworthy (l. 16). Boileau himself cannot lavish it on worthless objects (l. 108). The see-sawing between worthy praise and praise that is unworthy because of either the giver or the recipient induces an unease in the mind of the reader. In refusing to praise, Boileau sometimes uses language which casts doubt on the agreeableness of the enterprise: to praise Louis is 'd'un si grand fardeau la charge trop pesante' (l. 10), or 'le fardeau' with which his mind is 'accablé' (l. 136). Nothing will force Boileau to praise Louis, not even a reason: 'Il n'est espoir de biens, ni raison, ni maxime,/Qui pût en ta faveur m'arracher une rime' (ll. 113–14). Boudhors makes much of Boileau's refusal to mention Louis's patronage of letters. Line 113 seems a clear enough allusion, and one which in view of Boileau's reaction to the policy of *gratifications* borders on insolence. The poem rests on an evaluation it forces the reader to make of where Louis and Boileau stand in this difficult weighing of 'Les louanges d'un fat' (the praises of a fool) and 'celles d'un héros' (those of a hero) (l. 24).

None of this means that Boileau was satirising the King. The circumstances alone make this very unlikely. To circulate a lampoon on the King, even surreptitiously, would have been an act of near-treasonable folly. The *Discours* was published openly in 1665. And there is no doubt that, all in all, the poem comes over as a poem of praise. There is no mistaking the energy and rhythm of the panegyric in lines 115 and following:

> Mais lorsque je te vois, d'une si noble ardeur,
> T'appliquer sans relâche aux soins de ta grandeur...

What we have is a complex poem. Boileau has escaped from the simple alternative views that a poem can praise the worthy or condemn the vicious. He has arrived at a structure which can express conflicting truths and emotions and yet express an over-all meaning through the richness and subtlety this balancing makes possible. Boileau's enemy Cotin used the *Discours* as evidence that Boileau was indeed denigrating the King.[4] Adam is perhaps right in saying that Boileau saw the suggestion was plausible enough to be dangerous.[5] This is the penalty of the method. The *Discours* shows Boileau moving with increasing sureness towards a method of composing which will allow a poem to express a complex meaning, but to do so within the following difficult and conflicting imperatives: to satirise; to enable him to keep his peace with the authorities; and to praise what he finds praiseworthy without surrendering his judgment.

3

Satire IV is an attack on Reason. The word *raison* and its derivatives recur constantly in Boileau's writings, almost always to represent a positive value. Sometimes 'Reason' seems to represent the supreme positive value, as in the famous lines from *L'Art Poétique*:

> Aimez donc la raison: que toujours vos écrits
> Empruntent d'elle seule et leur lustre et leur prix.
>
> (I, ll. 37–8)

It was once assumed that Boileau was in some sense the poet of an Age of Reason stretching from Descartes to Voltaire and beyond, in opposition to the Romantic poets with their emphasis on intuition and emotion. Such simplistic ideas have long been discredited, and not only in relation to Boileau. Whatever his religious views in the 1660s, there is hardly a trace in Boileau of the knowing, self-satisfied Reason of the eighteenth-century Enlightenment or nineteenth-century rationalism, corroding traditional beliefs and institutions.

More recently, Brody has demonstrated in convincing detail some points of cardinal importance about Boileau's view of Reason. He has shown that, for Boileau, *Raison* is often a kind of informed sensitivity which enables the critic to sense the merit of a work of literature by an act of almost physical perception.[6] Reason 'enlightens' the critic. It is linked with 'Descartes's "lumière naturelle" – a fugitive reflection on earth of the "lumière pure, constante, claire, certaine… et toujours présente" of beatific vision – the "clarté" which for Boileau guarantees the infallibility of the ideal critic's "raison" is but a secularisation of that primal *clarté* by which human reason is made spiritually sentient.'[7]

Satire IV was undoubtedly born in a *libertin* environment. According to Brossette, it was sparked off in Boileau's mind by conversations with Molière and the Abbé La Mothe le Vayer on the theme that all men are mad. This sounds like a half-understood and sanitised version of what Molière and Le Vayer perhaps held as a serious philosophical position. Le Vayer's father was a Pyrrhonian, who held that certainty was an impossibility and rational demonstration therefore an illusion. Molière may or may not have accepted this. What does seem to emerge from his works is a sympathy for the natural and wayward realities of human impulse and a scorn for the abstract constructions which try to override it. This view and Pyrrhonism are perhaps not far apart, if we put them in their historical context. The late sixteenth century and the seventeenth saw a great effort by the Catholic Church to regularise and impose its world-view. This world-view was underpinned by the rationalism of Scholastic philosophy, to which Cartesian rationalism could seem to be affiliated. Opponents of this authoritarian trend, which made its weight felt in all departments of life, could see themselves as opposed by this monstrous apparatus claiming to be justified by demonstrative Reason. Reason would then be a natural target for a counter-attack.

Adam has also suggested that this theme was congenial to the Jansenists, and that their common opposition to the prevailing ideology caused both *libertinage* and Jansenism to be appreciated in certain circles.[8] We will come back to this point. In relation to *Satire IV*, it is enough to note that Reason is here, in modern terms, something more like Dogma. It is the universality of assumptions, rather than reasonableness, which is in question.

This comes out in the antithetical structure of the poem, which Boileau emphasised in his revisions. The opening lines pose a question: why does even the maddest man think that he alone is right? Then there follow paragraphs on two pairs of opposites: the pedant and the ignorant fop (ll. 5–18) and the bigot and the *libertin* (ll. 19–28). Boileau then exclaims, with some scandalous references to contemporaries, that he can never list all the types of folly, and that instead he can assert:

> pour rimer ici ma pensée en deux mots,
> N'en déplaise à ces fous nommés sages de Grèce,
> En ce monde il n'est point de parfaite sagesse:
> Tous les hommes sont fous, et, malgré tous leurs soins,
> Ne diffèrent entre eux que du plus ou du moins.
>
> (ll. 36–40)

He then develops his characteristic metaphor of journeying and losing one's way. After this, he emphasises the theme of paradox, already adumbrated in 'ces fous nommés sages de Grèce'. Lines 46–58 state the thesis that it is precisely our own vice and folly that we set up as wisdom. This is illustrated, in the final version, by another pair of contrasting portraits, the miser and the spendthrift (ll. 60–71), and then, again in the final version, by a man who brings the contrast together in one person: the gambler who thinks the miser and spendthrift both mad (l. 72), but who himself makes luck his religion (ll. 74–6), and who when he loses goes truly mad and threatens Heaven (ll. 77–84). The poem then turns to less violent lunacies, instancing Chapelain's itch to be a poet (ll. 90–102). The concluding section (ll. 103–28) defends the proposition that self-deception is often the best form of happiness, illustrating it by the story of the madman who heard the songs of the blessed spirits until he was cured.

Satire IV is an amusing poem, but it does not rise much above the level of a *jeu d'esprit*. Perhaps it appeared more daring at the time, when Boileau's enemies talked of immorality and blasphemy, and cried scandal at his attack on Reason. Boileau found it prudent to remove three lines which were too close to Molière's dangerous thoughts:

> Jouissez des douceurs que demande votre âge,
> Et ne vous plaignez pas ces innocents plaisirs
> Dont l'argent, tous les jours, peut combler vos désirs.[9]

Two points, nevertheless, deserve remark. The earlier versions did not include the characters of the spendthrift and the gambler, but did have a long passage comparing the miser to Tantalus, expanded from five lines of the *First Satire* of Horace's First Book. If Boileau was aiming at inviting his readers to savour an 'Imitation of Horace', he abandoned this in favour of introducing portraits which are structurally more relevant.

More interesting is the passage on Chapelain, which is the liveliest in the poem:

> Chapelain veut rimer, et c'est là sa folie.
> Mais bien que ses durs vers, d'epithètes enflés,
> Soient des moindres grimauds chez Ménage sifflés,
> Lui-même il s'applaudit, et, d'un esprit tranquille,
> Prend le pas au Parnasse au-dessus de Virgile.
> Que ferait-il, hélas! si quelque audacieux
> Allait pour son malheur lui dessiller les yeux,
> Lui faisant voir ces vers et sans force et sans grâces,
> Montés sur deux grand mots, comme sur deux échasses,
> Ces termes sans raison l'un de l'autre écartés,
> Et ces froids ornements à la ligne plantés?
> Qu'il maudirait le jour où son âme insensée
> Perdit l'heureuse erreur qui charmait sa pensée!
>
> (ll. 90–102)

These lines convey a meaning of some complexity. As Brody has shown, the complaint against Chapelain is that his elevated tone is spuriously based on *grands mots*,[10] and this fault is often linked in Boileau's mind with a lack of that illumination by reason that could 'dessiller les yeux' (l. 96).[11] Boileau's method owes nothing to a reasoned critique; we need never have read a word of Chapelain's work to laugh at Boileau's attack. The method is to create a picture of sublimely unwitting idiocy. Chapelain is mad, and tranquilly strides on to Parnassus in front of Virgil, even though smaller men whistle at him like schoolboys. He is a clown striding along on stilts (l. 98). He lacks the gift of reason, just as the elements of his verse are stuck on perversely, in defiance of reason. The denunciation of 'Reason' is here made in the name of Reason, and not spelled out discursively but conveyed through this startling picture. In this passage, at least, we see Boileau achieving the transformation from rhymed philosophy to poetry.

4

Satire V (Sur la Noblesse) and *Satire III (Le Repas Ridicule)* can both be dealt with rapidly, although they are of very different value.

In seventeenth-century France, *noblesse* gave not only social prestige but also legal and fiscal privileges. The concept is difficult to define in modern terms.[12] It was certainly not synonymous with belonging to one of the great aristocratic families. It was not necessarily incompatible with what we probably tend to think of as *bourgeois* occupations, for instance, a career in Law or as a public official. There was a recognised *noblesse de robe*. 'Nobility' could be obtained by direct gift of the king, or by becoming the holder of one of the more important offices under the Crown (by outright purchase or by payment of a tax which was in effect a purchase price). Boileau was not born *noble*, but claimed to be. Many years after the writing of *Satire V*, the genealogist who validated the Boileaus' nobility was condemned as a forger. Boileau had almost certainly bribed him.[13]

Satire V is an entertaining poem, but lacks substance. Addressed to the Marquis de Dangeau, one of Boileau's few friends at Court at this stage, it expounds the stock themes of the worthlessness of hereditary nobility if unaccompanied by virtue, with side swipes at heraldry, the lordly ways of impoverished nobles with their creditors, and the expedient of marriages with the daughters of rich self-made men. In form, it is a straightforward homily, enlivened by a rather mechanical example of Boileau's characteristic peripeties. He becomes passionate, imagines his audience's reaction, and falls into a dramatic dialogue with the listener:

> Il faut avec les grands un peu de retenue.
> Hé bien! je m'adoucis. Votre race est connue.
> Depuis quand? répondez. Depuis mille ans entiers,
> Et vous pouvez fournir deux fois seize quartiers:
> C'est beaucoup.
>
> (ll. 69–73)

Satire III is of a different order. It consists of a lively description of an absurd meal, at which a helpless guest is treated to equally grotesque food and conversation. It is one of the most comic of all Boileau's poems, in the sense of provoking laughter, and also, one would have thought, the most easily accessible. Indeed, comment would be superfluous, if it had not so often been misunderstood.

One of the results of the failure of late nineteenth- and early twentieth-century critics to take Boileau seriously was that they had to find strange reasons to account for the impression made by a poem like this. It used to be solemnly maintained that his merits lay in his realistic descriptions of seventeenth-century life and in his comments on contemporary authors. *Le Repas Ridicule* certainly describes 'low' objects in convincing detail:

> Deux assiettes suivaient, dont l'une était ornée
> D'une langue en ragoût, de persil couronnée;
> L'autre, d'un godiveau tout brûlé par dehors,
> Dont un beurre gluant inondait tous les bords.
>
> (ll. 49–52)

It also contains comments on a number of authors. But there is nothing documentary about it. The poem is a wild puppet-show of grotesques, heightened by the presence of the sane and baffled guest. His meeting with the first two other guests sets the tone:

> Deux nobles campagnards grands lecteurs de romans,
> Qui m'ont dit tout Cyrus dans leurs longs compliments.
> J'enrageais.
>
> (ll. 43–5)

Vile dish succeeds vile dish, to the ecstasy of the other guests, until a drunken singsong begins, only to be interrupted by another *entrée*:

Et la troupe à l'instant, cessant de fredonner,
D'un ton gravement fou s'est mise à raisonner.
(ll. 159–60)

Literary criticism becomes a fantasia of nonsense, emitted by a Daumier-like caricature:

un des campagnards relevant sa moustache,
Et son feutre à grands poils ombragé d'un panache,
Impose à tous silence, et d'un ton de docteur:
Morbleu! dit-il, La Serre est un charmant auteur!
Ses vers sont d'un beau style, et sa prose est coulante.
La Pucelle est encore une œuvre bien galante,
Et je ne sais pourquoi je baille en la lisant.
(ll. 173–9)

The effect is like that of a farce by Molière, and the satire is indeed in dialogue form. Two details show how little Boileau is soberly reflecting his view of life around him. The commentators are unable to decide which of the two interlocutors, A or P, is supposed to represent the poet. Of rather more significance is that the remarks on literature are hard to interpret. One of the idiot guests complains that the Alexandre of Racine's play is not like the heroes of Quinault. Is this praise of Racine, or an attack? Despite three centuries of commentary, it is impossible to tell: but this makes no difference to our enjoyment. Boileau is not describing cookery among social climbers, or reading a lecture on contemporary literature. His poem is theatre of the absurd, and its Dionysiac and liberating joy is its meaning.

5

Boileau said farewell to satire with two of his finest works. The order in which they were written is uncertain, but they both belong to around 1667/8. *Satire IX* was published in 1668, followed by a *Discours sur la Satire*. This was presumably written after the poem, but may conveniently be taken first.

Boileau's earlier critical works had been of various kinds. *Le Dialogue sur les Héros de Roman* was an amusing squib. The *Dissertation sur Joconde* (if indeed by Boileau, which is not certain) was weightier. It argued that the real touchstone of literary worth was the pleasure experienced by any critic of taste. This appeal to the essentially intuitive criterion of taste is at least similar to what we find in Boileau. The important translation of Longinus may have been in progress during these years,[14] but remained unpublished until 1674. The *Discours* is disappointing, if we are looking for revelations from a master of satire about the secrets of his art. There is no positive defence of satire as a corrector of morals or scourge of vice, no attempt to develop an extended theory. The *Discours* is short – less than half-a-dozen pages – and entirely defensive. Boileau had offended many by his satire, and was perhaps in real danger: at best, of *bastonnade* by some great person's bullies; at worst of the fate of Le Petit.[15] The *Discours* tries to show, from Latin and French precedents, that satirists have traditionally had licence to attack individuals and to name names.

Although this might seem to be all there is to say about the *Discours*, Boileau's choice of tactics perhaps deserves comment. He feigns surprise that grand personages should have taken offence at what are only quarrels among poets. This contradicts Boileau's usual proud claims for the importance of literature, but has a significance for his defensive manoeuvres:

Mais j'avoue que j'ai été un peu surpris du chagrin bizarre de certains lecteurs, qui, au lieu de se divertir d'une querelle du Parnasse, dont ils pouvaient être spectateurs indifférents, ont mieux aimé prendre parti, et s'affliger avec les ridicules, que de se réjouir avec les honnêtes gens.

The appeal is to social prejudices: important people (with the power to harm) should not bother about the quarrels of their inferiors; if they will side with Boileau against his enemies, however (and here Boileau slides neatly sideways), they will be putting themselves in the socially desirable category of the *honnêtes gens*. At the end, Boileau uses a similar tactic, but more insolently. People who admire the poets he attacks suffer from two defects. They are eccentric: 'Faudra-t-il, pour s'accommoder à leur goût particulier, renoncer au sens commun?', and, worse, they are old-fashioned: 'Il leur fâche d'avoir admiré sérieusement des ouvrages que mes satires exposent à la risée de tout le monde et de se voir condamnés à oublier, dans leur vieillesse, ces mêmes vers qu'ils ont autrefois appris par cœur comme des chefs-d'œuvre de l'art.' In a refined society, these are more embarrassing than more serious failings. Boileau is aiming to get the *honnêtes gens* on his side, and to shame his enemies into joining them.

The positive defence of satire comes in *Satire IX* itself:

> La satire, en leçons, en nouveautés fertile,
> Sait seule assaisonner le plaisant et l'utile,
> Et, d'un vers qu'elle épure aux rayons du bon sens,
> Détrompe les esprits des erreurs de leur temps.
> Elle seule, bravant l'orgueil et l'injustice,
> Va jusques sous le dais faire pâlir le vice,
> Et souvent sans rien craindre, à l'aide d'un bon mot,
> Va venger la raison des attentats d'un sot.
>
> (ll. 267–74)

This is largely traditional stuff, though it has a number of interesting features, not least Boileau's characteristic stress on 'nouveautés' and his surprisingly bold assertion that only satire can make palatable the traditional functions of poetry. But there are two points which call for emphasis. First, the tone is serious. (The lines that follow shortly afterwards are another matter. We shall come to them in a moment.) This seriousness is not always evident in Boileau, and is not the only tone he could choose. We may compare him with an English Augustan. When Pope makes a case for the usefulness of poetry in general, he does so in terms which provoke an equivocal response:

> Of little use the man you may suppose,
> Who says in verse what others say in prose;
> Yet let me show, a poet's of some weight,
> And (tho' no soldier) useful to the State.
> What will a child learn sooner than a song?
> What better teach a foreigner the tongue?
> . . .
> Let Ireland tell, how wit upheld her cause,
> Her trade supported, and supplied her laws
> . . .
> Not but there are, who merit other palms;
> Hopkins and Sternhold glad the heart with Psalms;
> The boys and girls whom charity maintains,
> Implore your help in these pathetic strains:
> How could devotion touch the country pews,
> Unless the gods bestowed a proper Muse?
> Verse cheers their leisure, verse assists their work,
> Verse prays for peace, or sings down Pope and Turk.
> The silenced preacher yields to potent strain,

And feels that grace his prayer besought in vain,
The blessing thrills through all the lab'ring throng,
And Heav'n is won by violence of song.
                    (*Epistle to Augustus*, ll. 201–6, 221–2, 229–40)

The virtue of poetry for teaching languages (in a mock panegyric addressed to George II, who hated poetry and who according to his enemies had never bothered to learn English properly);
the praise of bad poets who turned the Psalms into metre; the
stress on the desirability of attacks on the Pope (in a poem by a
Roman Catholic called Pope): all are set in an ambiguous relation
to the emotional appeal of the last three lines.

If Boileau's lines have a more forthright tone than Pope's, the
view they put forward forthrightly is the same as Pope puts
forward ambiguously. They assert a direct and immediate social
function for poetry. Modern critics are often shy of admitting
that a poet's work may be affected by the belief that it performs a
real social function, but seventeenth- and eighteenth-century
critics were not. This belief seems important to Boileau. It is
implicit in *Satire I*, and becomes very strong in his late verse.
It forms an important element in neo-classical theory – indeed,
perhaps the cardinal element in neo-classicism, in that it provides
the justification for poetry in the face of those forces in seventeenth-
century culture which regarded literature with suspicion, as un-
truthful and immoral. We shall return to this point in connection
with the *Art Poétique*.

If this were all there were to his poetry, Boileau might not be of
much interest now, except as a historical curiosity: but there is
much more. As he continues *Satire IX* he moves onto a different
tack:

> C'est ainsi que Lucile, appuyé de Lélie,
> Fit justice en son temps des Cotins d'Italie.
>   (ll. 275–6)

This brings together strands which were separate in the *Discours*,
and introduces a new one. The satirist appeals to tradition; he
brings in the argument of social snobbery. The Roman aristocrats
supported Lucilius: the French aristocrats should support Boileau,
and so assimilate themselves to the Roman heroes. The 'Cotins
d'Italie' are shown as trivial in comparison with Boileau/Lucilius,
and, in the next couplet, with Boileau/Horace.

These lines also show, in a relatively muted form, a characteristic movement in the poem: what starts as a grave theme (the
moral worth of satire) slides into the ridiculous (the 'Cotins
d'Italie'). What follows repeats the same movement more vio-
lently, to farcical effect. Boileau introduces a statement of personal emotion, his own real emotion, or that of his persona:

> C'est elle qui, m'ouvrant le chemin qu'il faut suivre,
> M'inspira des quinze ans la haine d'un sot livre;
> (ll. 279–80)

and then goes on to speak, in almost religious terms, of his vow.
But then he decides to unsay his vow, and to calm his enemies:

> Puisque vous le voulez, je vais changer de style.
> Je le déclare donc: Quinault est un Virgile;
> Pradon comme un soleil en nos ans a paru.
> (ll. 287–9)

The hyperbole is grotesque, if we think of the reverence in
which Virgil was held; it is rather more than grotesque, if we
remember that Louis XIV was the 'sun' of official propaganda.
Then the praise of bad authors comes pattering out, to the dismay
of his 'Esprit' (l. 294), and the whole procedure explodes into
farce:

> Mais ne voyez-vous pas que leur troupe en furie
> Va prendre encor ces vers pour une raillerie?
> (ll. 295–6)

Nonsense gathers into a crescendo, and culminates in a wild
cacophony:

> Qui méprise Cotin n'estime point son roi,
> Et n'a, selon Cotin, ni Dieu, ni foi, ni loi.
> (ll. 305–6)

Here, surely, is one secret of the poem's life. It is constantly
being serious: it is studded with short passages whose power and
conviction are unmistakable. But, each time, the equilibrium tips,
and the poet is carried away on a torrent of farce. Boileau's
'Esprit' cannot rise to 'le Belge effrayé fuyant sur ses remparts'
(l. 42) without falling into the absurdity of 'Cotin et moi, qui
rimons au hasard' (l. 45). Boileau's satire may win fame at the
price of danger (ll. 79–86), but this leads to the ludicrous picture
of the dead epics rotting away in the bookshops:

Laissez mourir un fat dans son obscurité.
Un auteur ne peut-il pourrir en sûreté?
Le Jonas inconnu sèche dans la poussière;
Le David imprimé n'a point vu la lumière;
Le Moïse commence à moisir par les bords.
Quel mal cela fait-il? Ceux qui sont morts sont morts.

(ll. 89–94)

Boileau's enemies may talk sense when they say he is intemperate, 'croit régler le monde au gré de sa cervelle' (thinks he can order the world to his fancy), and imitates Horace (ll. 120–8), but they fall into absurdity when they say that Juvenal had attacked Cotin's sermons (l. 129). A poet might reasonably write an ode in the manner of Malherbe (ll. 251–4), but the references to the 'alarmed' waters of the Jordan and 'picking' the palms of Idumaea (ll. 255–6) propel us into the fantasy-world of complete nonsense:

Viendrai-je, en une églogue, entouré de troupeaux,
Au milieu de Paris enfler mes chalumeaux,
Et, dans mon cabinet assis au pied des hêtres,
Faire dire aux échos des sottises champêtres?

(ll. 257–60)

Boileau's art has a richness here which is often underestimated, perhaps because we no longer admit to a taste for grandiloquence. I do not think we can simply say that in his references to 'le Belge effrayé' and the 'phrases de Malherbe' Boileau is mocking grand language. Mockery is certainly present, but there is also a relish for sounding phrases which comes out in much seventeenth-century literature, and in Boileau himself. In *Satire IX*, if we cannot feel the love of grandiloquence which accompanies the mockery of the grand phrases, some details indicate its presence. The lines about 'Bellone' and 'le Belge' (ll. 41–2) are accompanied by Boileau's note about the King's conquest of Lille. This would have been tactless if only mockery was intended. The phrases about the Danube, Sion and Memphis (ll. 252–4) are specifically associated with Malherbe, and Boileau expressed elsewhere his admiration for Malherbe, especially the Malherbe who 'd'un héros peut vanter les exploits' (can praise a hero's exploits) (*L'Art Poétique*, I, l. 17). Rightly used, these phrases represent resources of *la grande poésie*. Greatness crumbles in the hands of fools. If we care for greatness, this is more than a joke.

The passage in *Satire IX* that set us on this line of thought
(ll. 275–6) also introduces the appeal to social snobbery. 'Social
responsibility' might better represent the seriousness of the attitudes set out in the poem. At one level, Boileau is getting the
reader on his side by flattery:

> Un auteur à genoux, dans une humble préface,
> Au lecteur qu'il ennuie a beau demander grâce;
> Il ne gagnera rien sur ce juge irrité,
> Qui lui fait son procès de pleine autorité.
>
> (ll. 187–90)

More subtly, the reader's power surpasses that of the greatest
of Ministers or the official organs of culture:

> En vain contre le Cid un ministre se ligue:
> Tout Paris pour Chimène a les yeux de Rodrigue,
> L'Académie en corps a beau le censurer:
> Le public révolté s'obstine à l'admirer.
>
> (ll. 231–4)

These famous and beautiful lines do more than flatter. They
also appeal to the reader to show independence. As such, they
form part of the poem's emphasis on moral strenuousness. It
sounds this note lightly in the first lines: the tone is humorous, but
the subject is moral self-examination:

> C'est à vous, mon esprit, à qui je veux parler.
> Vous avez des défauts que je ne puis céler.
>
> (ll. 1–2)

Later, the poem insists on Boileau's moral probity, which 'sait
de l'homme d'honneur distinguer le poète' (knows how to distinguish the man of honour from the poet) (l. 212). In this context
come the lines on Richelieu and *Le Cid*, then the defence of satire.
The final serious movement of the poem, before the last humorous
descent, stresses this theme of moral independence:

> Non, pour louer un roi que tout l'univers loue,
> Ma langue n'attend point que l'argent la dénoue,
> Et, sans espérer rien de mes faibles écrits,
> L'honneur de le louer m'est un trop digne prix.
>
> (ll. 311–14)

Elements in the poem recall *Satire VII*, and show the development of Boileau's art. The list of bad poets clearly recalls the similar list in *Satire VII*:

> Que vous ont fait Perrin, Bardin, Pradon, Hainaut,
> Colletet, Pelletier, Titreville, Quinault,
> Dont les noms en cent lieux, placés comme en leurs niches,
> Vont de vos vers malins remplir les hémistiches?
> *(Satire IX*, ll. 97–100)
> Faut-il d'un froid rimeur dépeindre la manie?
> Mes vers comme un torrent coulent sur le papier:
> Je rencontre à la fois Perrin et Pelletier,
> Bonnecorse, Pradon, Colletet, Titreville.
> *(Satire VII*, ll. 42–5)

Both lists were changed in various revisions of the poems, and have given the commentators much trouble. Some critics have been surprised at the obscurity of some of the names: the identity of Titreville, in fact, has never been solidly established. Boileau has also been criticised for his apparent irresponsibility in substituting names to suit the enmities of the moment. Both criticisms seem to me misconceived. Boileau is taking off into flights of nonsense (or, better, of absurdity, because his nonsense is bitterly serious). He needs names which represent current folly, but which at the same time are more universal. The technique is that of Beckett, when Lucky invokes the scientists and philosophers in *En Attendant Godot*: Voltaire figures alongside the plausible-sounding Steinweg and Peterman and the farcical Testu and Conard. Boileau is creating a phantasmagoria of dunces, using real names (Boursault), deformations of real names (Kainaut), or possibly real but certainly obscure names (what Boudhors calls 'l'introuvable Titreville' – the unfindable Titreville). The flight of fancy is the same in both Beckett and Boileau.

Satire IX, however, shows a greater sophistication than *Satire VII*. As in *Satire VII*, the method is dramatic. (Indeed, the poem begins and ends like a play.) In *Satire VII*, Boileau addresses his Muse, who is fictionally a different and higher being. *Satire IX* is addressed to his 'Esprit', a word which means much more than the modern 'wit', and in seventeenth-century usage often means 'mind'.[16] Boileau is arraigning his own mind – the sum of his mental faculties – and this prepares us for the serious elements in the poem. At the same time, the 'Esprit' is given a more intemperate energy than the Muse. The technique is that of the music-hall routine of the ventriloquist with a dummy which takes on an anarchic life of its own. In *Satire IX*, as in the music-hall, the dialogue starts with apparent seriousness, but keeps sliding into nonsense tinged with violence. The final movement brings this out clearly. Boileau fears physical assault. His 'Esprit' is undaunted. Boileau tries to reason, then stops his 'Esprit' from speaking: the dummy has gone too far, and is thrust back, protesting, into its box:

Qui peut... – Quoi? – Je m'entends. – Mais encor? – Taisez-vous.
(l. 322)

Satire IX shows Boileau's powers near their height. It shows his seriousness more profound, and his farce wilder, than ever before. It contains these opposites in a dramatic structure, and with a constant movement between seriousness and anarchy. Like drama, the poem proceeds largely by dialogue. Like drama again, the way it gets its effects is by playing on the constant involvement and tension between the performer and the audience conceived as a social unit, not as solitary individuals. The implicit function seems to be partly to encourage moral uprightness, partly to promote social cohesion. Indeed, perhaps the latter includes the former. To encourage social cohesion is to reinforce the values shared by society, and is thus in itself a moral act. At the same time, the evoking of this interaction between performer and audience gives pleasure. It therefore satisfies that other grand imperative of neo-classical doctrine, that poetry should please. In the audience's reaction to *Satire IX*, the apparently separate demands of neo-classical doctrine are reconciled. Laughter directed against vice is an act of social utility. The shared laughter of an audience is an act of social solidarity.

6

Satire VIII is almost as brilliant, but will be treated only briefly. As in *Satire IV*, Boileau is here apparently attacking Reason and proclaiming the wisdom of instinct. The dramatic element is strong, and much of the poem consists of dialogue or pseudo-dialogue. There is more than a suspicion of deliberate paradox.

Man is contrasted with the animals (ll. 23–34), but at the end an ass is made to say that Man is only an animal (l. 308), with a play on the meanings of 'bête' (both 'animal' and 'stupid').

Boileau's characteristic subtlety in presenting intellectual and emotional positions forcefully and then balancing them with equally powerful opposite positions is here perhaps less interesting than the unorthodoxy of some of the positions he appears to favour. His attacks on the traditional view of Man as affiliated to God by Reason had given Cotin and others weapons against him, and here he reiterates his paradoxes in a still more disturbing fashion. Reason is opposed to Wisdom. Man does not have Wisdom: he is inconsistent (ll. 35–54) and goes against nature to torment himself and his fellows (ll. 65–160). Man's trouble is said to be Reason, but it turns out to be the unreasonable behaviour into which listening to Reason can lead him:

> Réglé par ses avis, fait tout à contre-temps,
> Et dans tout ce qu'il fait n'a ni raison ni sens.
> Tout lui plaît et déplaît, tant le choque et l'oblige;
> Sans raison il est gai, sans raison il s'afflige.
>
> (ll. 253–6)

This ambiguity does not come from his Latin predecessors. Various details echo passages from Horace, Juvenal and Persius, but the over-all effect is of a poem addressing itself directly to contemporary French society. As well as attacks on such generalised figures as the complaisant husband or the miser, there are lively assaults on the money-minded (with perhaps a concealed attack on Colbert) in lines 181–230, and on medicine and the law in lines 135–50, 173–4, 291–2, and 295–302. Other attacks are harder to evaluate. One of the most memorable passages is the denunciation of Alexander the Great, 'cet écervelé qui mit l'Asie en cendre' (that half-wit who set Asia on fire) (l. 100). This seems to represent Boileau's personal view, as it recurs in other works and is not a seventeenth-century commonplace. Under Louis XIV it could appear offensive to the régime, but the classical guise here perhaps provides a slight cover: Boileau avoids any explicit contemporary application. The poem's attitude to theologians – another dangerous topic – is more ambiguous still. The 'Docteur' who studies the Bible and presents his work to a rich ignoramus seems to be described sympathetically, but it is difficult to believe that Boileau or his audience admired Duns Scotus (l. 229). The conclusion that 'un Docteur n'est qu'un sot' (a scholar is only a fool) (l. 230) may be ironic, but, as so often in Boileau, is double-edged.

These ambiguities, and the moral fervour that nevertheless is the main impression left by the poem, are often interpreted as reflecting the tone of the Lamoignon circle, which Boileau began to frequent at this time. Whether or not this is true, *Satire VIII* points to a change in emphasis in Boileau's work, which formally is marked most obviously by a change from the *Satire* to the *Épître*.

4

The early Epistles

When in 1696 Madame de Maintenon referred to the *Épître sur l'Amour de Dieu* as 'la satire de Despréaux', she showed the difficulty of drawing a line between Boileau's Satires and Epistles. Several of the Satires are cast in the form of epistles to named people; many of the Epistles are strongly satirical, and most contain satirical passages. Nevertheless, there is an implied difference between them, and Boileau's change of direction from the Satire to the Epistle seems to mark a step in his evolution.

Put crudely, the biographical explanation usually given is that the change is from rebel to establishment figure. There is clearly something in this. As we saw in Chapter 2, importance is often attributed to Boileau's introduction into Lamoignon's circle. On the social plane, the significance of this is hard to estimate. Boileau had had friends in high social circles before this, but among the more raffish members of the aristocracy rather than the staider *noblesse de robe*. (The letter of 1676 recalling how the Duc de Vivonne used to visit him is famous: 'Êtes-vous encore ce même grand seigneur qui venait souper chez un misérable poète, et y porteriez-vous sans honte vos nouveaux lauriers au quatrième étage?')[1] He was soon to move in more exalted circles still, but the tone of the group around Madame de Montespan was perhaps closer to that of his young days than to that of the Hôtel de Lamoignon.

From the religious point of view, it is also difficult to see the significance of Lamoignon's influence. Lamoignon himself was a man of some tolerance, at least in his social habits. His visitors included Jesuits and Jansenist sympathisers, and he apparently relished the gibes of free-thinking *érudits* like Gui Patin against *les moines*.[2] On the other hand, he was a member of the Compagnie du Saint Sacrament, and had the reputation of a *dévot*. He could be plausibly represented as one of Molière's models for

Tartuffe,[3] and played a rôle in attempting to suppress the play. Boileau's attitude seems to have been ambiguous. He remained friendly with both Molière and Lamoignon, despite the affair of *Tartuffe*. In the *Avis au Lecteur* prefixed to *Le Lutrin*, he says of Lamoignon: 'l'accès obligeant, qu'il me donna dans son illustre maison, fit avantageusement mon apologie contre ceux qui voulaient m'accuser alors de libertinage et de mauvaises mœurs'.[4] Socially and religiously, it may have been this guarantee of respectability that he valued in Lamoignon's friendship.

More important for my purpose is the apparent change about this time in Boileau's assumptions about the function of poetry. We can all probably agree that the change is in the way in which the Epistles approach the traditional tasks of 'pleasing' and 'instructing'. The *Satires* had instructed negatively, by attacking vice or folly. The *Épîtres* usually appear to aim at putting forward some positive view. The *Satires* please by their verve and malice. The *Épîtres* on the whole try to adopt a more urbane tone. But these generalisations take us only a little way. We need to look at the poems in detail, and then the matter appears more complex.

One element in the background is evident. If we accept Brody's reasoning from the evidence, Boileau was working on his translation of Longinus from at least about 1664, and had finished it perhaps in 1667.[5] In about the latter year he presumably began work on *L'Art Poétique*. There are traces of Boileau's preoccupation with this ongoing work in several of the early *Épîtres*; conversely, study of these *Épîtres* can throw light on what Boileau is doing in his translation and in *L'Art Poétique*.

This chapter will concentrate on the most important of them: *Épître I* and *Épître IV*. Between these two, it will be convenient to consider, in the order of their composition, *Épître III*, *Épître II* and the prose *Arrêt Burlesque*, not just because of their intrinsic merits but because of the light they throw on Boileau's other works. The last in the series is *Épître V*, written in 1674, the year of the publication of *L'Art Poétique*.

2

The history of *Épître I* (*Au Roi*) is complicated, and almost justifies Boileau's claim to be bad at flattery. Presumably written in

1668, after the treaty of Aix-la-Chapelle, it praises (in the words of its traditional sub-title) 'les avantages de la paix'. When it appeared in 1670, it was out of tune with the gathering mood of resentment against Holland and desire for military glory. It was severely criticised on literary grounds as well. Eventually Boileau revised it extensively, rewriting the ending and cutting out or modifying many of the earlier lines. It is uncertain whether Louis XIV took any notice of the poem. No sign of official favour appeared.

Whether or not Boileau intended the poem as flattery of the King, it is complex in its effect, and altogether a fascinating piece. It shows one of the most common impulses in Boileau's work: the desire to produce original and striking effects. He has so often been presented as the poet of common sense that it is worth stressing the value he placed on the extraordinary: he must 'sortir de la route vulgaire' (leave the common road) (l. 14) and write 'des vers tout neufs' (entirely novel verses) (l. 17). One of the ways in which he sought to be striking was to use the high style even on 'low' subjects. Many years later, in a letter to Maucroix, he was to praise himself for saying in this Epistle 'noblement et avec cette élégance qui fait proprement la poésie'[6] that the King had encouraged the manufacture of lace:

> nos voisins frustrés de ces tributs serviles
> Que payait à leur art le luxe de nos villes.
> (ll. 141–2)

Love of ingenuity frequently appears in his work, as well as a strain of bombast at the expense of truth or consistency. This strain appears in the revised final passage of the Epistle, when he addresses the King thus:

> Qui ne sent point l'effet de tes soins généreux?
> L'univers sous ton règne a-t-il des malheureux?
> Est-il quelque vertu, dans les glaces de l'Ourse,
> Ni dans les lieux brûlés où le jour prend sa source,
> Dont la triste indigence ose encore approcher,
> Et qu'en foule tes dons d'abord n'aillent chercher?
> . . .
> Un Auguste aisément peut faire des Virgiles.
> (ll. 151–6, 174)

His originality comes out in *Épître I* in three more significant ways, two of which seem the result of conscious calculation, and the third of which perhaps results from more obscure characteristics of his mind.

The first way is by striking deliberately independent attitudes. Commentators have sometimes seen the poem as an attempt to capitalise on the successes of Colbert's peace policy, and have criticised Boileau's timing. I am not sure that this is justified. Whether or not Colbert is thought of as favouring peace (he was to support, for commercial reasons, the Dutch war of 1672),[7] Boileau's attitude seems intentionally provocative. The attack on conquerors (ll. 95–102) recalls the passage on Alexander in *Satire VIII* (ll. 100–12); it also looks forward to *Épître V* (ll. 45–50) and the passage on conquerors in *Satire XI* (ll. 75–90). Something similar appears also in his prose: *L'Arrêt Burlesque* refers to Alexander as 'le feu roi de querelleuse mémoire' (the late king, of quarrelsome memory).[8] All this corresponds either to a conviction held by Boileau himself, or to one which he deliberately puts forward as part of his persona. In *Épître I*, we shall find plenty of indications that Boileau goes beyond praising the advantages of peace and attacks war as such, sometimes in terms insulting to the King. Conquerors 'Entre les grands héros...sont les plus vulgaires' (are the most common among great heroes) (l. 97), even if they are Bourbons (l. 100). Moreover, when Boileau came to revise his poem, his new ending did not do anything to praise war, and he retained the most savage attacks on wars of conquest.

Boileau's revisions bear on the question of the second way in which he seeks originality. This is by mixing grandiosity with deliberate familiarity of tone. The mixture shocked contemporaries. Not only does Boileau address the King in a very familiar fashion (ll. 35–6, for example), but he also mixes with his sounding phrases amusing gibes at other poets and (in the first version) a fable about Justice and the Oyster. Criticisms of this flouting of literary decorum are said to have made him revise the poem. Modern critics have on the whole agreed with Boileau's contemporaries about the fable. The other lines cut out are also partly 'low' in seventeenth-century terms, with their references in plain language to plain economic facts, yet partly in the *style noble*:

O que j'aime à les voir, de ta gloire troublés,
Se priver follement du secours de nos blés,
Tandis que nos vaisseaux, partout maîtres des ondes,
Vont enlever pour nous les trésors des deux mondes.

In the first version, Boileau expressed in advance his awareness of such reactions, and explained his purpose:

Mais quoi! J'entends déjà quelque austère critique
Qui trouve en cet endroit la fable un peu comique.

This shows at least that the mixture was deliberate, and he goes on to imply that the function of the Epistle is to help the King unwind.

It is difficult to know whether Boileau's third way of being original was part of a conscious strategy or not. One of the mysteries about the workings of creativity is how far conscious intentions appear in the completed work. In any case, my concern is with the work itself rather than its writer's psychology, and this third way of achieving originality is the one which gives *Épître I* its enduring vitality: the way in which its structure is used to express its meaning.

The opening lines are subtly balanced:

Grand roi, c'est vainement qu'abjurant la satire
Pour toi seul désormais j'avais fait vœu d'écrire.
Dès que je prends la plume, Apollon éperdu
Semble me dire: Arrête, insensé; que fais-tu?
Sais-tu dans quels périls aujourd'hui tu t'engages?
Cette mer où tu cours est célèbre en naufrages.
(ll. 1–6).

The emphasis on 'Grand roi' is at once answered by the stress on 'satire' as the rhyme-word. Boileau then represents himself in line 2 as making the semi-religious 'vœu' to write only for the King; but the alliteration of 'vais' and 'vœu' links back to 'vainement' in line 1. In the following lines, the prosaic 'Dès que je prends la plume' (l. 3) is followed by the intervention of Apollo, with his direct address to the poet. This direct speech gives him some of the immediacy of the Homeric god. Perhaps the martial references in the next line and the evocation of the sea (with embarkation as well, in the initial version) owe something to the episode in Book II of the *Iliad*, in which Athene stops the Greek host departing.

Whether or not this is so, Apollo's appearance here has some of
the liveliness and dignity laid down for machines in *Chant III* of
L'Art Poétique. The references to 'périls' (l. 5) and to embarkation
are also thematic: they warn the poet, and by doing so both link
and contrast him with Louis XIV and his war-like exploits, and
with Pyrrhus (ll. 61–2).

Boileau then lays emphasis on the need to be original: he could
easily write pompous odes, as others do, but 'une raison sévère'
(a strict reason) (l. 13) means that he must seek new paths.
A further reason is that he is especially vulnerable to criticism, as
he has attacked others in his Satires, and now intends 'des bons
vers nous tracer le modèle' (to describe the model for good poetry)
(l. 22) – probably a reference to his work on *L'Art Poétique*.
He then points out that it is idle for a poet to admire his own
works if nobody else does (poetry is a social act), and here his
assumption of easy familiarity with the King comes in, rather as
in the *Discours au Roi*:

> Il est fâcheux, grand roi, de se voir sans lecteur.
> (l. 36)

The closing couplet of this passage was more concrete in its
original context than today:

> Je laisse aux plus hardis l'honneur de la carrière,
> Et regarde le champ, assis sur la barrière.
> (ll. 41–2)

'Carrière' in seventeenth-century usage retains its connotation of
the run made by a horseman in a tournament. Here, Boileau
presents himself 'assis sur la barrière' watching the tournament.
Louis XIV at this time delighted in mock-tournaments, such as
the famous *carrousel* of 1664. By association, the couplet shows us
Boileau in the position of the humble but admiring spectator, and
the King among the 'plus hardis'. But this is not its main meaning: the lines are clearly a reference to Boileau watching scorn-
fully the antics of the bad poets. The implied link between the
foolhardy poets and the King sets up a current of meaning which
goes against the ostensible aim of praising.

In the next movement, the image which Boileau picks out is
that of his watching the King from the sidelines: 'Des vertus de
mon roi spectateur inutile' (l. 46). His lines say that he will praise

the advantages of peace rather than the King's victories. The undertow of the verse goes against the surface movement, and produces a curious to-and-fro effect between praise and hinted blame, between the high style and the familiar. This is worth examining in detail.

Line 49 sets the oscillation going. To praise the King is a 'beau projet', and the note of uncertainty in 'projet' and the association of 'in vain' ('avoir beau') round the word 'beau' combine to suggest an element of doubt. This is compounded by the reference to Boileau's 'muse rebelle' at the end of the line. The muse is refusing to obey Boileau; but the association of 'rebelle' with the usual political meaning of rebellion against the King suggests a certain hostility of the poet to his fine (vain) project.

The tone then rises in an impressive line:

> La paix l'offre à mes yeux plus calme et plus serein.
>
> (l. 52)

Immediately, the tone changes to become Boileau confidential and man-to-man:

> Qui, grand roi, laissons là les sièges, les batailles.
>
> (l. 53)

The other poets who praise Louis's wars are shrugged aside with colloquial scorn: 'Qu'un autre aille en rimant renverser les murailles' (l. 54), and Boileau blandly dissociates the King from their antics: 'sur tes pas marchant sans ton aveu' (following in your footsteps without your permission) (l. 55). They are so daft that they get themselves covered 'de sang, de poussière et de feu' (with blood, dust and fire) (l. 56), which is also just what heroes do. In a line that combines colloquialism with the epic style: 'A quoi bon, d'une muse au carnage animée' (l. 57), their muse is turned into a comic virago. The next line introduces a rebuke to the King under the guise of a compliment: his 'valeur' (courage) is 'déjà trop allumée' (already too much on fire). But because of the way in which Boileau has manoeuvred the situation, it is hard for the King to take offence. Boileau assumes that, just as they have laughed together at the bad poets, they will now as men of good sense sit down to enjoy the good things of life:

> Jouissons à loisir du fruit de tes bienfaits,
> Et ne nous lassons point des douceurs de la paix.
>
> (ll. 59–60)

After this, we have one of the liveliest passages in the poem, the story of Pyrrhus and the counsellor who tries to dissuade him from wars of conquest:

> Pourquoi ces éléphants, ces armes, ce bagage,
> Et ces vaisseaux tout prêts à quitter le rivage?
> Disait au roi Pyrrhus un sage confident,
> Conseiller très sensé d'un roi très imprudent.
> Je vais, lui dit ce prince, à Rome où l'on m'appelle. –
> Quoi faire? – L'assiéger. – L'entreprise est fort belle,
> Et digne seulement d'Alexandre ou de vous:
> Mais, Rome prise enfin, seigneur, où courons-nous? –
> Du reste des Latins la conquête est facile. –
> Sans doute on les peut vaincre: est-ce tout? – La Sicile
> De là nous tend les bras; et bientôt sans effort,
> Syracuse reçoit nos vaisseaux dans son port. –
> Bornez-vous là vos pas? – Dès que nous l'aurons prise,
> Il ne faut qu'un bon vent, et Carthage est conquise.
> Les chemins sont ouverts: qui peut nous arrêter? –
> Je vous entends, seigneur, nous allons tout dompter:
> Nous allons traverser les sables de Libye,
> Asservir en passant l'Égypte, l'Arabie,
> Courir delà le Gange en de nouveaux pays,
> Faire trembler le Scythe aux bords du Tanaïs,
> Et ranger sous nos lois tout ce vaste hémisphère;
> Mais, de retour, enfin, que prétendez-vous faire? –
> Alors, cher Cinéas, victorieux, contents,
> Nous pourrons rire à l'aise, et prendre du bon temps. –
> Hé! seigneur, dès ce jour, sans sortir de l'Épire,
> Du matin jusqu'au soir qui vous défend de rire?
>
> (ll. 61–86)

The setting is the seashore, with Pyrrhus' ships about to embark. The setting (and the rhymes 'bagage'/'rivage') recall Apollo's intervention to stop Boileau embarking on praise of the King in lines 3–6, with its rhymes 't'engage'/'naufrage'. As in line 4 Boileau was 'insensé', so here the counsellor is 'très-sensé' (l. 64). By implication, Boileau is now the wise counsellor (converted by Apollo, the inspiration of poetry) restraining the 'roi très-imprudent' (Pyrrhus/Louis) from embarking on another 'beau projet': 'L'entreprise est fort belle' (l. 66). The following lines include some in the *style noble*: 'Faire trembler le Scythe aux bords du

Tanaïs,/Et ranger sous nos lois tout ce vaste hémisphère' (ll. 80–1). The dominant tone, however, is sprightly and colloquial, with enjambement and conversational rhythms; and Boileau revised them several times to get their easy flow just right. The moral is pointed sharply, with a change of register from the safe distance of history to the abuses of Louis's own Court:

> Le conseil était sage et facile à goûter.
> Pyrrhus vivait heureux s'il eût pu l'écouter;
> Mais à l'ambition d'opposer la prudence,
> C'est aux prélats de cour prêcher la résidence.
>
> (ll. 87–90)

This jolt is intended to bring the lesson home to the King, as is evident from Boileau's haste in the next lines to praise him for what he was himself most proud of: his application to *le métier de roi*. This passage of praise, however, is salted with another compliment of decided ambiguity. Among heroes, conquerors 'sont les plus vulgaires' (are the most common) (l. 97), and among these 'La Seine a des Bourbons' (l. 100). True, the Bourbons are paralleled by the Caesars, but also by the 'goths, vandales, gépides' who issue from the 'fanges Méotides' (marshes of the Mæotis) (ll. 101–2). To the classically minded and aristocratic society of seventeenth-century France, these associations were in all probability more insulting than they are to us. Nor is Boileau's equivocation in this passage yet over: he holds up to the King the example of Titus, but the last line of the paragraph introduces a note which, though perfectly in accord with his argument (there aren't many reigns like Titus'), has a sinister ring:

> Le cours ne fut pas long d'un empire si doux. (l. 115)

Again Boileau dances away from the point of danger. Of course, he needn't think about these remote historical references when Louis XIV is before his eyes (l. 116). The praise of Louis's moderation in victory appears firm and unambiguous, and may well have been sincere, though Boileau's preoccupation still seems to be with the novelty of his finding this subject for praise:

> Et c'est par là, grand roi, que je te veux louer.
> Assez d'autres, sans moi, d'un style moins timide,
> Suivront aux champs de Mars ton courage rapide.
>
> (ll. 124–6)

In the original version, the association of noble and familiar styles was kept up in a variant (already quoted) which followed the present line 142.

At this point, we come to a bifurcation between the earlier and revised version. The final version (from 1672 onwards) has forty lines of panegyric. They are certainly a skilful example of the *style noble*, often rising to real eloquence. One splendid line induces a little unease, as it seems not only false but also in contradiction to a more realistic line it recalls in *Satire I*:

> Un Auguste aisément peut faire des Virgiles
>> (*Épître I*, l. 174)
> Mais sans un Mécénas à quoi sert un Auguste?
>> (*Satire I*, l. 86)

Another fine line may have helped to germinate a finer line in *Athalie*:

> Des ans injurieux peut éviter l'outrage.
>> (l. 181; cf. *Athalie*, II, v, l. 496)

The end is modest and tactful, and shows Boileau using his reputation as a plain speaker to vouch to posterity for the honesty of his praise of the King. It is interesting also, as we shall note in connection with *L'Art Poétique*, that he contrasts the truth of history with the frankly incredible 'fables' (l. 185).

The original ending, however, may interest us still more, whatever fastidious critics, at the time and later, have thought of it. After a reference to Louis's reform of the law comes the fable of the oyster. The merits of these lines will be considered when we come to *Épître II*, together with the speculation that in them Boileau is trying to teach La Fontaine how to write fables. Here, its introduction may be in part due to a desire to flatter Lamoignon, who was associated with the King's legal reforms. But this can be only part of the reason. Its relevance to the Epistle is in its theme. Litigation is a form of warfare: 'la bataille' in line 49 of *Épître II*. The recommendation of Justice in the last line of the fable is, 'Vivez en paix.' (Live in peace.) This is nicely in keeping with a poem on the advantage of peace over war.

In the original version, the poem ended with the coda already noted, in which Boileau defended his use of 'la fable un peu comique'. The apology is clumsy, and the style sometimes clumsier still:

> Grand roi, je m'aperçois qu'il est temps de finir.
> C'est assez: il suffit.

The transition is nevertheless characteristic of Boileau, and of his poem. From the grand references to Horace, Augustus and Louis XIV, he comes back to contemporary satire: the Marquis who, 'plein d'un grand savoir chez les dames acquis' (full of great learning acquired among the ladies), reacts absurdly to *Tartuffe* and *Andromaque*. This recalls the transition in lines 87–90 from the story of Pyrrhus to 'les prélats de cour'. Although Boileau, with his customary deference to the public (especially his aristocratic admirers) rewrote the ending, his first version was carefully integrated with the themes and movement of the poem as a whole.

What, then, are we to make of *Épître I*? It is undoubtedly a fine poem, but I would like to draw attention to points in it which are often ignored. The epistolary form clearly seems intended to mix moral lessons with an agreeably urbane entertainment, as has often been remarked. But the deliberate mixture of high and low styles – one of the hallmarks of Boileau – seems intended to strike by its novelty, as do the independent views expressed. These are conscious strategies, and so partly is the advantage taken of the scope which this variety allows for making boldly critical points and then slipping away from them before the reader can take offence. In these ways, Boileau's technique allows him to perform the function of telling useful truths, but at the same time to please. That is, the poem is able to say things that could not otherwise be said without giving offence: even, perhaps, without danger to the poet. Less consciously, however, the structure of Boileau's poem, with its echoes of themes and words, its counterpointing of associative meanings against the prose meaning, is performing this function in a rather different sense. The poem's meaning is more than its ostensible message, and resides in the structure of its words and images. In this deeper sense, the function of the poem is to say what could not be said in any other way.

3

In *Épître III* (*Sur la Mauvaise Honte*) we see a new aspect of Boileau. It is one of the dullest of his poems, and has a subject which is easily summarised: a false sense of our dignity makes us choose the worse rather than the better path, and this is the real source of human misery. Much of the writing is slack, and over-loaded with feeble adjectives:

> Des superbes mortels le plus affreux lien,
> N'en doutons point, Arnauld, c'est la honte du bien.
> Des plus nobles vertus cette adroite ennemie
> Peint l'honneur à nos yeux des traits de l'infamie,
> Asservit nos esprits sous un joug rigoureux,
> Et nous rend l'un de l'autre esclaves malheureux,
> Par elle la vertu devient lâche et timide
>
> (ll. 15–21)

or inertly repetitive in its patterns:

> Le chardon importun hérissa les guérets,
> Le serpent venimeux rampa dans les forêts,
> La canicule en feu désola les campagnes,
> L'aquilon en fureur gronda sur les montagnes.
>
> (ll. 67–70)

Abstractions abound:

> L'avare, des premiers en proie à ses caprices,
> Dans un infâme gain mettant l'honnêteté,
> Pour toute honte alors compta la pauvreté:
> L'honneur et la vertu n'osèrent plus paraître;
> La piété chercha les déserts et le cloître.
>
> (ll. 78–82)

Not all the poem is as bad as this. But in these passages, *Épître III*, which was written at the beginning of the 1670s, looks forward to some of Boileau's last works. It is not an accident that in *Épître III* we already find the monotonous versification, the abuse of abstractions, the pedestrian narratives we find in *Épître XII* (*Sur l'Amour de Dieu*) and the last two *Satires*. The subject of the poem is indeed all too easy to summarise in a simple statement. Boileau himself does so:

> Des superbes mortels le plus affreux lien,
> N'en doutons point, Arnauld, c'est la honte du bien
> . . .
> C'est là de tous nos maux le fatal fondement.
>
> (ll. 15–16, 27)

All the rest is amplification and illustration. The devices of poetry are used to dress up a theme which could equally well be expressed in prose. The purpose of the exercise is to put over as effectively as possible a moral lesson. Boileau refers explicitly to his methods:

> Moi-même, Arnauld, ici, qui te prêche en ces rimes. . .
>
> (l. 86)

This is one very simple way of putting into practice the neoclassical precept that poetry should fulfil a moral purpose. And *Épître III* suggests a factor at work which favoured this simple interpretation. The poem is an attack on those, Protestants, freethinkers, or others, who by an act of personal judgment deny a truth vouched for by impersonal Reason or by authority:

> Oui, sans peine, au travers des sophismes de Claude,
> Arnauld, des novateurs tu découvres la fraude,
> Et romps de leurs erreurs les filets captieux.
>
> (ll. 1–3)

Hors de l'Église, point de salut: those who do not accept received doctrine are condemned as 'innovators'. The lines suggest a linking of moral and intellectual failings: unorthodox opinions are 'sophistries' and amount to 'fraud'. This illuminates the background to *L'Art Poétique*. Boileau is writing in the context of a dogmatic system which claims to possess the truth, and according to which failure to accept this truth is not simply a mistake, but a sign of intellectual muddle and wickedness.

4

Two minor works may be briefly noticed here. Though very different, both throw sidelights on Boileau's development at this time.

The first is the prose *Arrêt Burlesque*, a mock ruling by the Paris Parlement forbidding the teaching of non-Aristotelian doctrines in the university. It reminds us of the danger of accepting too easily some common generalisations about Boileau. At this stage of his career he was bent on becoming respectable: yet *L'Arrêt Burlesque* shows him attacking orthodoxy with brisk irreverence. His use of the word *raison* usually refers either to what is generally accepted, the *consensus gentium*, or to a quality of rightness in thought or expression which the sensitive critic intuitively recognises: yet in *L'Arrêt Burlesque*, 'la raison' is very much the Reason of the eighteenth-century *philosophes*. It is linked with experiment and with scientific discovery, and is opposed to the revived Scholasticism which underpinned the revived Catholicism of the Counter-Reformation Church. Scholasticism is condemned as no more than the use of meaningless words:

bannir des Écoles de Philosophie les formalités, matérialités, entités, virtualités, eccéités, Pétréités, Policarpéités, et autres êtres imaginaires, tous enfants et ayant cause de défunct Maître Jean Scot leur père. Ce qui porterait un préjudice notable, et causerait la totale subversion de la Philosophie Scolastique dont elles font tout le mystère, et qui tire d'elles toute sa subsistance.[9]

We are also accustomed to think of Boileau as an Ancient. Here, he is a Modern, preaching science and rationalism and mockingly presenting Reason as banned for being 'ami des nouveautés'.[10] This is far from the scorn of 'novateurs' in *Épître III*. Boileau's Modernism does not perhaps go very deep. In his various revisions he seems to lump together Cartesians and Gassendists, for example, as if they were much the same. Nevertheless, the Modernism is certainly there, and the piece has a decidedly Voltairean ring.

There is, however, an element in *L'Arrêt Burlesque* which marks it off from a squib such as *De l'Horrible Danger de la Lecture*, and which recalls not so much Voltaire as Rabelais. This is Boileau's delight in words, manifested in his tumbling synonyms and lists:

Fait défense au sang d'être plus vagabond, errer ni circuler dans le corps, sous peine d'être entièrement livré et abandonné à la Faculté de Médecine...Et en cas de guérison irrégulière par icelles drogues, permet aux médecins de ladite Faculté de rendre, suivant leur méthode ordinaire, la fièvre aux malades, avec casse, séné, sirops, juleps, at autres remèdes propres à ce; et de remettre lesdits malades en tel et semblable état qu'ils étaient auparavant; pour être ensuite traités selon les règles, et s'ils n'en réchappent, conduits du moins en l'autre monde suffisamment purgés et évacués.[11]

This exuberance is common in Boileau, as a manifestation of his emotional nature and joy in language. Twenty-five years later, we find it in his letter of 3 June 1693 to Racine, who had been canvassing for the preferment of one of Boileau's brothers:

M. l'Abbé Dongois est entré dans ma chambre avec le petit mot de lettre que vous écrivez à Madame Racine et où vous mandez l'heureux, surprenant, incroyable, prodigieux, ravissant, admirable, étonnant, charmant succès de votre négotiation.[12]

Épître II (*Contre les Procès*) provides a warning against accepting other generalisations. The first is the modern view that Boileau is not the promulgator of literary doctrines, but merely had the knack of expressing common opinions succinctly without really understanding them. *Épître II*, apparently referring to his work on *L'Art Poétique* at this time, is obviously to be taken only half-seriously when it complains of the difficulty of setting out the 'règles ennemies' for bad authors (l. 2), or of making them submit to Boileau's 'lois' (l. 3), which are based on Reason (l. 4), or of preaching 'la réforme au Parnasse' (l. 6). Nevertheless, the fact that these things can be said by Boileau, even half-humorously, in this way, suggests that there is something in them. The fable of the oyster has been seen as an attempt to demonstrate the rules of fable-writing ignored by La Fontaine. Critics have usually thought the fable unsuccessful. I am not sure about this: it reads amusingly enough, and Pope thought it worth translating, into a version which catches its brisk and dry humour exactly.[13] The very dryness of the style emphasises the point which Boileau is making: if a fable is to teach a moral lesson, it should be clear and direct. This suggests a different aesthetic from La Fontaine's, but fits very well with the emphasis on rules, reason and didacticism in the opening section of the poem.

This brings us to a second point worth making. We sometimes take too literally Boileau's statement in *Satire VII*: 'souvent j'habille en vers une maligne prose' (l. 61), and generalise it into a statement that he wrote his poems by deciding their prose sense and then dressing it up in verse. The assumption is that in *Épître II* Boileau is rhyming an introduction on the theme of litigation simply to avoid wasting the fable removed from *Épître I*. In Clarac's words, 'Obligé de détacher sa fable de l'épître au roi, il compose, pour la recueillir, au début de 1673, l'insignifiante épître II'.[14] Adam's view is similar: 'Mais parce qu'il tenait à sa fable, il imagina d'écrire, peu après 1674, une épître qui est, dans les recueils, la IIe, et où il introduit par une transition sans génie les vers qu'il ne se décidait pas à supprimer.'[15]

These interpretations of the circumstances may or may not be true, but they omit reference to the essential question, which is the thematic structure of *Épître II*. Boileau starts with the theme of his 'laws' and the 'reason' which informs them; he is going to 'reform' poetry, as Louis XIV and Lamoignon reformed the laws. Lignières then calls ('appelle', l. 9, and the verb brings to mind the legal term 'appeal') for a combat, a combat which is a form of trial. Boileau lets him 'Punir de mes défauts le papier innocent' (l. 16), words which again refer to legal processes. The poem then proceeds to preach the social virtue of a peaceful life, which leads naturally to the fable. The fable itself recommends not simply refraining from litigation, but peace, and rebukes foolishness: 'Des sottises d'autrui nous vivons au palais' (l. 51), a foolishness which is the opposite of the 'reason' of Boileau's 'laws'. The poem builds up a subtle structure of meaning round the opposites peace/strife, reason/folly. It springs from the same complex of ideas and emotions that lay at the root of *Épître I*. It is hardly surprising that the fable which helped to express this same meaning in *Épître I* now falls into place here.

5

In composing *Épître IV* to celebrate the French crossing of the Rhine in 1672, Boileau had some immediate objectives of which we can be fairly sure. One was to attract the favourable notice of the King. Another was to extend his range into a field of poetry nobler than either satire or the more informal type of Epistle. *Le Passage du Rhin* has affinities with epic, and in its use of machines it seems an experiment to test the theories in *Chant III* of *L'Art Poétique*. Apart from its intrinsic merits, *Le Passage du Rhin* is of special interest because of the questions it confronts head-on. How can poetry deal with a serious contemporary event? How can it invest modern history with the prestige of high poetry? How can the narrative of a contemporary event continue the tradition of Classical epic? What is the relationship of poetry and truth, and what implications does this relationship have for the use of poetic 'ornaments'?

The reputation of *Épître IV* has gone through many vicissitudes. In its own day it succeeded at Court, though it was much criticised for lack of elevation by Boileau's enemies. In the eighteenth and nineteenth centuries, opinion tended to stress more and more its stilted and artificial character: its serious elements came to seem pompous and contrived. Modern French scholars have usually seen it as a failure. Adam calls it 'cette pièce médiocre', and sees its light ending as the sign of 'une faiblesse d'inspiration qui ne réussit pas à s'élever sans effort et à se maintenir à une certaine hauteur de ton'.[16] Clarac's view is that 'l'épître guerrière annonce l'*Ode sur la prise de Namur*. Boileau n'avait la tête ni épique, ni lyrique.'[17] English and American critics have often stressed the playful element which is undoubtedly present in Boileau, even in his apparently solemn works, and *Épître IV*, which mixes lightness with solemnity, has benefited from this approach. The most brilliant examples of this approach have been provided by France.[18] His starting-point for his study of Boileau's poetry is the question which in my view is the really important question for Boileau: 'How does he reconcile his passion for truth with the fictions of his poetry?' In his analysis of *Épître IV*, France emphasises the tongue-in-cheek quality of the poem and sees the epic machinery as pastiche.[19]

France's view seems to me nearer the truth, but it avoids the problem of the poem's seriousness. The circumstantial evidence, for what it is worth, suggests that the poem was meant to be taken seriously. Apart from Boileau's wish to gain the King's favour, it would be strange if the serious parts were meant as burlesque, in a poem designed to be read at Court, among the friends and relatives of those killed in the fight. According to Brossette, Boileau turned to the real heroic of *Épître IV* as a relief from the mock heroic of *Le Lutrin*. Many of Boileau's contemporaries and their eighteenth-century successors seem to have taken the epic portions as an authentic attempt at the grand style. In the original *Avis au Lecteur*, Boileau refers humorously to 'l'histoire du fleuve en colère, que j'ai apprise d'une de ses naïades, qui s'est réfugiée dans la Seine', but it would be unjustifiable to take as mockery the following reference to the 'mânes de M. de Longueville' (spirit of M. de Longueville) and the 'plus illustre sang de l'univers' (most illustrious blood in the universe).

This *Avis au Lecteur* perhaps gives clues to the meaning of the poem, as France suggests, in that it not only mingles the serious with the self-deprecating but also touches on the question of truth in poetry. It is on these two aspects that the following discussion will concentrate.

The poem begins with Boileau's difficulties over writing a panegyric on the King's Dutch wars (ll. 1–38), and then (ll. 39–143) tells the story of the crossing of the Rhine: it ends humorously, with a wish (ll. 144–72) that Louis would make his conquests in Asia, where the names of the towns are more poetic. The crucial question is how far the epic central section aims at grandeur, and how far it is pastiche.

That Boileau echoes formulae from his butts Chapelain and Brébeuf proves nothing. It is clear enough that he agreed with Chapelain's aim of producing *la grande poésie*, using striking effects and tending to a moral end. What he objected to in Chapelain was the awkwardness of his style, his incongruous use of *pointes*, and his inability to vary his tone sufficiently to keep his readers awake. We should be hard put to it to criticise *Épître IV* on these grounds. Boileau's objections to Brébeuf were to his unreasonable exaggeration, 'qui regarde plus la pensée que les mots' (letter to Brossette, dated 9 October 1708).[20] Again, this is not a feature of *Épître IV*, at least in its serious portions. What does come out strongly in Boileau's poem is the imitation of Homer and Virgil, not only in the machinery but in individual lines. When he describes Louis XIV in terms borrowed from Homer: 'Il a de Jupiter la taille et le visage' (l. 57), it seems unlikely that he is joking, and I think the line remains impressive.

These things are a question of taste, but I find many of the lines authentically serious in their movement and phrasing:

> Le Rhin tranquille, et fier du progrès de ses eaux
> (l. 40)

> Sous les fougueux coursiers l'onde écume et se plaint
> (l. 124)

> Un bruit s'épand qu'Enghien et Condé sont passés.
> (l. 132)

This prompts an examination of the humorous sections.

Boileau's exordium does three things: it flatters the King (who can conquer faster than Boileau can write); it mocks the Dutch (by mocking the lack of euphony of Dutch place-names); and it provides a protective device against those who may mock Boileau or his departure from his earlier stance of attacking grandiloquent poets: 'Vous savez des grands vers les disgrâces tragiques' (l. 37).

The first of these three effects is clearly relevant to the poem as a whole, but so are the other two. The mockery of the Dutch reappears in the attack on their lack of courage (ll. 75–90). This leads up to the final turning-point of the poem:

> Du fleuve ainsi dompté la déroute éclatante
> A Wurts jusqu'en son camp va porter l'épouvante.
> Wurts, l'espoir du pays, et l'appui de ses murs;
> Wurts...Ah! quel nom, grand roi, quel Hector que ce Wurts!
> Sans ce terrible nom, mal né pour les oreilles,
> Que j'allais à tes yeux étaler de merveilles!
> Bientôt on eût vu Skink dans mes vers emporté
> De ses fameux remparts démentir la fierté;
> Bientôt...Mais Wurts s'oppose à l'ardeur qui m'anime.
> Finissons, il est temps...
>
> (ll. 141–50)

The Dutch (in fact, German) general is described in Homeric terms: 'l'espoir du pays, et l'appui de ses murs' (l. 143), but then Boileau exclaims that the name disqualifies him from being Hector. We perhaps forget too easily the scorn of royal, Catholic and aristocratic France for the republican, Protestant and bourgeois Dutch – their commerce, art and language all equally undignified. *Épître IV* is in part a satire against the Dutch, and in it Boileau is trying yet another 'voie nouvelle' by mingling high seriousness and satire. The mockery of the Dutch names forms one link between the serious section and the beginning and end. But Boileau's attitude is not simply scorn. In the last twenty lines of the poem, Dutch cacophony is contrasted with Classical euphony. But Asia, however 'en beaux mots partout riche et fertile' (everywhere rich and fertile in beautiful words) (l. 158), is nevertheless 'sèche et stérile' (dry and sterile) (l. 157), by comparison with the rich abundance of Holland evoked earlier, when Boileau had his river-god urge the Dutch:

. . .la faux à la main, parmi vos marécages,
Allez couper vos joncs, et presser vos laitages. . .

(ll. 89–90)

The language in which Boileau couches his praise of Asia, with its deliberately empty exaggerations (reminiscent of Brébeuf) of 'cent peuples altiers' (a hundred proud peoples) (l. 155) and 'des rimes à milliers' (rhymes in thousands) (l. 156) and its deflation of Classical grandeur: 'd'Ilion la poétique cendre' (the poetic cinders of Ilium) (l. 162), warns us not to take it solemnly. The closing expectation that Louis will arrive in triumph at the Hellespont in 1674 is obviously meant to raise a smile.

The attempt to insure in advance against hostile critics seems to me to derive from the same complex of emotions. It is in part a warning that the tone of the poem is mixed. It is also a sign that Boileau is using a device that often appears in his work: the rapid alternation between seriousness and apparent frivolity, so that the reader is continually forced to be alert in his responses. As so often this effect is compounded by Boileau's use of himself or his persona. We must hear about his troubles in fitting Dutch names into verse, but at the same time enjoy his virtuosity in doing so. We must be carried away into thinking that Louis is a Classical hero, but we must also see that he is not one (any more than Wurts is a Hector), and therefore recognise that it is absurd to expect him 'dans deux ans aux bords de l'Hellespont' (in two years on the banks of the Hellespont) (l. 172).

Our second theme is the poem's relation to truth. The *Avis au Lecteur* implies a direct relationship: poetry is history, and when the poet has more up-to-date information he will revise his poem. But the humorous reference to the naiad 'réfugiée dans la Seine' suggests something different: poetry has its own truth. In many ways (ignoring for the moment the machines), Boileau keeps very closely to the facts. Louis marches towards the Rhine, which is stormy (l. 55). He personally superintends the crossing (ll. 97–9), and the names of those who crossed are given. There is nothing exaggerated in this, even if Boileau did not have full information: at least one modern historian has given as much credit to the King as Boileau does.[21] The poem even mentions, at the price of some awkwardness, the King's provision of boats (ll. 115–16). We may compare the poem with the prose *Éloge*

Historique du Roi sur ses Conquêtes depuis l'année 1672 jusqu'en 1678, which Racine composed in 1684, possibly with Boileau's help.[22] The prose if anything exaggerates more than the poem, and omits the prosaic detail about the boats.

Despite this care for the truth, there is evidence of Boileau's desire to distance his subject-matter, to lift it into a more timeless realm. This is, of course, evident in his use of the usual devices of the *style noble*: 'mousquet' for 'fusil', 'coursiers' for 'chevaux'. It perhaps comes out in the use of the classical-looking 'Tholus' for the Tolhuis of geography (and of the *Éloge Historique*). More obviously still, it comes out in the use of epic machinery, to which we will come later. But Boileau has taken precautions against those who may find this elevation incongruous. Just as lines 37–8 try to pre-empt the criticism that he is now attempting what he attacked in others, so the first part of this introduction to the serious central section of the poem emphasises the artificial heightening he is using:

> Muses, pour le tracer, cherchez tous vos crayons:
> Car, puisqu'en cet exploit tout paraît incroyable,
> Que la vérité pure y ressemble à la fable,
> De tous vos ornements vous pouvez l'égayer.
> (ll. 32–5)

The opposition between 'vérité' and 'fable', and the implication that history is truth and poetry is fable, are interesting for Boileau's conception of poetry, as we shall see in his discussion of epic in *L'Art Poétique*.

We now come to the use of machinery, which has so often been attacked. Its first function seems clear: to dignify the subject-matter. The device of a river-god who takes human form to encourage the Dutch was perhaps more appealing in the seventeenth century, which was used to the convention of applying the trappings of Classical mythology to contemporary figures in poetry, painting and sculpture. It may have seemed especially appealing to Boileau, with his love of Homer and Virgil and his sense of the Classical tradition. We may be more favourably disposed to his solution if we consider the importance of the aesthetic problem he faced. Modern literature often stresses documentary accuracy, but the artist still needs to generalise and heighten it in some way, to remove it from mere imitation of the surfaces of life and to give it some wider significance. Some of the modern devices are at least no more successful than Boileau's, and in principle they are often similar.

Although this seriousness is present, there is another aspect brought out by France when he refers to pastiche. The introduction of the Rhine god has touches of humour: he is sleeping 'au bruit flatteur de son onde naissante' (to the flattering sound of his nascent stream) (l. 42); he is described, accurately but with some lack of dignity, as an 'humide roi' (damp king) (l. 47). There is a note of petulance in his annoyance at Louis's past and present victories (ll. 63–8). France singles out the following lines:[23]

> A ces mots essuyants sa barbe limoneuse,
> Il prend d'un vieux guerrier la figure poudreuse.
> Son front cicatrisé rend son air furieux.
>
> (ll. 69–71)

But I doubt if pastiche is quite the word. We need to savour the sly humour, but not at the expense of taking the grandeur as a joke. The address of the Rhine god to the Dutch is followed by one of Boileau's striking lines:

> La honte fait en eux l'effet de la valeur.   (l. 96)

Boileau then passes straight on to 'Louis en personne' and the nobles who led the crossing – some of whom died. It is hard to see all this as mockery.

There is, in fact, a doubleness about the whole epic passage. And here, I think, we see one source of the life of the poem. The humorous opening section is joking about the very serious matter of Louis's conquests. In doing so, it does the opposite of what it says it is doing: Boileau makes lively verse out of words he complains will not fit into verse. In the epic central section, the seriousness is real enough, but is flavoured with sly digs at the Rhine god, who in turn scolds the Dutch (ll. 86–90). The final section is ostensibly serious about Louis's further conquests and the superior virtues of Classical antiquity for poetry (so different from the intractable material of Holland). But in fact it is obviously a joke, and the sly digs are this time about Classical antiquity (with its sterile plains and poetic cinders). Boileau is

once again at his game of provoking differing responses in rapid
succession, and always moving on before we can feel settled
enough to reproach him. It is by these means – including his use of
epic machinery – that he is able to transpose the factual narrative
into the world of imagination, without being inaccurate, but at
the same time without being ridiculous or boring. I think this
shows poetic ability of a high order.

Indeed, it suggests a further point. Perhaps because of Boileau's
reputation as a technician, and as a critic interested in such
questions as the proper style for each kind of poetry and
whether supernatural machinery should figure in modern epics,
we tend to think of his use of machinery and of changes of tone as
devices. The effect of *Épître IV* certainly derives from a complex
mixture of tones. I think we should be ready to see this as an
expression of an underlying attitude to experience rather than as
an assemblage of contrivances. In part, this underlying attitude
may be a reflection of Boileau's temperament. But I do not think
this explanation is sufficient. I think both the tone and the technique of Boileau's poetry are related to important facts about the
nature of neo-classicism and its views on the proper functions of
poetry.

6

Épître V, on the importance of self-knowledge, is a smooth and
charming poem, but minor. It requires mention here only for two
points which bear on Boileau's preoccupation with poetry and
morality and poetry and truth. As Adam has remarked, it shows
the closeness of Boileau's thought to Montaigne's,[24] and Brossette
says Boileau was reading Montaigne at the time.[25] There is indeed
an attractive tentativeness about the moral attitudes expressed.
Boileau is not preaching received opinion, but engaged in a search:
'Je songe à me connaître, et me cherche moi-même' (l. 26).
Boileau represents himself, characteristically, as highly prizing
mental power and knowledge: 'l'esprit et le savoir' (l. 96), and
seeing right reason as a stable middle course: 'De la droite
raison je sens mieux l'équilibre' (l. 102). But, also character-
istically, moral achievement is something that is recognised by the
heart:

> si, dans le beau feu du zèle qui m'enflamme,
> Par un ouvrage enfin des critiques vainqueur,
> Je puis sur ce sujet satisfaire mon cœur...
>
> (ll. 142–4)

As for truth, Boileau makes a famous series of errors when he refers to astronomy:

> Que, l'astrolabe en main, un autre aille chercher
> Si le soleil est fixe ou tourne sur son axe...
>
> (ll. 28–9)

An astrolabe is hardly a suitable instrument for the purpose, and it is quite possible for the sun to be a fixed star and to turn on its axis. Boileau was criticised at the time for these mistakes, but he never bothered to put them right. His insouciance shows that when he stresses the importance of truth (which he often links with *le savoir*, 'knowledge') he is not so much concerned with factual accuracy as with a grasp of moral and psychological truth. If his astronomical references are sufficient to make his point clear to his audience, that is enough. And in this he is not departing from neo-classical doctrine. As Chapelain said when reproached with an error in a reference to falconry: 'en tout cas il n'y aurait qu'une erreur de volerie, non pas de poésie...Aristote a déjà absous les poètes qui pèchent en matière non-poétique.'[26]

5
A reading of *L'Art Poétique* (1)

The title *L'Art Poétique* may suggest that the poem is a technical manual. In view of Boileau's reputation as a neo-classical poet, it may also suggest that the poem is a systematic treatise setting out neo-classical doctrine. At least by implication, these were the views assumed both by Boileau's eighteenth-century admirers and by his nineteenth-century detractors. As views, they are not self-evidently absurd. In this chapter, however, I will approach *L'Art Poétique* from a different angle, and one more typical of recent criticism: from the consideration of the poem as a dramatic event.

We know that Boileau gave readings from *L'Art Poétique* in various salons from 1672 onwards. There is no doubt that the poem was intended primarily to be read aloud in such circumstances. The element of dramatic recitation is important in Boileau, and nowhere more than here. In a brilliant article, Orr has demonstrated the subtlety and daring with which Boileau uses language in a way which exploits the possibilities of a poem intended to be heard – including the possibilities offered by puns and like-sounding words and phrases.[1]

What is less certain is how far this social context allowed Boileau to use the structure of his poem to express his meaning. The organisation of his material is bound to be considered important by every author, and seventeenth-century literary theory fully recognised *la disposition* as of fundamental importance. Twentieth-century criticism of poetry tends to go beyond this, and to see structure as the main means of expression in a poem: structure is meaning. It is not absurd to suppose that this approach to reality is characteristic of the poet, of the man who temperamentally inclines to organise his experience into patterns which give him satisfaction in a particular way, and that it is this temperament which makes him a poet rather than, say, a philosopher or a scientist. But such a man is still influenced by his social and literary context, and may modify his strategy in accordance with it. In the case of works read before a salon, it is often assumed that over-all structure makes no effect, and that brilliant local effects are all-important. As a generalisation, this is perhaps too sweeping. An intelligent audience will presumably accept that structure is important, even if not easily grasped in the conditions of a salon reading, and will try to make allowances for this. Plays or extracts from plays were frequently read in seventeenth-century salons,[2] and it can hardly be doubted that the importance of dramatic structure was as thoroughly accepted then as at any time since.

We do not know whether Boileau read, or expected to be able to read, the whole of *L'Art Poétique* at one sitting. This would take only about an hour and a quarter; not impossibly long (society audiences flocked to sermons lasting much longer) but probably too long for comfort in the more relaxed atmosphere of a salon. Clearly, Boileau did read, and expected to read, separate passages in isolation: he gave readings while the work was in progress, and read to Louis XIV at least the passage on the ages of man (*Chant III*, ll. 373–90). I will assume, provisionally at least, that the structure of *L'Art Poétique* is of some importance, but that this structure is dictated only partly by Boileau's internal needs; that is, by his artist's instinct to organise his material so that structure expresses meaning. It was equally dictated by his assumption that he must adapt to the requirements of social inter-course and therefore, by his need to achieve variety, to 'égayer sa matière' (enliven his subject-matter), to provide brilliant set-pieces.

2

The first lines of *L'Art Poétique* must have been carefully calcu-lated, and are surely important in directing our attention when we read the poem to ourselves as a complete work. Whether Boileau ever read it in public as a single connected work, there can be little doubt that at some stage he announced to a gathering that this was the opening of his *Art Poétique*, and that he weighed the effect these lines would produce on an audience. There is plenty of evidence that Boileau was good at reading in public, and enjoyed this quasi-dramatic situation. As we have already seen often enough, his earlier poems are often based on a method rather like that of drama, and contain a large element of play-acting.

One factor Boileau must have had in mind when calculating the effect of his opening lines is the expectations of his audience. They would have known of earlier *Arts of Poetry*, at least by repute. Aristotle was a name of awesome authority, though very few people could read his *Poetics* in the original, and to study the numerous Latin translations and commentaries would be the mark of a pedant rather than an *honnête homme*. The first published French translation did not appear until 1671.[3] Cultivated readers would probably know of the prose treatises of La Ménardière and Colletet, but were hardly likely to expect anything so technical and dull; and, in any case, Boileau's work was poetry, not prose. Possibly some of them knew of Vauquelin's *L'Art Poétique* (1601) as Boileau himself probably did.[4] Everyone would know of Horace's verse *Epistula ad Pisones*, and some of the men if not the women probably knew it quite well. In view of Boileau's reputation as an author of Satires and Epistles, no doubt this was the model that most helped to form their expectations.

What might this lead the audience to expect? Vauquelin's beginning makes his purpose plain:

> Sire, je conte ici les beaux enseignements
> De l'art de poésie, et quels commencements
> Les poèmes ont eu; quels auteurs, quelle trace
> Il faut suivre qui veut grimper dessus Parnasse.
>
> (Book i, ll. 1–4)

Horace's opening is apparently different: he starts with a picture of a chaotic monster, and invites his friends to laugh at a poet who produces a similar jumble in words. The method is satirical, and might be expected to be followed by Boileau, but the implication is didactic in the same way as Vauquelin's more straightforward opening: Horace knows when people are writing poetry badly, and can tell them how to write it better.

Boileau's opening is not at all the same. There is the bold title, *L'Art Poétique*, then the first couplet:

> C'est en vain qu'au Parnasse un téméraire auteur
> Pense de l'art des vers atteindre la hauteur.
>
> (*Chant I*, ll. 1–2)

Here is a poem whose title implies that it teaches how to write poetry; here are the first two lines saying that poetry – or, at least, elevated poetry – cannot be written at all. The emphasis falls immediately on 'en vain'. The author evoked is 'téméraire', and although he is thinking of the heights he will never get there.

It is worth stressing that Boileau is writing specifically about 'l'art des vers'. Neo-classical critics were well used to the idea that poetry is co-extensive with imaginative literature, not with verse. Chapelain certainly regarded drama as poetry (*la poésie représentative*), but thought it should be in prose.[5] In the Preface to Books xiii–xxiv of *La Pucelle* he spells out his position in relation to the epic:

> quant aux vers et au langage ce sont des instruments de si petite considération dans l'épopée, qu'ils ne méritent pas que de si graves juges s'y arrêtent...la pureté de la diction, le nombre du vers et la richesse de la rime ne font que l'habillement du corps poétique, qui a les sentiments et les actions pour membres, et pour âme l'invention et la disposition.[6]

As so often, Boileau's critical ideas echo Chapelain's. In a letter of 10 November 1699 to Brossette, for instance, we find him accepting quite naturally that the author of *Télémaque* is a poet, and that the *Odyssey* is a 'roman'.[7]

As Brody points out, the next lines of the poem insist that to write well the poet needs not only 'native poetic potential (*génie*), which is not uncommon', but something harder to define: 'a secret source of poetic effectiveness which is extremely rare'.[8] Much of *L'Art Poétique* revolves around this indefinable centre, which is felt for the first time in the opposition in lines 3–5 between the 'influence secrète' and 'génie'.

Boileau then uses a device which is characteristic of his strategy in this poem: direct address to his audience: 'Ô vous donc qui, brûlant d'une ardeur périlleuse' (l. 7). Rather, it is an address to the would-be writer, and the listener in the salon or the reader has to decide whether it applies to him. Nature, says Boileau, knows what people are good at (ll. 13–18); it is Man who often does not know himself, and therefore goes wrong (ll. 19–26). Lack of self-knowledge leads to absurdity: the bad poet lives a disordered life in taverns (ll. 21–2), writes on the walls (l. 22), and goes rudely and inappropriately (l. 23) rushing after Moses into the desert (l. 25). In *Épître V*, Boileau had been concerned to save his reason

on 'cette mer que nous courons' (this sea on which we sail)
(*Épître V*, l. 35). Here, the end of the bad poet's 'career' (in all
senses) is 'running to drown himself' (l. 26).

It is against this background of rapid and mindless motion that
we are asked to respond to one of Boileau's most famous passages.
He begins with firm, plain language, marked by strong pauses and
repeated 'k' and 't' sounds which slow the rhythm further:

> Quelque sujet qu'on traite, ou plaisant, ou sublime,
> Que toujours le bon sens s'accorde avec la rime;
> L'un l'autre vainement ils semblent se haïr;
> La rime est une esclave et ne doit qu'obéir.
> Lorsqu'à la bien chercher d'abord on s'évertue,
> L'esprit à la trouver aisément s'habitue;
> Au joug de la raison sans peine elle fléchit
> Et, loin de la gêner, la sert et l'enrichit.
> Mais, lorsqu'on la néglige, elle devient rebelle,
> Et, pour la rattraper, le sens court après elle.
> Aimez donc la raison: que toujours vos écrits
> Empruntent d'elle seule et leur lustre et leur prix.
>
> (ll. 27–38)

We shall consider in a moment the semantics of some of these
terms. My concern at present is with the structure of the passage
and its effect on us. The opening couplet comes over, I think, as
an emphatic utterance, given an extra edge by the strong and
unexpected linking of 'pleasing' (or 'joking') with 'lofty', and
'good sense' with 'rhyme'. Boileau treats le bon sens and la rime
as two persons – we might rather say two dramatic figures.
They are a couple, linked by hate, and there is a strong implication
of the absurdity of the situation: 'L'un l'autre vainement ils
semblent se haïr', as though they are a mismatched husband and
wife in a Molière farce. The next line makes it a master/slave
relationship. As is the way with the slaves of Classical comedy
(or the valets in Molière), la rime can be useful, but requires
watching. Rhyme is a slippery customer, but with practice and
hard work on the master's part it can be forced to work for him.

Although le bon sens and la raison apparently mean almost
the same thing, the switch from the one term to the other prepares
us to think something is slipping about. This prepares us for the
following lines in which stability achieved gives place to mad
motion. Rhyme rushes away, and sense runs after her (ll. 35–6).

The use of the two terms *le bon sens* and *la raison* is part of Boileau's strategy. *Le bon sens* is a positive quality which everyone except a few eccentrics possesses: 'la chose du monde la mieux partagée'. For anyone not to claim it would immediately brand them as socially defective. The phrase has familiar, comforting undertones, such as *le bonhomme, le bon Dieu. Raison* is slightly more elevated. Brody is surely right to say that here in *L'Art Poétique* as elsewhere in Boileau it is closer to the associations of 'avoir raison' ('to be right') than of 'reason' in the sense of abstract ratiocination.[9] But in poetry the writer can manipulate the associations of words only to emphasise one aspect rather than another. He cannot completely suppress the other associations. (Poetry would lose its special richness, perhaps its *raison d'être*, if he could.) Behind Boileau's use of *raison* there remains the rational faculty of the Schools, the supreme mark of the human mind. In using the two terms, Boileau is drawing us into sharing a scale of values. *Le bon sens* is a cosy, sociable virtue: of course we all share in it. It is also 'reason', the quality of being right – a delightfully flattering notion, but one that begins to impose on us grave responsibilities. It is also absolute, eternal Reason, which sees all things and enables man to link himself to the order of the universe. In the whirligig of his verse, with its sudden stops to make comforting assertions of stability, Boileau is jolting us into grasping the stable principle he holds out to us. In his metaphors of journeying along a thorny and slippery road, he is mirroring the journey he is taking us on: from the easy laughter of the social occasion to a contemplation of grave matters. Once we accept *le bon sens*, 'voilà, nous sommes embarqués' (there, we are on the way); we are brought to accept Reason itself as our guide. And this Reason is indeed an absolute: the worth and brilliance of literature come from her alone, and then are only borrowed (l. 38).

The rest of *Chant I* consists mainly of passages of three types: direct admonitions on what to avoid and what to aim for in writing; a history of the 'Parnasse français'; and the reactions of good and bad poets to good and bad critics. They will be discussed here in that order, which corresponds roughly (but not exactly) to their order in the poem. Boileau's comments on good and bad poets and critics prompt reflections on his technique in this poem, which may throw light on the order of the topics treated in *Chant I.*

Modern critics have often been unkind about Boileau's negative and positive injunctions. The *faux brillants* of concetti (ll. 39–44), long-windedness (ll. 49–63), a too-uniform style (ll. 69–74), burlesque and 'low' language (ll. 79–97), exaggeration (ll. 98–102), obscurity (ll. 143–54) are all condemned, and their opposites praised; great stress is laid on the need to respect the language (ll. 155–62), and to write melodious and flowing verse (ll. 103–12), and on the value of careful workmanship (ll. 163–74). We can all concede the merit in the *vers maximes* which Boileau sometimes achieves, especially when he makes them exemplify what they preach: 'Qui ne sait se borner ne sut jamais écrire' (l. 63) is doubly appropriate in its concision and in its placing as a rebuke to long-winded poets. Orr has demonstrated in detail the complexity of Boileau's language. The most striking example is perhaps in the passage on *pointes* in *Chant II* (ll. 105–38), in which he plays with an astonishing range of the meanings the word 'pointe' can have in different contexts, some of them highly specialised. But here in *Chant I* the same skill is evident – as in the puns on 'nez' and 'nés' in lines 73–4, or on 'odieux' and 'Ô dieux' in line 110.[10]

Beyond this, disagreement sets in. Boileau's detractors see his admonitions as banal and often confusingly expressed. His defenders usually claim that he is not enunciating precepts, but expressing memorably his own perceptions of the creative process. They point out that Boileau sees obedience to his precepts more as removing obstacles to the aesthetic response than as positive means for achieving it:

> Le vers le mieux rempli, la plus noble pensée
> Ne peut plaire à l'esprit, quand l'oreille est blessée.
>
> (ll. 111–12)

Perhaps more illuminating is the point which modern critics have emphasised: the quality of paradox, as evidenced in lines 45–8:

> Tout doit tendre au bon sens; mais, pour y parvenir,
> Le chemin est glissant et pénible à tenir;
> Pour peu qu'on s'en écarte, aussitôt l'on se noie.
> La raison pour marcher n'a souvent qu'une voie.

Here, 'reason' is both the traveller and the goal.[11] This is not
the only paradox. Boileau demands variety:

> Heureux qui, dans ses vers, sait d'une voix légère
> Passer du grave au doux, du plaisant au sévère.
>
> (ll. 75-6)

This is the Boileau we have often met in the Satires and
Epistles, with his constant leaps between jokes and seriousness.
But he also demands unity:

> Il faut que chaque chose y soit mise en son lieu;
> Que le début, la fin, répondent au milieu;
> Que d'un art délicat les pièces assorties
> N'y forment qu'un seul tout de diverses parties.
>
> (ll. 177-80)

These paradoxical commands are linked to the idea of the
difficulty, even danger, of trying to write well. Banal or not, his
prescriptions show the razor edge on which the poet must walk:

> Un vers était trop faible, et vous le rendez dur;
> J'évite d'être long, et je deviens obscur;
> L'un n'est point trop fardé, mais sa Muse est trop nue;
> L'autre a peur de ramper, il se perd dans la nue.
>
> (ll. 65-8)

This last phrase brings us to the dangers the poet runs,
'brûlant d'une ardeur périlleuse' (burning with a dangerous
ardour) (l. 7). Some of these are social: he puts his readers to sleep
(l. 72), his works are relegated to the provinces (l. 94), he is
exposed to 'la censure publique' (public blame) (l. 183). But the
real danger is that he will lose the precious faculty of 'Reason',
and so take off on that wild career in which he loses himself in
the clouds (l. 68) or drowns himself (ll. 26, 47).

These points have often been noted, and do much to illuminate
and justify Boileau's procedure. Nevertheless, they seem to me to
leave many questions unanswered about why L'Art Poétique is
cast in a didactic form – indeed, why it takes the form of an
Art Poétique at all. I would remark on two points which may
take us further: Boileau's association of intellectual with moral
failings; and the use he makes of the social setting for which his
poem was written.

Traditionally, Boileau was regarded as an apostle of Reason, and the critics took sides for or against his intellectualism. More recently, the stress has been on the intuitive nature of his judgments and the way in which he himself stresses an intuitive perception of 'rightness'. This is the main argument of Brody in his *Boileau and Longinus*. Although this view is a necessary corrective to the old one, we should not lose sight entirely of the intellectualism of Boileau's approach. The characteristic danger threatening the bad poet is madness. The 'reason' which he loses is no doubt the power to act in a healthy manner in a normal social environment, but it is also 'reason' in the sense of the ability to conduct himself rationally. A failure to write well, however, is also bound up with morality. Lack of sense, or of knowledge of the proper way of writing, is discussed in the language of ethics, or even of religion:

> Surtout qu'en vos écrits la langue révérée
> Dans vos plus grands excès vous soit toujours sacrée.
> En vain vous me frappez d'un son mélodieux,
> Si le terme est impropre ou le tour vicieux;
> Mon esprit n'admet point un pompeux barbarisme,
> Ni d'un vers ampoulé l'orgueilleux solécisme.
> Sans la langue, en un mot, l'auteur le plus divin
> Est toujours, quoi qu'il fasse, un méchant écrivain.
>
> (ll. 155–62)

A clumsy phrase is 'vicieux'; a solecism is 'orgueilleux', evidence of the greatest of all sins; a writer who makes these mistakes is 'méchant'; that is, 'worthless', but also 'evil'. By contrast, the positives are sanctified by religion: 'révérée', 'sacrée', 'divin'. Literary faults are moral faults, the result of lack of self-knowledge:

> Mais souvent un esprit qui se flatte et qui s'aime
> Méconnaît son génie et s'ignore soi-même.
>
> (ll. 19–20)

The moral quality of intellectual clarity comes out most forcefully in lines 147–54, with their attack on those who cannot think straight. The clinching line is celebrated:

> Ce que l'on conçoit bien s'énonce clairement.
>
> (l. 153)

Brody is surely right to insist that this does not mean that Boileau wanted the poet to formulate his thought first, then put it into verse.[12] Nevertheless, the quality of being able to produce the right

conceptions depends on a basic rightness of mind which is suscep-
tible to 'Le jour de la raison' (the light of reason) (l. 149).

My second point, the use Boileau makes of the social setting,
has been touched on in connection with the Satires. In *L'Art
Poétique*, more obviously than in his earlier poems, Boileau is
making an appeal to the social prejudices of his audience. The
poet (Saint Amant) who 's'ignore soi-même' (lacks self-knowledge)
spends his time in taverns (l. 22). The burlesque spoke the
language of the markets (l. 84). The contagion of burlesque rose
from the socially inferior Provinces to the middle classes. The
Court for a time was affected, but was soon 'désabusée' and sent
such language back to the lower orders from which it came.
Good poetry is associated with what is *noble*, and the social connotations of the word cannot be ignored: 'Le style le moins noble
a pourtant sa noblesse' (l. 80).

Whatever the arguments about Boileau's general precepts, there
has been almost unanimous condemnation of his historical
passages in this Canto. As modern scholarship has shown – and
as was for the most part knowable when Boileau wrote – the
account of French poetry in lines 113–40 is seriously inaccurate.
It is not true that in the Middle Ages: 'Le caprice tout seul faisait
toutes les lois' (l. 114), and the versification of mediaeval French
poetry was not haphazard.[18] Marot did not write triolets, or
invent the strict rondeau; the account of Ronsard is unjust; and
Malherbe did not dominate the development of French poetry in
the way Boileau implies.

These criticisms are no doubt justified, though in part they
reflect not so much the superiority of our knowledge over Boileau's
as the difference in our prejudices. To a seventeenth-century
audience, mediaeval French poetry would pass as 'irregular',
even if they were able to appreciate its conventions; Ronsard's
poetry did fall from favour after his death; Malherbe did embody
an ideal of *la grande poésie*. Rather than debate the historical
accuracy in detail, it may be profitable to look at the function of
this account rather closely.

One clue is the passage on the burlesque (ll. 81–97), to which
historically minded scholars have also objected. Whatever the
accuracy of Boileau's account of the burlesque, we can single out
two factors. It is near enough to the truth to be plausible to

Boileau's audience. It also has a didactic function. By showing how 'low' literary habits rose from their socially unacceptable beginnings to infect polite society, and how polite society finally rejected them, it offers a paradigm of how Boileau expects his audience to behave: they are to show their social superiority by rejecting what he points out to them as 'low'.

His account of French literary history has a similar function. It is not history, but a myth: the 'low' Middle Ages have given way by degrees to the high style of the 'auteurs de ce temps' (authors of this age) (l. 140). To be effective, a myth must have villains and heroes, and yet be plausible. The now-unfashionable Ronsard and the admired Malherbe fill these rôles to perfection. Ronsard is described in terms reminiscent of Chapelain on his stilts in *Satire IV*: he is 'trébuché de si haut' (cast down from such a height) (l. 129). His faults are pedantry and pride: a mixture of the social, moral and literary. Malherbe appeared in the early part of the poem as the writer of heroic odes (l. 17), not, for instance, as the writer of the *Consolation à du Périer*, or of vigorous pornography. Similarly, in this passage he is associated with social and moral grandeur. As has been pointed out, he is associated with power: 'D'un mot mis en sa place enseigna le pouvoir' (l. 133).[14] He has constrained the Muses to obey the rules, not of literature, but of the aristocratic code of duty (l. 134). He is wise ('sage'), and his language offers nothing rough to the 'oreille épurée' (refined ear) of the now-refined audience. We may be reminded of Boileau's cavalier attitude to scientific detail in *Épître V*: plausibility is more important to him than accuracy.[15] Perhaps more appropriately still, we may think of the machinery in *Épître IV*: Boileau is raising his precepts to a more important level by associating them with a tradition.

The third and final topic treated in the rest of *Chant I* is the interaction between the poet and his audience. The author should submit his works to scrutiny by his friends (ll. 183–92). A flatterer shows himself by the exaggeration of his praise (ll. 193–8). A foolish author resists even justified criticism, and finds fools to admire him (ll. 209–32). These passages exhibit some of the characteristic devices of Boileau's best work: paradox (the false friend is kind, the kind friend severe); dramatic dialogue (the repartee between the foolish author and his critic); and the clinching *bon mot*: 'Un sot trouve toujours un plus sot qui l'admire' (l. 232).

They also show three other features which are important in Boileau's thought, and in his strategy in *L'Art Poétique*. First, there is the emphasis on the moral effort required to write well. The poet must face the pain of self-knowledge (l. 186) and give up pride (l. 189). His friends must combat his failings ('défauts') and the moral connotations of this are reinforced by the adjective applied to these severe critics in line 188: 'zélés'. 'Zèle' and 'zélé' are most often used in connection with religious zeal. Secondly, the social element is emphasised, and this time with a strong hint of criticism of the aristocracy. There are fools not only in the provinces and among the bourgeoisie, but close to the highest in the land (ll. 228–30), and these also are 'zélés' for their own version of the truth.

It is here that we come to a last point, and one which I think shows most clearly what Boileau is about. The final section (from line 183 to the end) yields its full value if we read it in the light of the reactions it provokes in an audience: that to-and-fro of emotion between the reciting author and his hearers, or (less immediately) the poet and his reader. The section starts sternly, with a reference to fear: 'Craignez-vous pour vos vers la censure publique?' (l. 183) and an injunction to self-examination. The tone lightens with its picture of the flatterer: in a ceremoniously polite society in which salon *habitués* tried their hand at rhyming and read their verses to each other, it is not difficult to imagine the uneasy smiles that this could provoke. If any of Boileau's audience had been guilty of such behaviour, whether as poet or as critic, their unease would prepare them to receive the firm lessons in lines 199–207, which depict the candid critic. After this, Boileau gives them their reward, in the form of the lively farce of the obstinate poet. But in this, and right up to the end of the Canto, he continues his manipulations:

> De ce vers, direz-vous, l'expression est basse, –
> Ah! monsieur, pour ce vers je vous demande grâce,
> Répondra-t-il d'abord. – Ce mot me semble froid;
> Je le retrancherais. – C'est le plus bel endroit! –
> Ce tour ne me plaît pas. – Tout le monde l'admire.
> Ainsi toujours constant à ne se point dédire,
> Qu'un mot dans son ouvrage ait paru vous blesser,

C'est un titre chez lui pour ne point l'effacer.
Cependant, à l'entendre, il chérit la critique;
Vous avez sur ses vers un pouvoir despotique,
Mais tout ce beau discours dont il vient vous flatter
N'est rien qu'un piège adroit pour vous les réciter.
Aussitôt il vous quitte; et, content de sa muse,
S'en va chercher ailleurs quelque fat qu'il abuse:
Car souvent il en trouve: ainsi qu'en sots auteurs,
Notre siècle est fertile en sots admirateurs;
Et, sans ceux que fournit la ville et la province,
Il en est chez le duc, il en est chez le prince.
L'ouvrage le plus plat a, chez les courtisans,
De tout temps rencontré de zélés partisans;
Et, pour finir enfin par un trait de satire,
Un sot trouve toujours un plus sot qui l'admire.

(ll. 211–32)

At first, the audience can enjoy themselves, and feel reassured. They are not fools, because Boileau identifies them with the wise critic whom the foolish author spurns: '*Vous* avez sur ses vers un pouvoir despotique' (l. 220). The audience can then laugh happily at the statement that: 'Notre siècle est fertile en sots admirateurs' (l. 226), who are supplied by 'la ville et la province' (l. 227). But here a note of uneasiness comes back. The aristocracy and the Court are perhaps not fools themselves, but the enemy is within the gates and close to them: 'Il en est chez le duc, il en est chez le prince', and 'chez les courtisans' (ll. 228–9). The 'zeal' of the good critic (l. 188) is grotesquely paralleled by that of the supporters of bad writing. The final epigram is not without ambiguity. We can hardly avoid admiring Boileau's verve in this passage, and we can imagine the laughter of his audience. But, again, there is an unsettling hint. Our admiring laughter may be checked in mid-course when we remember what Boileau is saying: that admiration may be a sign of folly.

This ability to play on the reactions of his audience seems to me to explain much about the first Canto. Its structure is based on continually inviting a comfortable reaction and then unsettling the audience by provoking a different one: hence the jumping about from subject to subject; the paradoxical assertions, the offering of a lump of sugar and then a bitter pill. This method of writing indicates more than a simple wish to 'égayer sa matière'. It is an expression of a determination to question the audience's social and moral preoccupations and so to bring them to a more strenuous self-awareness; to bring them, in fact, to that state of keenly functioning sensitivity which Boileau sees as the precondition of good writing.

3

Chant II is the weakest in the poem, and can be discussed briefly. It is interesting mainly for the light it throws on the purpose of *L'Art Poétique*. Critics sympathetic to Boileau have on the whole emphasised his concern with the creative process, or with the interaction between an author and his audience, rather than with rules. Some doubt is cast on the accuracy of this modern view by his insistence, in the opening lines of *Chant I*, on 'l'art des vers', where the associations of 'art' are with 'technique', and verse is limited to poetry rather than standing for imaginative writing in general. With *Chant II*, it is hardly possible to maintain the view that Boileau is not concerned with rules as definitive. To a large extent, Boileau is doing what the writer of a systematic treatise on neo-classical theory might do: discussing separate types of poem, arranging them in order, and describing the characteristics of each. There is little of the dramatic to-and-fro, the playing with the psychology of composition and appreciation, which we find in *Chant I. Chant II* is mainly precept or description (though we should not underrate the suppleness of Boileau's art even here: Orr has drawn some of his most striking examples of Boileau's puns and word-play from this Canto).

Despite this verbal liveliness, there is a slackness about the treatment of some of the *genres*. It is difficult, for instance, to feel that Boileau had much time for the Pastoral, and the passage on it (ll. 1–37) is vague and confused. We therefore have to ask ourselves why Boileau found it necessary to write 204 lines on matters that did not interest him. The most likely explanation is the obvious one: that he did in fact think of himself as laying down the law for writers and readers.

Chant II nevertheless exhibits the same attitudes as the rest of the poem. There is the same emphasis on the almost impossible nature of the poet's task. For the Pastoral: 'Entre ces deux excès, la route est difficile' (l. 25). In line 94, 'Un sonnet sans défauts vaut seul un long poème', but line 96 informs us that 'cet heureux phénix est encore à trouver'. The basic requirement is for the emotional integrity needed to portray emotion (ll. 44–57). The vogue for *pointes* was due to 'le vulgaire' (l. 107), and was banished by 'Reason'; like the fools in *Chant I*, admirers of *pointes* still lurk in the Court (ll. 130–2), but they are buffoons, and – worse, in a worldly society – unfashionable. The bad poet lacks self-knowledge, and the moral discipline that follows from it; his pride betrays him into absurd behaviour (ll. 195–204).

Two other themes are especially prominent. First, factually accurate history is rejected in favour of a parabolic pseudo-history, sometimes making use of historical material, sometimes not. In lines 73–81, Boileau gives a broad enough hint of what he thinks of historical accuracy in poetry: he mocks the writers of odes who are 'maigres historiens' who follow 'l'ordre du temps' (chronological order) in 'leur vers exact' (their accurate poetry). He then passes (via the evocation of Apollo as the god of inspiration) to a striking piece of mythical history which shows Apollo inventing the sonnet to plague French poets. After this, it is hardly surprising that his history of Roman satire (ll. 145–67) is vague and partially inaccurate. It is near enough the truth to be plausible, and Lucilius, Horace and the rest, like Ronsard and Malherbe in *Chant I*, appear as representatives of particular positions rather than as historical figures. The purpose seems to be to justify the various types of satire, and the whole passage is an amplification of the statement in abstract terms which introduces it:

> L'ardeur de se montrer, et non pas de médire,
> Arma la Vérité du vers de la Satire.
>
> (ll. 145–6)

The second prominent theme is morality. In part, the moral theme is the need for emotional integrity already mentioned: to write good love poems, one must be in love. Boileau is being genuinely moral here, not prudish: Orr has pointed to the pun on bad poets 'erecting' themselves into lovers in line 48.[16] More directly, this theme comes out in the requirement that verse should not be immoral. This is attributed to the desire for moral purity of both the poet's audience (ll. 176–7) and Boileau himself (ll. 179–80). This linking of morality to the values of polite society has implications for literary technique: 'la pudeur des mots' (the modesty of the words) (l. 178) must soften the immoral idea. There is an ambiguity here, as if Boileau is tempering his hatred of sham in the interests of social conformity. But there is no ambiguity about the injunction to shun impiety. It is not only wrong to make God 'le sujet d'un badinage affreux' (the subject of a hideous jest) (l. 188). It is also literally dangerous, and in a reference to the Le Petit case (l. 190) Boileau explicitly threatens the atheist with the torture and death prepared for him by the régime.

There is a further aspect of *Chant II* which has often been discussed. The choice of minor *genres* seems arbitrary, in that it covers such things as the rondeau and the vaudeville.[17] This seems to argue a desire to extend the empire of the rules into even the smallest corner of literature. 'Il faut, même en chansons, du bon sens et de l'art', says line 191, and this follows closely on the Le Petit passage, suggesting that the opposite of atheism is the 'bon sens' and 'art' taught by Boileau. Critics have often discussed why *Chant II* omits all mention of the Fable. The point is interesting, and will be considered later. I would only remark at this stage that *Chant II* also ignores the formal didactic poem, although this too was a recognised Classical form, and is mentioned with honour in *Chant IV* (ll. 157–62).

6

A reading of *L'Art Poétique* (ii)

Boileau is presumably offering his audience something of importance in *Chant III*, as it is much the longest (428 lines out of a total
of 1100). The importance comes in part from the magnitude of its
subject, the three great *genres*, Tragedy, Comedy and Epic. What
springs more intimately from the experience of reading the poem
is the special urgency of much of the verse. Clarac has remarked
that the lines on Christian 'machines' in the Epic (ll. 193–208)
are 'passionés et précis, ils ont l'accent de la polémique',[1] and
many of the lines on Tragedy and Comedy stand out as especially
memorable, in a poem full of memorable lines. One sign of the
intensity of Boileau's involvement in this Canto is the emphasis on
matters of literary theory which were under active debate at the
time, another important element in the poem, but one which is
even more prominent here than in the other Cantos. I hope to
show some reasons why *Chant III* is of such importance to what
Boileau is saying, but they are not obvious from an inventory of its
contents.

The structure also offers difficulties. The distribution of lines
gives the greatest importance to the Epic (175 lines), then to
Tragedy (159 lines), then to Comedy (94 lines). This is the
traditional order of precedence. It is not clear why Boileau does
not follow this order in his presentation, as Rapin did in his
Réflexions sur la Poétique d'Aristote (also published in 1674).
Perhaps this is a question which should not bear too much weight,
as one of Boileau's concerns appears to be to 'égayer sa matière'
and distinguish his poem from a pedantic dissertation. Nevertheless, there are some indications that the order is significant, or at
least fits in well with the larger purpose of the poem, and I hope to
show what these are. My approach will be to examine *Chant III*
in detail in the order in which Boileau arranged it.

The first eight lines are striking:

> Il n'est point de serpent ni de monstre odieux,
> Qui, par l'art imité, ne puisse plaire aux yeux:
> D'un pinceau délicat l'artifice agréable
> Du plus affreux objet fait un objet aimable.
> Ainsi, pour nous charmer, la Tragédie en pleurs
> D'Œdipe tout sanglant fit parler les douleurs,
> D'Oreste parricide exprima les alarmes,
> Et, pour nous divertir, nous arracha des larmes.
>
> (ll. 1–8)

They make a point which derives from Aristotle, and which is often stressed in neo-classical theory: that the artistic representation of even the most unpleasant object can give pleasure. They cite Tragedy as an example. The opening, with its 'serpent' and 'monstre odieux', perhaps creates a slight *frisson*, but this is soon allayed by the 'pinceau délicat' and its 'artifice agréable', which makes the unpleasant object 'un objet aimable' in line 4. The mixture of unpleasantness and rather insipid elegance is striking, especially when the most frightful thing (l. 4) becomes an 'objet aimable' (which, in the language of the salons, meant 'a person to whom one is sexually attracted'). The paradox by which Tragedy compels us by magic force ('pour nous charmer', l. 5) to take pleasure in sadness (l. 8) may seem banal, but the way it is expressed is curious. The elegant phrasing and the reference to tears (seventeenth-century audiences wept at tragedies) place us firmly in the context of contemporary society. At the same time, the subject matter takes us into a different world. 'Oreste parricide' (l. 7) was too shocking a subject for the French seventeenth-century stage; no play on the murder of Clytemnestra by Orestes appears in Scherer's list.[2] Racine introduces the 'alarmes' of Oreste in *Andromaque*, but he is careful not to mention matricide.[3] The only Oedipus play of the century is Corneille's. It passes quickly over 'Œdipe tout sanglant',[4] and describes him blinding himself in heroic disdain at the gods' injustice; Corneille in his *Avis au Lecteur* and *Examen* explains that he played down the physical aspect as much as possible, to avoid upsetting the ladies.[5] Boileau is yoking together elegance and sentiment – qualities prized by his audience – with the Greek directness their taste rejected. As so often in Boileau, the liveliness of the lines comes from the game he is playing with his audience. First, their favourable reaction is stimulated by apparent flattery of their taste; secondly, Boileau introduces another set of values which they normally reject, so producing a slight shock; and, finally, the neatness of his expression leaves them with the choice of accepting his discreetly offered modification of their views or classing themselves with fools and boors by rejecting it.

Having performed this manoeuvre, Boileau again hastens forward with reassurance. He is not lecturing them about Greek barbarities or the obscurities of Aristotle, but encouraging the writers of fashionable entertainment: 'Où tout Paris en foule apporte ses suffrages' (l. 12); and 'tout Paris' here means *tout Paris*, in the sense of 'Parisian high society', rather than 'everyone who lives in Paris'. The emphasis in lines 15–37 is on pleasure, emotion and making things easy for the audience. There is no point in a 'scène savante' (l. 20) or 'raisonnements' (l. 21): the spectator is in charge (ll. 22–4), and everything must be arranged so that he can enjoy himself. Boileau's shifts of pronoun show his strategy: the dramatists are 'vous' (ll. 9, 11, 15, 20, 23, 24); the audience are 'nous' (ll. 18, 19), and Boileau is one of them (ll. 26, 29, 32, 33).

It would be tedious to go through the rest of the section line by line, but I think that to do so would show the same features: the to-ing and fro-ing between the appeal to contemporary taste and the invocation of Classical rule or antecedent, and the emphasis on pleasure for the audience. It may be more fruitful to ask three questions crucial to an evaluation of *L'Art Poétique*. First, what is the content of Boileau's doctrine? Second, how far is he attempting to teach a doctrine? Third, what use does he make of the precepts he adapts from Classical sources?

The first question has been answered by many scholars. Boileau is perfectly in accord with the views established by Chapelain and other theoreticians forty years before *L'Art Poétique* appeared. Many of his formulations can be paralleled almost word for word in Chapelain's unpublished jottings in his *Discours sur la Poésie Représentative*:

La poésie dramatique ou représentative a pour objet l'imitation des actions humaines, pour condition nécessaire la vraisemblance, et la merveille pour sa perfection...
Du judicieux mélange de la vraisemblance et de la merveille naît l'excellence des ouvrages de ce genre-là ...

Ils [the poets] ont particulièrement égard à faire parler chacun selon sa condition, son âge, son sexe; et appellent bienséance non pas ce qui est honnête, mais ce qui convient aux personnes, soit bonnes, soit mauvaises, et telles qu'on les introduit dans la pièce...

Tout cela [the unities and other rules] fondé sur la condition de vraisemblance, sans laquelle l'esprit n'est ni ému ni persuadé...

Le plus digne et plus agréable effet des pièces de théâtre est lorsque par leur artificielle conduite le spectateur est suspendu de telle sorte qu'il est en peine de la fin et ne saurait juger par où se terminera l'aventure...

Dans le premier [acte] les fondements de l'aventure se jettent; dans le second les difficultés naissent; dans le troisième le trouble se renforce; dans le quatrième les choses penchent vers le désespoir; dans le cinquième le nœud se démêle avec vraisemblance par des voies imprévues, d'où resulte la merveille.[6]

Boileau insists in lines 47–52 on *le vraisemblable*: what is generally probable or acceptable. This is in line with orthodox doctrine. Corneille was unusual in arguing in favour of representing *le vrai*: what actually happened, however unlikely or unpalatable. This is the only point on which Boileau overtly opposes Corneille's theory or practice, whatever he said later. There is no reason to believe, as is often suggested, that Boileau is here championing Racine's technique against Corneille's. If anything, the stress on exciting plots with surprise endings is in line with Corneille's theory and practice rather than Racine's. The remarks on clear expositions (ll. 27–37) might reflect on Corneille, but are very general. The references to characters introducing themselves as 'Oreste' or 'Agamemnon' are not necessarily allusions to Racine's practice. Oreste's introduction of himself in *Andromaque* is indirect, in the usual neo-classical manner. *Iphigénie* was being written at the same time as *L'Art Poétique*, and the play was not performed until after the poem was published. One poet may of course have been influenced by the other's work from his knowledge of it before it was made public, but we know little of their relations at this time, and the influence could have been either way; indeed, it is equally plausible that the two poets were prompted by their common source in Euripides. In any case, it is not certain that Boileau approves of characters introducing themselves so crudely. If he was thinking of Euripides, this is not a good sign: Euripides is omitted from the account of Greek Tragedy in lines 61–80. The tone of the verse suggests scorn for such an obvious device, and there are parallel cases where Boileau says one fault is so bad that he prefers the opposite but less exasperating one:

> J'aime mieux Bergerac et sa burlesque audace
> Que ces vers où Motin se morfond et nous glace.
> *(Chant IV,* ll. 39–40)

Although unsurprising in itself, Boileau's preference for *le vraisemblable* over *le vrai* (l. 48) is interesting in its context. In other contexts, his use of the term *le vrai* and its cognates is strongly positive.[7] As Genette has remarked, the seventeenth-century concept of *vraisemblance* refers essentially to a code of social conventions.[8] Despite the opening flourish of *Chant III,* lines 9–158 firmly relate Tragedy to the conventions of French seventeenth-century polite society. In Boileau, as in Chapelain, even the surprising and marvellous effects of poetry *(la merveille)* arise from the pleasing results of the author's ingenuity in manipulating *vraisemblance.* There is no hint of any numinous or metaphysical element. This comes out strongly in the passages on the history of Tragedy in Greece and France (ll. 61–92). History is used in Boileau's customary way, as material for a parable. The history of Greek Tragedy is a parable of progress towards good taste. From being 'informe et grossière en naissant' (shapeless and rude at its origins) (l. 61), it received polish at the hands of Sophocles (ll. 75–80).

The myth of French Tragedy has a more complicated purpose. There are only two passages in the section on Tragedy where Boileau the moralist shows his claws. One is the grudging admission of love in serious plays (ll. 95–7), followed by the injunction: 'que l'amour, souvent de remords combattu,/Paraisse une faiblesse et non une vertu' (ll. 101–2). In the account of the French theatre, there is no mistaking the note of scorn for the 'troupe grossière' (uncivilised troupe) who:

> sottement zélée en sa simplicité,
> Joua les Saints, la Vierge et Dieu, par piété.
> Le savoir, à la fin dissipant l'ignorance,
> Fit voir de ce projet la dévote imprudence.
> On chassa ces docteurs prêchant sans mission...
> (ll. 85–9)

The myth again shows the progress of elegance, but with an additional point: the theatre is of a different order from the

Church, and must not meddle with holy things. As Orr has shown, 'joua' here has the double meaning of 'acting', and also 'playing with, mocking',[9] which points up the division of kind between the theatre and religion. Boileau's point seems close to that of the sixteenth-century playwright and neo-classical theorist Jean de la Taille, who objects to the representation of the crucifixion of Christ on the stage, as it will be seen to be only feigned.[10] The implication again is that the two orders are distinct: religion is the truth, and the theatre is only fiction. This opposition of the two orders of value is perhaps inherent in all neo-classical doctrine, and it comes out clearly in Boileau.

Our second question was how far Boileau is teaching anything in this section. It is often said that his precepts are banal. Perhaps, as precepts, they are, but it is worth examining how Boileau puts them to work. A typical passage is at the end of the section on Tragedy. It begins (ll. 145–50) by evoking the aptitude of audiences for criticism, which is brought concretely before us. An author:

> trouve à le siffler des bouches toujours prêtes.
> Chacun le peut traiter de fat et d'ignorant:
> C'est un droit qu'à porte on achète en entrant.
> (ll. 147–50)

The wretched author is also brought dramatically before us, alternately cringing and stretching before his tormentors (ll. 151–152). The next lines contain some of the banalities often complained of, but in the context they take on the tone of the impossible demands made by the chorus of critics:

> Qu'en nobles sentiments il soit partout fécond;
> Qu'il soit aisé, solide, agréable, profond...
> (ll. 153–4)

The sing-song of the lines evokes the chanting of the crowd, but in line 155 Boileau changes the tone. A line which starts as a continuation of the shouting begins to put forward a more sharply positive view: 'Que de traits surprenants sans cesse il nous réveille', and the last word is also a reminder to us to wake up and listen critically. The next line springs forward with one of Boileau's characteristic metaphors of motion: 'Qu'il coure dans ses vers de merveille en merveille', and the passage ends with what Edelman rightly calls one of Boileau's most beautiful lines:

Et que tout ce qu'il dit, facile à retenir,
De son ouvrage en nous laisse un long souvenir.[11]

(ll. 158–9)

Analyses such as Edelman's of the essentially dramatic nature of Boileau's technique refute some of the attacks of those who see *L'Art Poétique* as a haphazard collection of commonplace advice. But there are other points which need an answer, and which friendly critics tend to shy away from. What is Boileau getting at when he enunciates rules for the would-be poet? Why does he attach importance to rules at all? How far is he telling his readers to frame their judgments on the basis of the rules?

A test case is the passage on the unities. Apparently, Boileau is linking observance of the three unities to an absolute code sanctioned by Reason:

Mais nous, que la Raison à ses règles engage,
Nous voulons qu'avec art l'action se ménage;
Qu'en un lieu, qu'en un jour, un seul fait accompli
Tienne jusqu'à la fin le théâtre rempli.

(ll. 43–6)

In context, things are slightly more complex. Nowhere in *L'Art Poétique*, or elsewhere in his extant works, does Boileau use the normal seventeenth-century argument that the unities of time and place, for instance, are reasonable because they assimilate the dramatic location and time as closely as possible to the single place and few hours of theatrical performance. Nor does he adopt the secondary seventeenth-century argument stressed by many modern scholars, to the effect that the unities are sensible because they prevent breaks in the dramatic illusion. Both arguments are open to the obvious objection that they misunderstand the nature of the audience's acceptance of the illusion. We can perhaps deduce from Boileau's works, as Brody and others have done, that he regarded rules as negative helps, enabling the author to avoid solecisms which distract the reader's attention. Brody seems to me convincing when he points out that for Boileau, Reason often means something like 'practised taste'.[12] There is definitely a variety of personal taste – perhaps possible only in societies with a fine sense of nuance – which finds satisfaction in the neatness implicit in the ideal of the unities. Boileau's passage is set explicitly in the context of the tastes of French society:

Un rimeur, sans péril, delà les Pyrénées,
Sur la scène en un jour renferme des années.
Là, souvent le héros d'un spectacle grossier,
Enfant au premier acte, est barbon au dernier.

(ll. 39–42)

The emphasis is on 'grossier'. The contrast is with what
'we' – Boileau and his audience – prefer: 'Mais nous,...Nous
voulons...' (ll. 43–4). What may be all right in Spain will not do
in the refined culture which you and I share, dear reader. There
is an element here of the attitude of the nineteenth-century
European: the natives may wear loin-cloths and eat with their
fingers, but we use knives and forks and wear trousers, as God
intended.

The analogy brings out a serious point. We might say simply
that Boileau's tactic is social: he is getting his readers (or his
audience) on his side by flattering their prejudices. But we have to
go further than this to understand his thought, and a more serious
cultural comparison may help. When Soames and Dryden translated this passage, the phrasing they chose is revealing:

But we, that are by Reason's Rules confin'd,
Will, that with Art the Poem be design'd...
(*The Art of Poetry*, Canto III, ll. 471–2)[13]

This is the typical English view: the rules are a constraint, a
discipline, something willed rather than natural, even something
arbitrary. Boileau's emphasis is different. To follow the rules is an
engagement, a contract, an obligation voluntarily entered into to
live according to the code of Reason. It is a mark of a superior
civilisation, and of the self-discipline which alone makes civilisation possible. Here we do see Boileau making something like an
absolutist claim. It links him not only with Chapelain and the
view of neo-classical rules as 'dogmes d'éternelle vérité', but also
with Voltaire and his assumption that France had discovered the
eternal laws of Reason (which underlies so much of Voltaire's
criticism of Shakespeare). *L'Art Poétique*, also, implies the claim
that the values of French society are right in an absolute sense.
'*Raison*', with its overtones of not only 'practised taste' but also
'the rational faculty' (what makes Man human and turns his soul
to God) is a strong positive in Boileau's work. In this short passage,
Boileau is doing several things. He is giving his audience the

pleasure of feeling their own superiority confirmed; he is giving them the more purely aesthetic pleasure of satisfying the same taste that savours the unities by the neatness of his formulation; and he is discreetly but firmly asserting that this social superiority and this taste are reflections of an eternal order which sanctions them both.

Our final question asked what use Boileau makes of the precepts he adapts from Classical sources. *Chant III* is full of examples, and the section on Tragedy contains some of the most famous. Sometimes they are close imitations of well-known tags from Horace:

> L'esprit n'est point ému de ce qu'il ne croit pas.
> Ce qu'on ne doit point voir, qu'un récit nous l'expose.
>
> (ll. 50–1)

More remarkable are those which summarise ancient critics more obliquely, as in the case of the opening passage, which is loosely based on Aristotle. One example is the passage on the Aristotelian pity and terror:

> Que dans tous vos discours la passion émue
> Aille chercher le cœur, l'échauffe et le remue.
> Si d'un beau mouvement l'agréable fureur
> Souvent ne nous remplit d'un douce terreur,
> Ou n'excite en notre âme une pitié charmante,
> En vain vous étalez une scène savante.
>
> (ll. 15–20)

On one level, this may seem a vulgarisation of a difficult doctrine, but I think this judgment is inadequate. The lines seem concerned to achieve a union between the interest of a worldly audience in playgoing and the apparently remote discussions of scholars on a text which, however famous and however often quoted, was unlikely to have been read by most of Boileau's audience. What appears at first glance as vulgarisation may have several functions in this poem. It may give an educated but unscholarly audience the feeling that they are being put in touch with the thoughts of professional intellectuals. It may show the intellectuals' theories at work in what is at first sight no more than a fashionable entertainment in a salon. It may also make the audiences at the entertainment mindful of the great tradition behind it.

A comparison may help to clarify Boileau's strategy in his use of Classically based passages. In 1674, Racine was able to congratulate himself that his audiences 'ont été émus des mêmes choses qui ont mis autrefois en larmes le plus savant peuple de la Grèce'.[14] This makes an important critical claim: that the parts of *Iphigénie* imitated from Euripides made their effect because they appealed to human reactions common to the centuries of Pericles and Louis XIV. We may or may not agree with this claim, but it is an important element in neo-classicism, and perhaps in any theory of culture.

In *L'Art Poétique*, the appeal may be partly to the principle that Racine invokes: the fact that Horatian or Aristotelian passages can be brought into a modern context provides for the author and for those few who are sensitive to the Classical tradition a strengthening awareness of continuity with the past, and a reassurance that the Classical values are eternally valid. But the main effect is surely to evoke among the audience that sophisticated but less compelling reaction that we find in the salon rather than the theatre. The conscious allusions to famous dicta which even an unscholarly audience will recognise may encourage a slight feeling of superiority. More important, they perhaps create a feeling of solidarity. This underlines Boileau's strategy in *L'Art Poétique*, which is to weave a fine web by which a powerful social élite – and, by extension, each individual who reads the poem – is drawn into a wider intellectual élite of all the centuries, who can strengthen each other by precept and example to keep civilisation precariously safe against folly.

Here I think we have a clue to the significance of the poem, and one that shows how its characteristic features work together to convey its meaning. Boileau's continual to-ing and fro-ing between Classical tradition and contemporary taste; his pictures of sliding and perilous motion; his emphasis on the difficulty of achievement; his rapid shifting between pronouns; his habit of pulling his audience one way, only to jolt them by suddenly changing direction: all these fall into place if we see them as part of Boileau's incitement to us to join in a desperately difficult endeavour: the task of keeping civilisation afloat on the restless and dangerous sea of unreason.

2

This view of the poem suggests one reason why in *Chant III* Tragedy precedes Epic. With Tragedy, the gap between tradition and contemporary fashion was more easily bridged. *Tragédies* were enjoyed by Boileau's audiences, and were written within a framework believed – however mistakenly – to be based on Classical rules and precedents. Epic was a different matter. The great effort to provide France with an *Aeneid* had been made in the 1650s.[15] It had produced boring poems such as Scudéry's *Alaric* (1654) and Chapelain's *La Pucelle* (1656), which Boileau insistently mocks. After these failures, a cultivated audience might in theory respect the Epic (just as nineteenth-century audiences might in theory admire efforts at Tragedy) but in practice did not look to it for enjoyment. Boileau therefore starts with a *genre* which appeals to his audience, before tackling one they find boring and old-fashioned.

He starts his account of the Epic, then, with a need to win his audience over, and this determines how he goes about it. Epic, we are told, has an even loftier air than Tragedy, and in presenting its narrative:

> Se soutient par la fable et vit de fiction.
> Là, pour nous enchanter, tout est mis en usage.
> (ll. 162–3)

Right down to line 309, where the closing paragraph of the section begins, Boileau constantly reiterates two themes: that Epic is fiction; and that it must delight its audience. As though to pre-empt the protest that epics are boring, each verse paragraph insists on their function of giving pleasure:

> ...Le poète s'égaye en mille inventions
> Et trouve sous sa main des fleurs toujours écloses
> (ll. 174, 176)

> C'est là ce qui surprend, frappe, saisit, attache
> (ll. 188)

> C'est d'un scrupule vain s'alarmer sottement,
> Et vouloir aux lecteurs plaire sans agrément
> (ll. 225–6)

> Voulez-vous longtemps plaire et jamais ne lasser?
> (l. 245)

> De figures sans nombre égayez votre ouvrage
> (l. 287)

> Partout il [Homer] divertit et jamais il ne lasse.
> (l. 300)

Even allegory, which is often thought of as a means of moral instruction, is presented as a means of giving pleasure (ll. 163–72, ll. 226–32). Classical mythology is a source of pleasure (ll. 221–4), and so are Classical names (ll. 239–40). Christian machinery is forbidden because it does not give pleasure:

> De la foi d'un chrétien les mystères terribles
> D'ornements égayés ne sont pas susceptibles.
> L'Evangile à l'esprit n'offre de tous côtés
> Que pénitence à faire et tourments mérités.
> (ll. 199–202)

To show the Devil howling against God does not give pleasure (ll. 205–6); if Tasso did so, the pleasure given by his poem derived not from this but from the episodes of chivalry and love which had 'de son sujet égayé la tristesse' (lightened the gloom of his subject) (l. 216).

Boileau seems at times almost to ask that epics should be funny. His emphasis is on grace, lightness and decoration, but the way in which he uses 'riante' (something like our modern English 'delightful', but also 'laughing') sometimes suggests he is recommending comedy:

> Mais dans une profane et riante peinture   (l. 219)
>
> Que tout y fasse aux yeux une riante image   (l. 288)
>
> J'aime mieux Arioste et ses fables comiques
> Que ces auteurs, toujours froids et mélancoliques,
> Qui, dans leur sombre humeur, se croiraient faire affront
> Si les Grâces jamais leur déridaient le front.
> (ll. 291–4)

At the same time, Boileau insists that epic poetry is fiction:

> Ce n'est plus la vapeur qui produit le tonnerre,
> C'est Jupiter armé pour effrayer la terre
> . . .
> Ainsi, dans cet amas de nobles fictions,
> Le poète s'égaye en mille inventions.
> (ll. 167–8, 173–4)

The word 'fiction' appears four times (ll. 162, 173, 203, 326): *vraisemblance*, a great watchword of neo-classicism, is not mentioned at all. The Epic presented a problem for French neo-classical critics, who recognised that epic poetry should be bold, but found this difficult to reconcile with *vraisemblance*. Chapelain attempts a rationalisation in the Preface to the first twelve books of *La Pucelle*:

> J'ajouterai que la poésie, et principalement celle qui chante les héros, étant toute figurée et toute hyperbolique...déroge à cette exacte vraisemblance qu'on voudrait exiger du poète, suivant la doctrine d'Aristote mal entendue...Ce qui a obligé ces grands génies [Homer and Virgil] d'en user ainsi, contre la vraisemblance ordinaire, a été pour donner un air plus majestueux à leurs poèmes.[16]

This fits in well enough with Boileau's insistence on the need for epics to be surprising, striking and attractive. What does not appear in Boileau, however, is the thought which I have omitted from the Chapelain quotation above. Chapelain says that this departure from 'la vraisemblance ordinaire' is really justified by the moral aim. Epic poetry exaggerates in order to teach or inspire. It 'cherche à élever les cœurs aux actions extraordinaires, en donnant de grandes idées de celles dont elle traite, afin que, s'ils n'y peuvent atteindre, ils les suivent au moins d'aussi près que leurs forces le peuvent souffrir'.[17] If Homer and Virgil go against 'la vraisemblance ordinaire', it is 'pour mieux porter les hommes aux entreprises possibles, par l'image de celles qui sont même au-dessus de la possibilité'.[18]

Boileau deals with the difficulty in another way, and one which brings him surprisingly close to Ronsard. In the *Avertissement* to his abortive epic *La Franciade* (1572), Ronsard says that his poem is not history, but a novel: 'bref, ce livre est un Roman comme l'Iliade et l'Aenéide'.[19] For Boileau, *fiction* is associated with the Novel, which he says in *L'Art Poétique* is such an inferior *genre* that the rules of reason hardly apply: 'Dans un roman frivole aisément tout s'excuse;/C'est assez qu'en courant la fiction amuse' (ll. 119–20). Many years later, he was to refer to the *Odyssey* as a 'roman', adding that it instructed the reader.[20] There is very little, however, in *L'Art Poétique* that even hints at instruction as the main aim of the Epic. (The reference to profiting from Homer

in line 308 – 'C'est avoir profité que de savoir s'y plaire' – is
decidedly ambiguous.) Boileau insists as heavily as he can that the
fictions of Epic are to give pleasure, and that they are untrue.

In lines 177–92, he gives an example of how fiction is more
interesting than fact, and contrasts the poet with the historian:
again, like Ronsard.[21] The most striking passage, however, is
where he explicitly contrasts poetry with truth. The fictions of Epic
are 'songes' (l. 235) with that word's strong seventeenth-century
connotations of absurd and immoral delusions. We have only to
think of: 'Voilà de vos Chrétiens les ridicules songes' (*Polyeucte*,
l. 1199) or: 'Ô songe peu durable!/Ô dangereuse erreur!'
(*Athalie*, ll. 843–4). The contrast is with the 'Dieu de vérité' (God
of truth) of Christianity (l. 236), just as in lines 203–4 the contrast
is between the 'mélange coupable' (blameworthy mixture) of
fiction and the 'vérités' of the Gospel. Here Boileau the moralist is
strongly present. There is more than an indication that poetry is
foolish, even 'coupable'. The accent is on 'De la foi d'un chrétien
les mystères terribles' (l. 199), and the corollary of 'pénitence à
faire et tourments mérités' (l. 202), and the urgency of the verse
shows that the point is important. In my view, it is of crucial
importance to an understanding of *L'Art Poétique*, and it will be
discussed further in the next chapter.

In this section on Epic, the insistence on its fictional character,
the comparison with the frivolous Novel, the playing down of
any moral aim, combine to suggest that Boileau rates it below
Tragedy. If so, the order of subjects in *Chant III* would correspond to Boileau's order of precedence. The order is that of three
degrees of seriousness. Tragedy rests on *vraisemblance*, the idealised and philosophical conception of what is lifelike; Epic rests on
fiction, the productions of the imaginative faculty, which Boileau
prized highly, but not as highly as *la raison*; Comedy, as we shall
see later, rests on *vérité* in the sense of observation of actuality –
an estimable quality, but to the seventeenth-century mind less
elevated than either *vraisemblance* or the dignity of *nobles fictions*.

Boileau gives the impression throughout this section of being
somewhat on the defensive. There are several possible reasons for
this: awareness that no great modern French epic exists to throw
a bridge between the contemporary salon and the Greek and
Roman past; anxiety lest his audience should therefore find Epic

a pedantic and boring subject; consciousness of the inadequacy of his own presentation of this grandest of the *genres* as merely amusing fiction; or uneasiness at the profound implications of *le merveilleux chrétien*. In one passage, there is perhaps a hint of personal embarrassment concealed behind his frequent device of carrying his readers rapidly along and then confusing them by seeming to change direction. Heroes must be heroic, he says, but they must have faults (ll. 246–8). This echoes Aristotle, and is not an unusual position in neo-classical criticism. But they must be like Caesar, Alexander, or Louis – a surprising juxtaposition of Louis XIV with *défauts*, and one which momentarily reminds us of Boileau's earlier attacks on Alexander. Then he retrieves his position by contrasting such heroes with 'un conquérant vulgaire' (l. 252) – that is, until we remember lines 95–102 of *Épître I*, with their 'conquérants' who are 'vulgaires', and equal praise of Bourbons, Caesars and barbarians. Then, as usual, Boileau swings round. Narratives must be concise, he says, using one line; descriptions can be longer if properly handled, he goes on, and takes eleven lines to say it. We may think the lines go on too long, and are too much concerned with details. If we do, Boileau has got there before us:

> Sur de trop vains objets c'est arrêter la vue.
> Donnez à votre ouvrage une juste étendue.
>
> (ll. 267–8)

These rapid swings act as a defensive technique. It works here, with his precepts, just as it did earlier, with his 'now-you-see-it-now-you-don't' remarks about the King.

At the end of the section (ll. 311–34), the appeal to the audience is again made unobtrusively but artfully. Epic poetry needs long and hard work. Haphazard inspiration will not do, and leads to ridiculous hopping about. The bad poet (like Chapelain in *Satire IV*) is fatuously pleased with his own productions, which are all the while mouldering sadly in the bookshop. 'Tristement' (l. 332) shows the bad epics are not what Boileau is recommending but in fact the opposite (cf. l. 216). Boileau's audience have the good sense to prefer pleasure, and not to be mad. He confidently takes them aside and assumes his and their identity of interest, suggesting that they leave the bad epics to the worms and dust:

Laissons-les donc entre eux s'escrimer en repos,
Et, sans nous égarer, suivons notre propos.

(ll. 333-4)

This we will now do.

3

The short section on Comedy (ll. 335-428) takes up a number of themes, which are adumbrated in the introductory history of Greek Comedy. This is plainly a parable. Few seventeenth-century play-goers could have known Aristophanes' works at first hand, and Menander, who is held up as the model, was known only in fragments, much scantier fragments even than we possess to-day.

Boileau's parable shows how moral and aesthetic progress go together. At first, malice and insolence traduced wisdom, wit, honour and merit for the amusement of 'un vil amas de peuple' (a low crowd of the populace) (ll. 339-44). The magistrates then forced poets to be wiser, and Comedy began to 'instruct' and 'please' by proper means (ll. 345-52). Against this background of morality imposed by the law to the benefit of art, Boileau recommends the comic poet to study the life around him (ll. 359-72) and to remember that there are nevertheless certain general patterns of behaviour which characterise people at different ages (ll. 373-90).

There is something piquant about Boileau, the poet who originally, 'né moqueur, par mille jeux plaisants,/Distilla le venin de ses traits médisants' (ll. 337-8), and now become 'plus sage' (wiser) (l. 347), as the friend and eulogist of Lamoignon, reciting this passage in front of his illustrious audience. The piquancy is no doubt intended, as he now comes to a touching passage in which he applies his precepts to the comic theatre of his day. As a young man, he had been notoriously a friend of Molière. At the time of *Tartuffe*, he had found himself in an ambiguous position between the friend of his disreputable youth and his new protector Lamoignon, who was certainly trying to use the authority of the magistracy to make the stage more moral. Lamoignon, indeed, was thought by some to have been the model for Tartuffe.

Whatever Boileau's attitude then, there is no doubt where he

stands now. He draws a pointed contrast between aesthetic distinction based on observation on the one hand, and immoral
buffoonery to please the people on the other. Perhaps Molière
could have been the first of comic poets if he wished. Instead, he
preferred buffoonery (ll. 393–400). The prize goes, not to Molière,
but to Terence (ll. 415–20). The denunciation of comedy which
stoops 'De mots sales et bas charmer la populace' (l. 404), and of
the 'grossière équivoque' (smutty double-meanings) and 'saleté'
(dirt) which please the public of the Pont Neuf, clearly bears on
the comedy of Molière, the 'ami du peuple' (friend of the lower
classes) who had 'sans honte à Térence allié Tabarin' (shamelessly
linked Terence with Tabarin) (ll. 395, 398). Tabarin had performed 'dans une place' (in a public square) (l. 403), in fact the
Place Dauphine.[22] Molière had been criticised for his 'saletés'
and 'grossière équivoque' in *L'École des Femmes*.[23] Boileau
opposes to the bad comic poet the author who is 'agréable'
(l. 421); Molière, he tells us, had abandoned 'l'agréable' (l. 397).
In later life, Boileau claimed to have been the model for Molière's
Alceste. If he claimed this at the time of *L'Art Poétique*, there is
again a piquancy in his reference to 'l'auteur du *Misanthrope*'
(l. 400): this is one more example of his equivocal self-deprecation
for dramatic purposes. But if his audience were waiting to see
which way he jumped, he leaves them in no doubt. Morality and
pleasing the right people are the touchstones of Comedy. Molière
is inferior to Terence.

4

Morality and social solidarity are two themes of *Chant IV*.
The third theme, which Boileau uses to link them, is money.

The Canto opens with another of his parables. This story of the
doctor turned architect is no doubt in part a satire on Claude
Perrault, and probably Boileau's audience enjoyed the allusion.
As a satire, however, it has a strange conclusion: the praise of the
architect seems sincere. Rather than looking for contemporary
satire, we should perhaps investigate the functions of the passage
in the framework of the poem as a whole. Two points seem to me
important. First, the doctor has presumably followed conscien-
tiously his 'art inhumain' (l. 21). It is not he, but his 'science',
which is 'suspecte' (l. 23). That is, when he follows the rules, he

does harm. When he turns architect, nothing direct is said about rules. He 'semble né dans cet art' (seems born to this art) (l. 13), and 'la règle' (the rule) which he then uses (l. 22) is a simple instrument in the service of his talent. The point is made with Boileau's customary neatness. Having described the rules, he is subordinating them to something more important, but the rules are useful nonetheless, as instruments.

The second point is that Boileau insinuates gracefully what his theme is now to be. Underneath the gaiety of the fable, there is a moral question. The doctor is described as an 'assassin' (l. 2), and his crimes are convincingly if amusingly set out. That this is more than a joke is indicated by a detail that has nothing to do with gibes against medicine. The doctor is a 'savant hâbleur' (l. 2), an accomplished boaster. This links him with many of the bad poets in the poem: the madman with his 'voix insolente' (insolent voice) (*Chant I*, l. 23), the 'follement pompeux' (foolishly grand) author of pastorals (*Chant II*, l. 13), the 'auteur altier' (arrogant author) of *Chant II*, l. 197, the foolish epic poet of *Chant III*, ll. 270–4, quite as much as the explicitly boastful 'poète orgueilleux' of *Chant I*, l. 129 and the 'auteur intraitable' (obstinate author) of *Chant I*, l. 208. Boastful pride is a sign of lack of *raison*, as these passages show. Pride is the first sin, and the cause of Man's fall from 'rightness'. The association of murder and pride indicates the moral condemnation implicit in Boileau's fable, and in its concluding line he makes use of the ambiguity in 'bon' and 'méchant' to express this point and link it with the need for technical skill which is emphasised in *L'Art Poétique*. 'Skilful' and 'unskilful' are also 'good' and 'evil'.

Most of *Chant IV*, from line 25 to line 192, is straight sermonising. Boileau continues to manipulate his pronouns to indicate his complicity with his audience, but his approach is direct, even rude:

> Son exemple est pour nous un précepte excellent.
> Soyez plutôt maçon, si c'est votre talent.
>
> (ll. 25–6)

His aristocratic hearers are to take up a mechanical trade, and the blunt 'maçon' is used instead of the nobler 'architecte'.

The variant to lines 34–8 underlines Boileau's method. The original version is lively in the manner of the early Satires:

> Les vers ne souffrent point de médiocre auteur:
> Ses écrits en tous lieux sont l'effroi du lecteur:
> Contre eux dans le Palais les boutiques murmurent.
> Et les ais chez Billaine à regret les endurent.[24]

The change of direction after the first line, the comic exaggeration of the rest, prefigure the 'burlesque audace' which line 39 half-praises and half-damns. In 1701, Boileau replaced these lines with a straightforward series of statements on bad authors in his plain didactic style. But in this part of the poem he does not entirely eschew dramatic effects elsewhere. In lines 44–8, he raises an uneasy smile in his audience: he tells those who admire his readings before publication that often the work when it appears is disappointing.

He then summarises and emphasises (ll. 49–84) two points he has made earlier: that fools must not be listened to, but that 'un censeur solide et salutaire' must be consulted. The tone is almost scolding:

> Je vous l'ai déjà dit, aimez qu'on vous censure.
>
> (l. 59)

The fool shows 'orgueil' (pride) (l. 62), with its Christian associations of the deadliest sin. He is a 'subtil ignorant' (subtle ignoramus) (l. 62), uses 'vains raisonnements' (empty arguments) (l. 65), has a 'faible raison, de clarté dépourvue' (feeble reason, bereft of light) (l. 67), his sight is 'débile' (weak) (l. 68) and his advice dangerous (l. 69). Those who listen to him drown (which, in Boileau's universe, signifies loss of reason).[25] The true judge is severe, and the author shows in a very bad light, with his self-deception, his 'doutes ridicules' (absurd doubts) and his 'esprit tremblant' (wavering mind) (ll. 75, 76). The true judge has a moral authority which enables him to dispense the author from following the 'règles prescrites' (rules laid down) on occasion (ll. 77–80).

This stern recapitulation leads up to some of Boileau's strongest and most plainly didactic verses:

> Auteurs, prêtez l'oreille à mes instructions.
> Voulez-vous faire aimer vos riches fictions?
> Qu'en savantes leçons votre Muse fertile
> Partout joigne au plaisant le solide et l'utile.

> Un lecteur sage fuit un vain amusement,
> Et veut mettre à profit son divertissement.
>
> (ll. 85–90)

There is a characteristic alternation between moral severity and a more relaxed attitude when Boileau emphasises that the depiction of love is allowable (ll. 97–100), and again when he advises the poet to behave as an agreeable social being (ll. 121–4), but the dominant tone is moral:

> Aimez donc la vertu, nourrissez-en votre âme:
> En vain l'esprit est plein d'une noble vigueur;
> Le vers se sent toujours des bassesses du cœur.
>
> (ll. 108–10)

We now come to a section of sixty-eight lines (ll. 125–92) in which Boileau talks about money. There is nothing perfunctory about this section. The fervency of the moral denunciation (ll. 130–1, 169–70, 173–8) is unmistakable, and inspires some of Boileau's most trenchant lines. The long mythical history of poetry (ll. 132–66) is based on Horace, and brings nothing new (though we may note that Boileau, unlike Horace, explicitly mentions in lines 157–8 the usefulness of Hesiod's didactic poetry). But the myth leads up to another denunciation of avarice as the source of literary degradation:

> Mais enfin l'indigence amenant la bassesse,
> Le Parnasse oublia sa première noblesse.
> Un vil amour du gain, infectant les esprits,
> De mensonges grossiers souilla tous les écrits.
>
> (ll. 167–70)

This is not in Horace, and is an unexpected feature. The verse gives two clues to its significance here. First, there is a stress on the immorality of loving money. Second, the love of money and the need for money are linked to social as well as moral baseness (ll. 166–7). The appeal is to a cultivated audience which would prefer glory to money. It is also an appeal to the aristocratic virtue of *gloire* (the 'laurels' of Apollo in line 178 recall the laurels of the successful general) against the commercial virtues. In stressing the subject of money, Boileau is linking his emphasis on morality to an appeal to the ideals of the Court and the salons.

It is by this means that Boileau arrives at the conclusion to his poem. This is a eulogy of Louis XIV, who 'Fait partout au mérite ignorer l'indigence' (l. 192). It is more than a eulogy, however. It evokes a picture in which all the poets, in their different ways, serve society in its different aspects. Louis is to be praised not only in grand verse: lesser poets will use his name in songs to be sung 'par la bouche des belles' (by the mouths of the fair sex) (l. 199), to amuse 'les ruelles' (fashionable literary gatherings) (l. 200), or to enchant the forests (l. 201), or even to sharpen epigrams (l. 202).

The conclusion modestly suggests Boileau's rôle in giving encouragement and advice:

> Vous me verrez pourtant, dans ce champ glorieux,
> Vous animer du moins de la voix et des yeux;
> Vous offrir ces leçons que ma muse au Parnasse
> Rapporta jeune encor du commerce d'Horace;
> Seconder votre ardeur, échauffer vos esprits,
> Et vous montrer de loin la couronne et le prix.
> Mais aussi pardonnez, si, plein de ce beau zèle,
> De tous vos pas fameux observateur fidèle,
> Quelquefois du bon or je sépare le faux,
> Et des auteurs grossiers j'attaque les défauts;
> Censeur un peu fâcheux, mais souvent nécessaire,
> Plus enclin à blâmer que savant à bien faire.
>
> (ll. 225–36)

Here, good and bad gold suggest good and bad verse, but also the good gold of Louis and the bad gold desired by avaricious poets. The 'défauts' of the 'auteurs grossiers' refer back to the 'grossière nature' of mankind before the advent of Reason in line 135. The final couplet presents Boileau as the *honnête homme*, modest but conscious of his own value. It concludes gracefully this final movement, which has brought together the elements the poem has developed: morality, aesthetic merit and social distinction converge in the communal effort to celebrate the achievements of civilisation, as manifested in the reign of Louis XIV.

7
The significance of *L'Art Poétique*

1

The central critical problem of any evaluation of Boileau is this: what are we to make of *L'Art Poétique*? The position I take is that *L'Art Poétique* is Boileau's greatest achievement, and of great historical significance: it is not only a master-piece, but shows how neo-classicism was enabled to function as a literary doctrine at the turning-point in European history, at the end of the seventeenth century and the beginning of the eighteenth. The discussion in this chapter will fall into four parts. The first will merely note the didactic character of the poem, and some of the issues this raises. The second and third will attempt to relate the poem to some wider considerations. Finally, I will sum up my interpretation, and discuss the implications of it for some other views of Boileau.

Traditionally, *L'Art Poétique* was regarded as a statement of neo-classical doctrine. Clearly, in some ways it falls short of being a systematic treatise. It does not start with a consideration of the function of poetry, stressing its moral purpose. It does not discuss the nature and justification of the need to observe *vraisemblance* or *les bienséances*. In considering individual *genres*, it does not set out fully the means by which each inculcates morality – in Tragedy, by poetic justice and perhaps catharsis, in Epic by allegory, in all *genres* by explicitly moral maxims.

It is difficult, however, to deny another aspect of the poem which the traditional view emphasised: that in it Boileau is prescribing rules for poets. Although some neo-classical rules are omitted (for instance, Boileau does not attempt to define the lapse of imagined time permitted in an epic), there seems little reason to suppose that he is not laying down rules. Much of *L'Art Poétique*

– to put things at their lowest – at least seems to be couched in prescriptive terms:

> Quelque sujet qu'on traite, ou plaisant, ou sublime,
> Que toujours le bon sens s'accorde avec la rime
> *(Chant I*, ll. 27–8)

> Aimez donc la raison: que toujours vos écrits
> Empruntent d'elle seule et leur lustre et leur prix
> *(ibid.*, ll. 37–8)

> Quoi que vous écriviez, évitez la bassesse
> *(ibid.*, l. 79)

> Que ce style jamais ne souille votre ouvrage
> *(ibid.*, l. 95)

> Auteurs, prêtez l'oreille à mes instructions.
> *(Chant IV*, l. 85)

There is perhaps a note of self-mockery in some of this, as at the end of *Chant IV*, where Boileau offers the lessons he has learned from Horace (ll. 227–8), but the constant use of the imperative tells its own story. To quote from *L'Art Poétique* all the formulae on the pattern 'Do this', or 'Let this be done' would be to copy out half the poem.

It is no doubt true, as has often been urged,[1] that Boileau's ardent temperament prompted him to generalise his perceptions into universal statements: what Adam calls 'l'absurde emploi de *tout*, de *seul*, de *jamais* et de *toujours*'.[2] But when, outside *L'Art Poétique* itself, Boileau talks about what he is doing, he is quite clearly thinking in terms of instructing. The most formal statements are in his *Au Lecteur* prefixed to the *Œuvres Diverses* of 1674. As he explains, he had undertaken the translation of Longinus for his own instruction:

Mais j'ai cru qu'on ne serait pas fâché de la voir ici à la suite de la Poétique, avec laquelle ce Traité a quelque rapport, et où j'ai même inséré plusieurs préceptes qui en sont tirés.[3]

The Preface to the translation indicates what he had in mind:

J'ai songé qu'il ne s'agissait pas simplement ici de traduire Longin; mais de donner au public un Traité du Sublime, qui pût être utile.[4]

For good measure, the original 1674 Preface added a comment on Aristotle's *Rhetoric*: 'C'est un ouvrage d'une extrême utilité, et pour moi j'avoue franchement que sa lecture m'a plus profité que tout ce que j'ai jamais lu dans ma vie.'[5]

The *Discours sur l'Ode* confirms that by 'préceptes' inserted in *L'Art Poétique* he does mean precepts in the sense of rules:

> Ce critique, selon toutes les apparences, n'est pas fort convaincu du précepte que j'ai avancé dans mon Art Poétique, à propos de l'Ode... Ce précepte effectivement qui donne pour règle de ne point garder quelquefois de règles, est un mystère de l'art.[6]

There is nothing unusual in this emphasis on the possibility and necessity of laying down rules for poetry. Chapter II of the *Traité du Sublime* considers the argument that 'Le Sublime... naît avec nous, et ne s'apprend point', and 'que c'est une erreur de le vouloir réduire en art, et d'en donner des préceptes'.[7] Boileau's translation (which here faithfully reflects Longinus) expresses the normal neo-classical view that:

> quoique la Nature ne se montre jamais plus libre que dans les discours sublimes et pathétiques, il est pourtant aisé de reconnaître qu'elle ne se laisse pas conduire au hasard, et qu'elle n'est pas absolument ennemie de l'art et des règles. J'avoue que dans toutes nos productions il la faut toujours supposer comme la base, le principe et le premier fondement. Mais aussi il est certain que notre esprit a besoin d'une méthode pour lui enseigner à ne dire que ce qu'il faut, et à le dire en son lieu; et que cette méthode peut beaucoup contribuer à nous acquérir la parfaite habitude du Sublime.[8]

The assumption is exactly in accord with that made by Corneille at the beginning of his first *Discours*: 'Il est constant qu'il y a des préceptes, puis qu'il y a un art...'[9] In view of the evidence, there is surely every justification for the view taken by Voltaire of Boileau, 'ce maître de Parnasse':

> Qui, donnant le précepte et l'exemple à la fois,
> Établit d'Apollon les rigoureuses lois.[10]

Or by Vauvenargues:

> Boileau ne s'est pas contenté de mettre de la vérité et de la poésie dans ses ouvrages, il a enseigné son art aux autres.[11]

Or, from the standpoint of a different society, by Pope:

> The Rules, a nation born to serve, obeys,
> And Boileau still in right of Horace sways.[12]

There is also, I think, another powerful argument against the adequacy of those modern views which emphasise the personal element in *L'Art Poétique*, or see it, not as an aesthetic code, but as an expression of a given temperament in a given milieu. This is the peculiar nature of the poem's impressiveness and durability. Verlaine's *Art Poétique* expresses memorably and concisely an aesthetic position. So does Gautier's *L'Art*, and many another poem. None of these has imposed itself on people's minds in quite the same way. The question that needs to be answered is: What gives *L'Art Poétique* its importance? It does not score simply because it is longer or more comprehensive than Verlaine's or Gautier's. Many other *Arts of Poetry* have been longer and more comprehensive and been forgotten. Nor is *L'Art Poétique* pre-eminent among Boileau's works by the quality of its verse. Hervier, Adam and many others have pointed out its defects of padding, monotony of rhythm, repetition of formal devices, and so on. It is certainly not remarkable for much originality of thought. Bray demonstrated long ago, and others have since amply confirmed, that Boileau brought little new to neo-classical theory. To answer our question, we need to consider some more fundamental issues.

3

My starting-point will be some comparisons between Boileau and Montaigne. In a work of literature, the tone and temper of the writing are as much part of what is said as any ideas that can be separated from it. Brody is certainly correct when he demonstrates Boileau's reliance on his own critical responses, on the instantaneous, intuitive perception that enables the reader to recognise poetic quality: a quality which is a *je ne sais quoi* incapable of abstract definition. This is not far from Montaigne's comments on poetry:

A certaine mesure basse, on la peut juger par les préceptes et par art. Mais la bonne, l'excessive, la divine est au-dessus des règles et de la raison. Quiconque en discerne la beauté d'une vue ferme et rassise, il ne la voit pas, non plus que la splendeur d'un éclair. Elle ne pratique point notre jugement; elle le ravit et ravage.[13]

The preceding sentences in Montaigne, on the difficulty of judgment and the rarity of good critics compared with poets, are even closer to Boileau and to his position in the world of seventeenth-century French literature. Naturally, Boileau was an inheritor of the Renaissance and its Classical culture. Despite his care to maintain his stance of *honnête homme*, he was in many ways close to what the Moderns called a *philologue* in his love of Greek and Roman literature and his scorn for science. As Sayce has pointed out, his attitude to science in *Épître V* echoes the attitudes of the Renaissance humanists.[14] It is easy to find in Boileau other points of resemblance to the attitudes of Montaigne – for instance, condemnation of the Wars of Religion.[15] More generally, the scepticism of such pieces as *Satire IV* is in principle similar to ideas expressed by Montaigne.

Nevertheless, there is in Boileau, as in the seventeenth century generally compared with the Renaissance, a very different atmosphere from that in Montaigne. Montaigne's style, and seemingly his mental processes, are fluid, suggestive, so that his theme often 'se renverse en soi' (turns back on itself) until he wonders if anyone will grasp it.[16] Although Boileau's work is subtler and more ambiguous than it is sometimes given credit for, there is no doubt that it at least seems clearer, more dogmatic, more straightforward, a hostile critic might say more simplistic, than that of Montaigne. It is this aspect of Boileau – the legislator, the dogmatist, the teacher of good sense – which is the Boileau of tradition.

The traditional view may be partly mistaken, but it could hardly have been so powerful for so long unless it was based on something in Boileau's work, and certainly not on the content alone. Even when Boileau is expressing apparently open-ended ideas – the scepticism of *Satire IV*, the frequent insistence on the need to abandon the rules in the service of a higher mystery of art – we hear a confident, prescriptive tone.

The obvious reaction of the modern critic may again be to stress the personal element, to say that Boileau is by temperament more dogmatic than Montaigne. This is no doubt true, but it does not answer the basic question. There is a feeling in the work of Boileau, as often in the work of great writers, that the man, the milieu and the moment have come together in just the right way to favour a particular form of creation. It is hard to imagine that in the sixteenth or eighteenth century, any poet, however dogmatic in temperament, could have successfully cast his central work in the form of an *Art Poétique*. How did Boileau manage it?

We may make progress towards an answer by taking a passage from Montaigne which may seem to have nothing to do with *L'Art Poétique*, but which may help to pin down the seventeenth-century quality we are looking for. In *De l'Expérience* (*Essais*, Book III, ch. xiii), we find the following:

En la Chine, duquel royaume la police et les arts, sans commerce et connaissance des nôtres, surpassent nos exemples en plusieurs parties d'excellence, et duquel l'histoire m'apprend combien le monde est plus ample et plus divers que ni les anciens, ni nous ne pénétrons, les officiers députés par le Prince pour visiter l'état de ses provinces, comme ils punissent ceux qui malversent en leur charge, ils rémunèrent aussi de pure libéralité ceux qui s'y sont bien portés, outre la commune sorte et outre la nécessité de leur devoir.[17]

Why does this strike us as typical of the sixteenth century, rather than the seventeenth? One answer is the interested tone of the reference to China, and the relativist standpoint this implies. As Hazard pointed out, 'China' had a symbolic significance for seventeenth-century thought. Pascal's difficulty with all the implications of a true recognition of Chinese civilisation is evident. One basis of his apology for Christianity is what he calls its *perpétuité*: 'Cette religion...a toujours été sur la terre.'[18] 'Le Messie a toujours été cru. La tradition d'Adam était encore nouvelle en Noé et en Moïse.'[19] So China posed the dangerous possibility that an independent and older tradition existed.

Pascal's *Pensées* fascinate partly because of their incompleteness and paradoxical nature, and the reason for his difficulty with the concept of China is clearer if we turn to Bossuet. His *Discours sur l'Histoire Universelle* says nothing about China. It starts with the creation of the world, and proceeds through the Flood, Abraham and Moses up to the birth of Christ, picking the threads of Classical history up as it goes along. It then follows the history of the Roman Empire and the Catholic Church, and goes on to deal with the history of France up to Charlemagne. For a universal history, it is remarkably parochial. Voltaire was to poke fun at it by representing a Chinese scholar examining it and finding that it was only a tribal history of part of the Mediterranean world. We shall come back to Voltaire and China.

Bossuet is one of the important French seventeenth-century writers whose reputation has declined steadily. In part, this is due to the evident narrowness of his sympathies. But we should not underestimate the complexity underlying his dogmatism. If, in his *Discours*, he concentrated on Jewish and Classical history, this was not because nothing else was known. Montaigne's *Essais* show well enough that information (accurate or not) was available about China, Mexico and other civilisations, and about their chronologies. Pascal's difficulties were occasioned by Martini's history of China, which appeared in 1658, when Bossuet was thirty-one. Bossuet was well placed to know the latest work on the reliability of the Judaeo-Christian scriptures. He knew Spinoza's *Tractatus*, which appeared in 1670, and in 1678 was personally responsible for the attempt to suppress Simon's *Histoire Critique du Vieux Testament*. His selection of material for the *Discours* is dictated by his purpose, which emerges clearly from the structure of the work. Only the first part is a narrative of events. The rest is interpretation, as all serious history must be. The second part demonstrates the continuity of the Christian religion, and the third part interprets the rise and fall of empires as part of a divine plan. The *Discours* impresses as a construction, an assertion of values. Everything in it is subordinated to the extraordinary effort to bring everything into one system, and to make that system watertight, filling all history and allowing no chink through which doubts can infiltrate.

Here I think we have a clue to the characteristic power of seventeenth-century French Classicism. In the great writers of the age, there is certainly a pride in the achievements of their society, which they see as representing a universal norm. Other societies are either measured by it, or simply ignored. In this sense, the great writers are profoundly conformist: they are engaged in celebrating the virtues of their culture, which they see as characterised by Pascal's *perpétuité*. At the same time, their insights into human motivation are radically subversive of their ostensible values. The supreme example of this contradiction is Racine. But I think he represents, though in unusually pure form, the characteristic of French seventeenth-century literature which gives it its peculiar intensity: a tension between the social façade and the passion behind it, a sense of anarchy pressing against immovable discipline. If Bossuet seems to us less impressive, it is because he is more homogeneous. The emphasis is on one element only, the tendency to build a conformist system.

In this, I think Bossuet represents, more faithfully than the greater writers, a feature common in seventeenth-century French culture. Other traditions were active, even within the Church, but there is a strong trend in many spheres of life and thought to build a system designed to last for eternity. This is clearly one element in neo-classicism, and is reflected in the desire to legislate apparent in *L'Art Poétique*. It was once assumed that this tendency was one aspect of a general call to order reflecting Richelieu's establishment of absolutism. Modern research has disposed of this idea, at least in its simple form. It is easy to exaggerate the effectiveness of Richelieu's stabilising efforts. After his death, the central government's authority rapidly declined, until re-established by Mazarin and Louis XIV from the mid-1650s onwards. This slackening of authoritarian rule perhaps coincided with the development of a less rigorous temper in literature, but there is no sign of revolt against the rules as such.

A more plausible view is perhaps that a factor in the development of neo-classicism was the influence of the Counter-Reformation. Neo-classical critical doctrines were certainly developed in Italy at a time of increasing repression of new ideas, and came to France at the time of the great orthodox offensive against free thought, which Spink has called *la crise du libertinage*.[20] I have suggested elsewhere that the set of critical doctrines worked out by neo-classical critics may have functioned as a protective device, enabling poets to defend their activities as serious and moral in an age when they might incur the suspicion of the orthodox.

Whether or not there is truth in these views, they bear mainly on the establishment of neo-classicism in France. Only with difficulty can they explain why its doctrines continued to flourish in the latter part of Louis XIV's reign, in which religious orthodoxy may have become more repressive than in the middle of the century, but the shift towards Enlightenment attitudes among the intelligentsia is already evident. Still less do they account for some of the questions raised in Chapter 1. Why should neo-classical doctrines have continued to be warmly espoused in eighteenth-century France? Why were they so influential in Restoration and eighteenth-century England, with its different social, political and religious systems? My view remains that convention, fashion and politics are not sufficient to account for the facts.

A clue may be found if we return to Voltaire. Unlike the *Discours sur l'Histoire Universelle*, his *Essai sur les Mœurs* deals at some length with China. Indeed, chapter ɪ starts with it. The Chinese empire was vaster than that of Charlemagne; its history goes back before the Biblical date of the creation; its science is both accurate and ancient. The size of its population proves its antiquity, and it is foolish to say that the population of the world could have been replenished by a single family in the short time allowed for in the Bible after the deluge. In chapter ɪɪ, we are in the presence of the philosophic Chinese of the Enlightenment myth. Confucius was a sage, not a prophet, but the Chinese intelligentsia were Deists (like Voltaire). Despite the modest title of the *Essai*, we are nearer to Bossuet than Montaigne. There is none of Montaigne's subtle indirection, his free-floating curiosity which delights in human diversity and is willing to follow where its implications lead. Voltaire's language, like Bossuet's, is clear-cut, and his polemical purpose is unconcealed. Like Bossuet, he is asserting a system of values, though different ones. He, too, is in possession of the truth about the world, or at least a method of arriving at it. And neither in Bossuet nor in Voltaire do we feel a merely personal insistence. Bossuet has behind him the tradition of Catholic Christianity; in Voltaire we sense that he appeals with confidence to the growing forces of Enlightenment opinion.

This assertion of an intellectual system commanding wide assent and felt to be of the highest importance is fundamental. French commentators, perhaps starting with Boileau himself, certainly from Madame de Staël onwards, have often blamed Cartesianism for the decline of poetry. English critics have often blamed the same decline on the rise of rationalism and science, emphasising the secondary rôle implied for poetry in the views of knowledge put forward by Bacon, Hobbes, the Royal Society, Locke, and Descartes. This thesis is open to a number of objections. The list of leaders of seventeenth-century thought is so heterogeneous that it is hard to lump all its members together. Modern research has shown that the attitudes of Bacon and

Newton, at least, were a good deal subtler and more complex than used to be assumed. Descartes, who never fitted well with any of the others, now appears more clearly linked to Scholasticism and Counter-Reformation thought than was once implied. The thesis also ignores the importance of other trends of thought, such as revived Scholasticism, which must have seemed much more important at the time and which were at least as inimical to poetry.

Nevertheless, there is an element of truth in this view. The various thinkers named may have little in common, but there is a sense in which they fostered a common world-view. All, like Bossuet and Voltaire, seemed to inspire in their followers a feeling that here at last was a doctrine or method that made sense of the world and proposed an authoritative frame of reference. We may link this with the thesis that the reassertion of discipline by the Counter-Reformation Church influenced the growth of neo-classicism. What we find in these various cases is a more or less authoritative world-view which proclaims its own version of the truth, to which poetry, like everything else, is subordinate. It does not seem unreasonable to suppose that such a system might have the effect of devaluing poetry, or at least of forcing those concerned with poetry to work out some justification for it which will fit within the system.

To have this effect, an intellectual system must possess certain typical features. There seems to be, in Western thought at least, a recurring tendency to build systems which do possess these features. Whether their subject-matter is religion, or science, or politics, their characteristics are that they are thought of as in some sense absolutes; that they cover (explicitly or by implication) all aspects of life; and that they are formulated in such a way that each element requires acceptance or rejection. They require a plain 'Yes' or 'No': the Zen or Hindu 'Yes *and* No' or the reasonable 'Perhaps, but...' are alien to them. These systems have found it difficult to accommodate the claims of the arts, which are usually based on different attitudes to experience, and which evade these black and white alternatives. In practice, these systems tend to relegate the arts to second place, if not to reject them as 'untrue' or immoral. Christianity has tended to reject the arts as worldly vanities or incitements to sin (as in Puritanism and

Jansenism), or to harness them as adjuncts to the Faith (as the Counter-Reformation Church did). Nineteenth-century mechanistic science tended to regard the arts as mere decoration, or to require them to seek seriousness by conforming to the truth discovered by science. Communism has combined these attitudes, rejecting art, as did mechanistic science, as a frivolous distraction from the serious political business of life rather than from the scientific truth, or, like the Counter-Reformation Church, emphasising its rôle as propaganda for Communist rather than Christian doctrine.

Presumably the type of literary doctrine evolved, and how it operates, will vary according to the accepted world-view. In European culture, at least, there seem to be similarities between the literary doctrines in vogue at periods when a systematic world-view of this type has been generally accepted. The outstanding example is neo-classicism, but it is one of a family of theories which are based on similar mental patterns. As I have argued elsewhere, and as many others have done, neo-classicism finds its logical continuation in nineteenth-century naturalism, which reflects the dominance of materialistic science. In modern Marxist criticism, we can perhaps see a similar case to that of neo-classicism in the Counter-Reformation: the official ideologists lay down criteria for Social Realism, which (as befits a doctrine based on nineteenth-century scientific materialism) clings to the neo-classical principles of *vraisemblance* and moral utility.[21] In the Middle Ages, also, we find some features of literary doctrine which resemble neo-classicism. There is a proliferation of *Arts of Poetry*, the most famous being Geoffrey of Vinsauf's *Poetria Nova*. This explains in detail how a simple statement can be converted into poetry by elaborating the language. It resembles nothing so much as a *reductio ad absurdum* of Voltaire's famous letter of 20 December 1737 to the Crown Prince of Prussia, in which the same doctrine is expounded.[22] A well-known device of mediaeval poetry is allegory, by which moral truths can be taught delightfully. This doctrine also flourishes in neo-classicism. It is explicit in Chapelain's Prefaces to *La Pucelle*, and reaches its most systematic formulation in Le Bossu's *Traité du Poème Épique* (1675). Poetry must teach, and allegory is the most powerful method by which it can do so.

What I am arguing, then, is that an authoritarian theory of poetry will tend to be worked out and imposed when an authoritative view of the world is worked out and imposed (at least in principle) on all aspects of life; and that what is important for this process is the authoritarianism and pervasiveness of this world-view, rather than its specific doctrinal content. This is a more generalised version of the views that neo-classicism was in part a reflection of the authoritarianism of Richelieu, or of the Counter-Reformation Church. In the case of neo-classicism, this greater degree of generalisation makes some sense of the stability of the doctrine during the intellectual revolutions of the Enlightenment in France and of the Restoration and Augustan age in England. The attitudes implicit in Newtonian physics and *le progrès des lumières* formed a world-view every bit as comprehensive and sure of itself as that of Bossuet. Perhaps the shaking of tradition and the reliance on evidence from other civilisations made the formulation of rules for poetry impossible with the old confidence, but the clear imperatives of neo-classicism were as congenial to the new brisk rationalism as to the scholastic dogmatism of the Counter-Reformation. It is only when we come to the insistence on subjectivity which we find in Rousseau and the Romantics, and perhaps also the willingness to break the existing social order, that neo-classicism loses its self-confidence and dwindles to a reactionary cult.

Even if this generalisation has any validity, it does not in itself explain neo-classicism. We still need to investigate, for instance, how the critical doctrines functioned, whether as an extension of the dogmatism of the ruling world-view into poetry, or as a defensive measure for poetry against devaluation by a ruling system of values. I think the evidence strongly favours the latter interpretation.

In England, the neo-classical doctrine was never accepted as whole-heartedly as in France, and when an English poet does accept it his tactical reason is often obvious. In late sixteenth- and early seventeenth-century England, there was what an American scholar has rightly called 'the war against poetry'.[23] In this case, as he shows, the attack came from Puritanism, associated with a radical impatience with aristocratic frills and a proto-scientific thirst for unadorned, pragmatic truth. The counter-measure which at least two Puritan poets adopted was to espouse neo-classical doctrine. Sidney's neo-classical manifesto, probably written early in the 1580s, and first published in 1595, is explicitly a *Defence of Poesie* (or *Apologie for Poetrie*) and stresses poetry's moral utility.[24] Later, Milton came close to condemning poetry in the name of religion when, in *Paradise Regained* (Book IV, ll. 331–64),[25] he put in the mouth of Jesus an attack on Greek literature. But he left himself an escape hatch when he condemned Greek poems because they failed to fulfil adequately the neo-classical requirement: they are 'Thin sown with aught of profit or delight'. When, in the Preface to *Samson Agonistes*, he came to defend Tragedy, he did so by appealing to its moral aim, and to its superior value when written according to neo-classical precept: 'antient rule, and best example'.[26] By 1671, when these two poems were published, the thirst for unadorned truth was evident in the rise of science in England, and the cultivation of the plain way of writing and thinking recommended by the Royal Society. Writers like Dryden could turn to neo-classical doctrine as a defence for poetry against this new threat; and the late seventeenth and eighteenth centuries are the heyday of neo-classicism in England.

I would therefore take seriously the title of Sidney's essay. And, if we turn to seventeenth-century France, I think the evidence points the same way. One example seems to me especially suggestive, because it relates to a document which historians of literature often regard as marking a stage in the acceptance of neo-classicism in France: Jean Mairet's famous Preface of 1631 to his pastoral tragi-comedy *La Silvanire*. This deserves re-reading without preconceptions, because of the fascinating mixture of ideas it contains. Mairet starts his argument, not with rules, but with a curious series of statements in which he half makes, and half withdraws, the Classical and Renaissance claim that the poet is directly inspired by the gods:

Poète proprement est celui-là qui, doué d'une excellence d'esprit et poussé d'une fureur divine, explique en beaux vers des pensées qui semblent ne pouvoir pas être produites du seul esprit humain … je passe aux louanges de la poésie, qu'on ne peut nier être le plus digne de tous les arts, soit pour la noblesse de son origine, comme celle qui vient immédiatement du Ciel, soit pour l'excellence des beaux effets qu'elle produit.[27]

His purpose in the preface is illuminated by one of his sub-headings: *De l'excellence de la poésie*. But these ideas about poetry might have been more acceptable in the days of Renaissance neo-paganism than in the age in which they were written. In the eyes of the Counter-Reformation Church, they could only appear suspect. Mairet soon shies away from these potentially dangerous assertions to a statement of neo-classical principles. It is indeed an interesting pointer to the underlying consistency of neo-classicism throughout its long history that this early manifesto in France refers to the *je ne sais quoi* which signals poetic excellence, as well as to the necessity of rules. Mairet's preface is not so much a defence of the rules as a defence of poetry, and I would see this conjunction as a sign of the defensive function of the doctrine. What the pagan doctrine of inspiration could do in the Renaissance, the doctrine of neo-classicism will do in an age more dogmatically inclined.

If this defence is the function of the neo-classical rules, it does not, of course, explain why they took the forms they did. Study of the proximate factors is needed, and one of them is easily identified. Counter-Reformation Catholicism made an effort to rehabilitate the mediaeval synthesis of Christian and Aristotelian rationalism. New factors since the Middle Ages were the wider knowledge of and respect for the Classics, and the rediscovery of the *Poetics* of Aristotle. It is not implausible, as has been suggested by one of the most eminent scholars of the history of thought, that we should link together 'the new Aristotelianism in both philosophy and literary criticism'.[28] The *Poetics*, with their stress on verisimilitude and their search for a justification for poetry, certainly lent themselves to the purposes of critics during the Counter-Reformation and later, who almost all interpreted Aristotle in a moral sense. I do not think we should attribute this reverence for Aristotle to antiquarian sentiment, inability to think, or lack of knowledge of his meaning. That some unorthodox spirits (such as Racine) interpreted Aristotle psychologically rather than morally shows what could be done; that the moral view was nevertheless almost universally accepted shows that there were powerful underlying forces at work. Aristotle, interpreted as a dogmatist, could provide just what was needed in the environment of a dogmatic world-view. Indeed, Aristotle's statement that poetry is more philosophical than history contains the germ of all that any ideologue can desire.

It will be apparent from these reflections that I see not the slightest reason to underplay the importance of neo-classicism as a doctrine. Neo-classicism seems to me functionally related to the powerful tendency in Western thought during the sixteenth to the eighteenth centuries to erect dogmatic systems of the sort described. I would indeed argue that nineteenth-century naturalism, which is a logical continuation of neo-classicism, is related in a similar way to nineteenth-century materialistic science. I would see neo-classical doctrine as the most successful example of a defensive response to the dilemmas posed by such systems for poetry. Moreover, in some of the surviving forms of Christianity, but more potently in some of the variants of Marxist thought, such attitudes are still with us today, and express the same tendency to dogmatise and systematise. It is not surprising, therefore, that similar responses are still evident in modern theorising about the arts. It is difficult to regard neo-classicism as of only antiquarian interest when we consider the twentieth-century debates on commitment, or the social relevance of the arts, or drama as documentary, or the function of the arts in stimulating political awareness, or the need for ideological correctness. The specific neo-classical rules may no longer be accepted: but here we still see, very thinly disguised, the neo-classical debates on the moral function of art, and the need to observe *vraisemblance* and *les bienséances*, to justify the *dulcis* by means of the *utilis*.

Against this background, I do not think we should make too much of the gaps and inconsistencies of neo-classical doctrine. What is remarkable is the effort towards completeness and consistency, even at the expense of ignoring some awkward issues. These apparent blind spots may even reveal the consistency of the underlying world-view, as they do in Bossuet. They testify to the existence of difficulties, but also to the sensitivity that perceived them, and, more important, the determination to transcend them.

I therefore think it is not at all strange that in seventeenth-century France, in a society in which there was an immense collective effort to build up and assert a universal system of values, neo-classical doctrines should have been a focus of interest. It also seems to me understandable that a poet who, like Boileau, succeeded in writing an *Art Poétique*, should have found himself hailed as performing a task central to his culture. What does require some explanation is how he was able to write it so well: ideological correctness is usually dull.

4

One aspect of neo-classicism which has already been discussed is *vraisemblance*: the principle that art should present what is probable in normal circumstances. Although it appears under its own name only fleetingly in *L'Art Poétique*, further discussion of it may help towards understanding the poem's special quality.

As Genette has remarked,[29] *vraisemblance* is linked with another neo-classical imperative: the need to observe the *bienséances*, both in the sense of what is fitting to the objects represented (*les bienséances internes*) and in conformity with the expectations of the public and ordinary decency (*les bienséances externes*). The point which I think needs stressing is that both *vraisemblance* and *les bienséances internes* are in the last resort subsumed in *les bienséances externes*. The concept of what is normal is easily taken as what is normal in seventeenth-century society. Racine's attitude in his Preface to *Iphigénie* shows the process at work:

Quelle apparence que j'eusse souillé la scène par le meurtre horrible d'une personne aussi vertueuse et aussi aimable qu'il fallait représenter Iphigénie? Et quelle apparence encore de dénouer ma tragédie par le secours d'une déesse et d'une machine, et par une métamorphose, qui pouvait bien trouver quelque créance du temps d'Euripide, mais serait trop absurde et trop incroyable parmi nous?[30]

Conformity to the moral delicacy of a seventeenth-century audience is linked with subscribing to their world-view. In the seventeenth-century world-view, pagan gods are not real, and cannot intervene in human affairs, and therefore cannot do so in a serious play. Observing *vraisemblance* means ideological conformity.

Les bienséances internes may seem to lead in a different direction, as Classical heroes may naturally behave differently from seventeenth-century Christians. Indeed, this Classical legacy may help poets to escape from the straitjacket of contemporary morality. But in practice this legacy tends to be renounced in favour of observing *les bienséances externes*.

A clear example is suicide, which in Classical antiquity was considered often sensible and in some cases a striking proof of nobility, but which in Christian morality is strongly reprobated. We can trace a shift in its treatment. In Hardy's *Scédase*, the hero kills himself. This is in accordance with the Classical sources, and with Greek morality. Not only does the general emotional structure of the play invite us to approve, but Hardy introduces a speech specifically to tell us that it is praiseworthy.[31] Once neo-classicism is firmly established, the playwrights find themselves in a difficulty. In a notorious example, Corneille has a Christian martyr threaten to commit suicide because her God orders it.[32] The way in which Racine ignores this difficulty is one example of his way with neo-classical conventions, which is far less conformist than the Preface to *Iphigénie* would suggest. The more conformist Addison had trouble in his *Cato*. His hero commits suicide. This is not only in accordance with history – *le vrai*: it is also as *vraisemblable* as one could wish, in a Roman hero confronted with the defeat of all he stands for. Addison's treatment of this enables us to observe in action the conflict between *vraisemblance* as what is likely and *vraisemblance* as conformity to an ideology. Cato commits suicide, but regrets his action:

> And yet methinks a beam of light breaks in
> On my departing soul. Alas, I fear
> I've been too hasty.[33]

This brings us back to Boileau. He may not lay much stress on *vraisemblance*, but a constant preoccupation in *L'Art Poétique* is with morality. There can be little doubt that by this he means Christian morality. This central concern leads him into some difficult areas. First, there is an ambiguity between morality as Boileau seems to mean it in his more solemn moments, and the social morality of the *honnête homme*. A clear example is his discussion of love in Tragedy in *Chant III*, ll. 93–102. Second, there is the common neo-classical problem of the extent to which the truth of poetry conflicts with the higher truth of religion. These two problems had contemporary solutions which Boileau avoids in *L'Art Poétique*, an avoidance for which critics have often reproached him.

The first of these was antiquarianism. He could have followed Rapin in recommending tragedies on the Greek model, without a love-interest. This would have cut him off from the taste of his audience, and his refusal to do so has therefore led some to conclude that he was weakly going along with his contemporaries, content to be a salon entertainer rather than a critic. My attempts in the earlier chapters of this book to analyse how he gets his effects may have shown that the truth is rather different. There is a movement which occurs so frequently in his poetry as to suggest that it is part of the way his mind worked. This is for him to lead his audience to laugh or feel with him, and then suddenly to turn aside. He thus makes them examine their responses, to decide whether to follow him on his new track or continue on the old one. Similarly, his constant appeal to the equation of social with moral and intellectual worth is not simply flattery of his audience's snobbery. He induces too many uneasy feelings about nobility, too many reflections that fools are 'chez le duc' or 'chez le prince', for this to be plausible. I suggest that a better explanation is one that links this turn-about manoeuvre with his emphasis on a social function for poetry. In both cases he is urgently concerned with making real to himself and his audience the importance of building shared values which will bind together society, poetry and religion in a structure which holds firm against unreason. Unreason is the 'shipwreck' of society and of the individual mind: the ship is kept afloat by shared values based on self-examination.

It is this concern which dictates the structure of *L'Art Poétique*. I would not claim that this structure is rigorous, and in the circumstances in which it was intended to be recited the over-all form would probably count for little. Nevertheless, the poem does have an over-all shape that means something. It begins by talking of verse in general, and of that indispensable but most private element, the poetic faculty: the first duty of the would-be poet is to examine himself and to be sure that he has that faculty. The poem then moves through the *genres* which scarcely raise the question of public morality to those that do. *Chant IV*, as the climax of the poem, concentrates on the link between literature and public morality. It culminates in an essentially social gesture: the poets are to co-operate in a glorification of the social order. But the modest concluding lines are equally significant. Boileau ends, not with the glorification of Louis XIV, but with an assessment of his own limitations. The last lines pick up the themes of the opening section.

There is a second solution which Boileau did not adopt, one which many critics of the time accepted, but which *L'Art Poétique* carefully evades. The potential conflict between poetry and the truth of Christian doctrine and morality (or, in the eighteenth century, poetry and scientific truth) could, according to neo-classicism, have only one outcome. An impressive line of critics from Chapelain to Le Bossu insist that morality and doctrine must take precedence over poetry. A consequence from which they do not shrink is that the most serious poetry is allegorical. Its purpose must be didactic, and allegory offers a method for teaching delightfully. This is why, in *Chant III* of *L'Art Poétique*, the discussion of Christian machinery in the Epic is so crucial, and why I think we do wrong to shrug it aside as a polemical *hors d'œuvre*. When faced with the issue of poetry and truth, Boileau accepts the implication of his doctrine. His presentation is based on the assumption that there is a contrast between the 'vérités' and 'mystères terribles' of Christianity and the 'fictions', 'songes' and 'mensonges' of poetry. But he does not accept, or at least he evades, the simple allegorical solution. The penalty is a rather weak prescription that Epic should be amusing and ornamental. The difficulty is not solved, but at least he is saving poetry from being didactic in the simplistic sense.

There is one other point which may be relevant here. Various explanations have been advanced for why Boileau omits the Fable from his poem. The Fable is one example of a directly didactic *genre*. He also omits the Didactic Poem as such from his list of *genres*, although hallowed by the precedents of Hesiod, Lucretius and Virgil. I suggest two reasons for the omission. First, *L'Art Poétique* is itself a didactic poem. To write about the Didactic Poem in a didactic poem is to set up a baroque play-within-a-play tension which is at odds with the aesthetic Boileau is propounding. Second, it would expose a sensitive and central issue, which Boileau found difficulty in handling. According to neo-classical doctrine, all poetry is didactic, or ought to be. To discuss didactic-ism is to raise, more acutely, the problems raised in the section on Epic.

Let us now turn from morality to the rules.

From time to time, we hear of hoaxes by which eminent critics are fooled into praising poems which have consciously been pro-duced to show the absurdity of modern poetry. This is a salutary reminder, not only of the fallibility of critics, but also of the element of expectation that enters into appreciation. We bring, ready-formed, to the act of appreciation a range of possible responses within different terms of reference. The frames of reference and responses we use are selected because of the cues we pick up in the object. The assumption 'This is a modern poem' itself suggests a frame of reference and prepares a range of responses in the critic's mind. Genette quotes Cohen's example of how, if a newspaper story is set out as a poem, this purely typo-graphical change effects our response.[34] In neo-classical art, with its well-defined and explicit conventions, two effects in particular are made available to the artist. First, it is made fairly easy for him to evoke immediate recognition of the function of a poem: 'This is a *jeu d'esprit*', 'This is a panegyric.' As a result, neo-classic poets found it easier than we do to write social or public poetry which, however lacking in permanent qualities, fulfilled its function adequately for the purpose for which it was produced: the expectations of the audience met them half-way. Second, and this is surely a commonplace, the shared acceptance of neo-classical doctrine enabled the poet to produce subtle but powerful effects by departing or threatening to depart from the conven-tions.

This again brings us to Boileau's method. He does lay down rules with his frequent formulae saying: 'Do this', 'Don't do that', 'Let's do this', 'Let that be done'; but the emphasis is on creating the emotional context in which his audience can appreci-ate good poetry. This is surely one reason why he so often ex-emplifies what he is urging or condemning.[35] More than this, his method relies on the existence of the norms laid down by the rules. By writing within an obvious convention – satire, panegyric, moral advice – he sets up in the reader a frame of reference, but then, by changes of level and mood, shuttling between directness and irony, he forces the reader's mind to move around constantly, shuffling and re-examining his responses and frames of reference in order to keep up with the poem. This is the source of the astonishing vitality of Boileau's best work. As we read him, our minds do a lively dance, and we (rightly) attribute the liveliness to the poems which induced it.

The conclusion to be drawn from this discussion is the same as from the discussion of his treatment of poetry and morality. Far from being a superficial or incoherent summariser of the doctrine, Boileau is profoundly aware of its bases, uses and limitations. His art is founded, first, on his intuitive perception of the psychology of the aesthetic response; secondly, on his awareness that this response is conditioned by intellectual and social factors; and thirdly, on his conviction that the social, intellectual and aesthetic must be held together in a synthesis if cultural achievement is to be possible.

These three factors are complemented by a fourth, which is perhaps an aspect of the first. This, which seems to be founded on something in his temperament, is his quasi-dramatic method, which enables him to swing his audience to and fro and at the same time explore differing view-points on experience. He avoids, at least in the poems so far discussed, the didactic dullness implicit in neo-classicism and evident in the works of some of its exponents.

The importance of this quasi-dramatic element may lead to two further reflections. The seventeenth century in France, which so signally failed to produce a great epic, is one of the great ages of dramatic literature. The sense of human beings as *jouant la comédie* is very strong in its non-dramatic literature, in Pascal, La Rochefoucauld, La Bruyère, as well as Boileau.[36]

This dramatic element perhaps gives one clue to the importance of Jansenism for the great writers of the century. Much appears baffling in the history of Jansenism, which on the face of it might seem just another dispute on theology. Modern scholars have sought for some underlying factor to explain why this particular dispute should have assumed such importance. Adam has pointed out the importance of Jansenism to many Frenchmen as a symbol of opposition to an oppressive régime, or of French independence from Ultramontane domination. There is Goldmann's thesis that

Jansenism crystallised the dilemma of an office-holding class linked historically with the Crown but undermined in its functions by Royal absolutism.

No doubt there is something in these historical and sociological explanations. I would like to draw attention to the characteristic feeling-tone of Jansenism, and of writers influenced by it, which may be relevant to its effect on literature. The apparent obscurity of the grounds of controversy, with the famous unfindable Five Propositions; the endless stratagems of Jansenist apologists, driven from defence of Jansen's orthodoxy to the distinction between *fait* and *droit*, always protesting loyalty to Church and King, but always evading obedience to their wishes: all this suggests that the fact of opposition, the effect of being at an angle to prevailing orthodoxy, was the vivifying element in Jansenism for the writers under its influence. If there is truth in this suggestion, it indicates a link between Jansenism and the attitude that at first sight is its intellectual and emotional opposite: *libertinage*.

What characterised the *libertins* was not any common doctrines, or even any common view of life. Although many *libertins* professed beliefs that foreshadowed eighteenth-century Deism, the evidence points to a range of different beliefs, from magical pantheism through to stoicism, materialistic rationalism, or simple impatience with metaphysical subtleties. Life-styles varied from the proud assumption of the rôle of Magus, to the stance of the Epicurean philosopher, to a faith in the goodness of the life of the senses, and so on to uninhibited debauchery.

What these elements have in common is opposition to the conventional wisdom and morality of Counter-Reformation society, though usually mixed with an impulse towards conformity that is more than merely a prudent façade. What we find in the great writers of the century is a tension between their passionate acceptance of their society and a radical refusal to accept its conformism. Pascal, Racine and Boileau are all closely associated with Jansenism. La Rochefoucauld, La Fontaine, and even Molière, have links with it. At the same time, Molière and La Fontaine are certainly *libertins*. Racine probably, and Boileau possibly, had *libertin* sympathies in their youth, and were closely associated with *libertins*. Pascal's apologetics base themselves on an awareness of the *libertin* critique of Christianity. La Roche-

foucauld's personal philosophy may have been Christian, but the
Maximes present us with a secular world. Jansenism and seventeenth-century *libertinage* may seem far apart, and of very
different importance for the future, but the lives of the great
writers show them strangely intertwined.

This is not to argue that the true artist must be a rebel, whether
or not the rebels of his age are Jansenists or *libertins*. The evidence
suggests strongly that the greatest writers have been upholders of
the values of their societies, often members of the ruling circles or
under the direct protection and patronage of those who were:
Aeschylus, Sophocles, Virgil, Shakespeare, Corneille, Molière,
Racine. But the sensitivity and intelligence needed to write great
literature are unlikely to coexist with a capacity for unthinking
acceptance of prevailing opinions. Creativeness implies involvement with its material, but also distance from it. In strongly
authoritarian cultures, it is not surprising if we find that the great
writers are defenders of the régime, but that at the same time they
need intellectual elbow-room within which to function.

A second and final reflection brings us back to Boileau, *L'Art
Poétique* and the dangers of dogmatism. The discussion of Epic
in *Chant III* raised the crucial question of didacticism. Boileau
evaded it. In my view, this was because of the dramatic nature of
his imagination, perhaps assisted by a flirtation with *libertinage*
and by his Jansenist sympathies, which kept him slightly at an
angle to any orthodoxy. But it is the ability to stay at this angle,
rather than the content of his unorthodox views, which is important in this context. Jansenism, though unpopular with the
régime, exercised a remarkable hold on its supporters. Sympathy
with a persecuted ideology can, in principle, have the same per-
vasive and limiting effects on the individual mind as submission to
a more widely accepted orthodoxy. This is a point to consider in
Boileau's later, more overtly Jansenist, poems.

5

L'Art Poétique differs in nature from many, though not all, of
Boileau's other poems. Its purpose is to set out a doctrine on how
poetry should be written and appreciated, though there is some
equivocation on how far the rules apply to poetry which is merely

'fictions'. As the work of a poet, not a philosopher, it succeeds by acting out this doctrine rather than by statement. But the doctrine is there, and I do not think we should underestimate the seriousness with which it was offered and received.

A prose paraphrase of the doctrine as defined in *L'Art Poétique* would run something like this. In both writing and responding to poetry, the essential activity is self-examination. The poetic method, even in non-dramatic poetry, is akin to that of drama, with its stimulation of complex responses by objectifying possible positions. The intellectual and imaginative exercise induced by this method gives pleasure. Except in merely fictional poetry, the aim must be moral improvement. To escape from subjectivism, it is essential to use social and religious values as controls. To escape from the dangers of aesthetic caprice, poetry must follow accepted conventions: the rules. To obey the rules, however, is more than a badge of moral and intellectual self-discipline. It is an act of faith in the values of civilised society. It is also a sign that poetry, like other praiseworthy activities, partakes in that grand synthesis which reflects the unchanging rational order. As I have tried to show in Chapters 5 and 6, these ideas are all clearly present in the poem. They seem to me to form a coherent doctrine: what is more, it is fully consistent with neo-classical theory, of which it constitutes a sensitive exploration and restatement.

It follows from this interpretation that, in my opinion, some recent views of the poem are mistaken, or at least incomplete. Adam has said, for instance, that *L'Art Poétique* shows Boileau's lack of intelligence, and a failure to appreciate 'la ferme doctrine de Fleury et de Rapin', who had wanted poetry to be grand and primitive, as they conceived it to have been in Greek and Biblical times.[37] My view would be the reverse of this. *L'Art Poétique* shows Boileau's remarkable intelligence. One sign of this is his realisation that neo-classical doctrine, if it is to succeed in its function, must seem to be universally valid. Like Bossuet's, the scheme must be universal. Unlike Fleury and Rapin, Boileau sees that it is futile, and a denial of the purpose of the doctrine, to indulge in antiquarian dreams about a golden age or revivals of Greek Tragedy. He sees that the neo-classical principles must be demonstrated to work in the here and now, in French society in the seventeenth century. He sees that literary neo-classicism is part of an ideological structure, linked functionally with the social structure and its religion. Even his failings in *L'Art Poétique* come from this ability to get to fundamentals. His lines on the Epic show not so much his insufficiencies as one fundamental difficulty of neo-classicism: it marks out a space for poetry, but only within a type of world-view whose values must override those of literature.

It is also difficult to accept Moore's view of *L'Art Poétique*:

> Fortunately we need no longer be embarrassed by having to call these banalities great principles of art. It is now established that the *Art Poétique* was written for the salons, as an entertainment, by a well-known satirist.[38]

In my view, this misrepresents every significant point. Boileau's poem is certainly entertaining, but the subtle psychological warfare by which he activates his hearer's responses is part of an over-all strategy by which he upholds a serious position. To dismiss *L'Art Poétique* as an amusing party-piece is to mistake Boileau's tactics for his war-aim.

I would also propose an amendment to Brody's views. His *Boileau and Longinus* exposed the falsity of the traditional view at its most extreme: the caricature of Boileau as a proponent of abstract ratiocination measuring the quality of poetry by mechanical rules. He demonstrated Boileau's emphasis on reason as an informed taste, an ability to perceive intuitively that inner power 'qui enlève, ravit, transporte' in which the greatness of literature lies.

But this, in my view, does not go far enough. As Brody acknowledges,[39] in Boileau *raison* may mean Reason – the immutable intellectual truth about the order of the universe. I would add that *savoir* may mean 'knowledge' – in the sense of the possession of this truth, and of the knowledge of how to construct poetry in accordance with it. I would place much more emphasis than Brody on Boileau's view of neo-classicism as a body of rules, and to that extent would agree with the traditional view of him.

Brody also seems to take it as self-evident that 'Boileau was not one of those writers, like Montaigne or Hugo, who evolve.'[40] If we abstract from Boileau's works of different periods his critical principles, we may find, as Brody does, a remarkable consistency. But if we look at his poetic technique, I think we do find a development. The two aspects on which I diverge from Brody are in fact linked: the poetic technique changes because Boileau's view of how to fulfil the neo-classical function of poetry changes. We are dealing with a continuing process. *L'Art Poétique* shows a change in emphasis from the early Satires and Epistles. Development continues in his later work. It takes the form, as the next Chapter will try to show, of a progressive simplification of his approach to the writing of poetry.

In *L'Art Poétique*, however, Boileau's art is subtle and complex. And this leads to a last point on which I think some correction of long-held views is needed. It is true that we should be hard put to it to find in Boileau's poems a critical idea or a precept not already part of neo-classical doctrine. But it is surely misleading to think of him simply as expressing in a brightly clever way ideas already conceived by others. To write a poem is itself to create something new. In the case of *L'Art Poétique*, the very form of the poem brings something fresh to neo-classical doctrine. Earlier theorists had argued (often ineptly, it may seem to us nowadays) that poetry should have a moral aim, and must therefore be *vraisemblable* and follow the rules. By demonstrating, in the reactions it provokes in the audience, the self-examination from which poetry can start, and by relating this starting-point to the social fabric, *L'Art Poétique* puts the doctrine on a firmer basis. Its effect is to make the doctrine rest, not on argument, but on experience.

8

Complexity and simplification

I

Boileau was never to write anything surpassing *L'Art Poétique*, but a good deal of his poetry remains to be considered. It can be divided into three groups. First, there are the poems he wrote at the time he was working on *L'Art Poétique*, or soon after. These include his mock-epic *Le Lutrin* (published in part in 1674 and in full in 1683); *Épître IX* (*Le Beau et le Vrai*) written in 1675 and published in 1683; *Épître VI* and *Épître VII* (both written in 1677 and also published in 1683), which relate to the quarrel over Racine's *Phèdre*, in which Boileau offended many by his support of Racine; and *Épître VIII* (written in 1678 and published in 1683), which thanks the King for the appointment as Historiographer Royal. Then, some years later, came a group of poems related to the famous Quarrel of the Ancients and the Moderns and its repercussions. In 1687, Charles Perrault read to the Academy his poem *Le Siècle de Louis le Grand*, in which he praised modern authors at the expense of the great writers of antiquity. Boileau and other defenders of the Ancients took offence. In 1693 his Pindaric *Ode sur la Prise de Namur* was intended as a lesson to Perrault, who had attacked Pindar. In 1694, Boileau published *Satire X* (*Sur les Femmes*). He was no doubt partly influenced by the fact that cultured women tended to favour the Moderns. *Épître X* (*A Ses Vers*) and *Épître XI* (*A Son Jardinier*) were written around 1693, and published in 1698. In effect, they reply to the personal attacks on him by defenders of the Moderns.

The third group of poems is on explicitly moral and religious subjects: *Épître XII* (*L'Amour de Dieu*), written in 1696, published in 1698; *Satire XI* (*Sur l'Honneur*), written 1698/9, published 1701; and finally *Satire XII* (*L'Équivoque*), on which Boileau worked from 1702 onwards, and of which publication was forbidden by the King. All three poems are related to contemporary religious disputes. Boileau, although he insisted on his orthodoxy, took the side of the Jansenists in his insistence on the necessity of love for God and of the special gift of God's grace, and attacked what he thought of as the laxity of the Jesuits, with their emphasis on the power of the sacraments to offset the effects of human imperfection.

These three groups of poems correspond to three stages in Boileau's poetic evolution, and also to the stages in his decline. The first group represent some of his finest work, and the individual poems merit attention. The second group can be discussed more briefly: though sometimes powerful and attractive, they show a falling-off which may be related to the changing attitudes to poetry which they embody. The last group contain the least interesting of his works. They show the completion of the change in his approach to poetry, and at the same time a collapse in literary quality.

2

The volume of *Œuvres Diverses* in which *L'Art Poétique* was published contained also the first four Cantos of *Le Lutrin* and the translation of Longinus' *Treatise on the Sublime*. Although this book is not concerned with Boileau's prose, the translation of Longinus is too important to be ignored. It may have been begun by Boileau's brother Gilles, and Boileau had probably been working on it since 1663/4.[1] The scholarly *Remarques* which accompanied it were revised from time to time in response to points made by other scholars. The *Réflexions Critiques sur Quelques Passages du Rhéteur Longin*, which came out in two stages, in 1694 and 1713, are more loosely connected with the translation, but also display much Classical learning. The translation and its apparatus confirm Boileau's concern with the reader's (or listener's) spontaneous reaction to poetic quality. This is fully in accord with the views expressed in the *Dissertation sur Joconde* of 1664/5 (again almost certainly by Boileau, though just possibly by his brother Gilles):

Ces sortes de beautés sont de celles qu'il faut sentir, et qui ne se prouvent point... Mais après tout, c'est un je ne sais quoi; et si votre ami est aveugle, je ne m'engage pas à lui faire voir clair.[2]

Against this, however, we should remember that Longinus/ Boileau still insists on the rules. The Preface of the *Œuvres Diverses* of 1674, as already noted, together with the Prefaces to the translation, use formulae that can only mean that Boileau is thinking in terms of prescriptions for poetry.[3] The translation of chapter II makes use of the notion of 'the rules', and *Réflexion II* takes up a sentence from the same passage which stresses the importance of method:

Notre esprit, même dans le Sublime, a besoin d'une méthode, pour lui enseigner à ne dire que ce qu'il faut, et à le dire en son lieu.[4]

It is unavailing to debate whether Boileau is a devotee of rule, or alternatively of intuition. In the translation of Longinus and its related documents, as in *L'Art Poétique*, he is both. As so often with Boileau, we need to search for the point of view from which these apparent contradictions are resolved.

Nowhere is this more evident than in considering *Le Lutrin*. It is above all a comic poem. It recounts, with all the panoply of a mock-epic, the absurd quarrel between two ecclesiastics over the placing of a lectern. Much of the effect comes from the contrast between the banal subject and the heroic trappings. Even if we miss some of his Classical allusions, it is hard not to warm to Boileau's comedy. In *Chant II*, one of the characters, an amorous but cowardly wig-maker, is about to go off to install the lectern. His wife, echoing Virgil's Dido, begs him to stay. The husband's response depends partly on the reference to the convention by which the hero must rise above the blandishments of women, but more on the comic effect of the gap between heroism and reality:

> Ma femme, lui dit-il d'une voix douce et fière,
> Je ne veux point nier les solides bienfaits
> Dont ton amour prodigue a comblé mes souhaits;
> Et le Rhin de ses flots ira grossir la Loire
> Avant que tes faveurs sortent de ma mémoire.
> Mais ne présume pas qu'en te donnant ma foi
> L'hymen m'ait pour jamais asservi sous ta loi.
> Si le ciel en mes mains eût mis ma destinée,
> Nous aurions fui tous deux le joug de l'hyménée,
> Et, sans nous opposer ces devoirs prétendus,
> Nous goûterions encor des plaisirs défendus.
> Cesse donc à mes yeux d'étaler un vain titre:
> Ne m'ôte pas l'honneur d'élever un pupitre.
>
> (*Chant II*, ll. 38–50)

Again and again he brings off, with splendid gaiety, this trick of the double reference, of solemnity followed by a let-down.

But this is not the whole story. Although Boileau's 1683 *Avis au Lecteur* says the poem is 'un ouvrage de pure plaisanterie' (purely an amusing work) the *Au Lecteur* of the 1674 edition sets it in the context of a serious discussion on the Epic. Originally it was subtitled, not *Poème Héroï-Comique*, but *Poème Héroïque*. Half a joke, no doubt (*Le Lutrin* is 'une bagatelle'), but not more than half. In *Chant III* of *L'Art Poétique*, Boileau verges on saying that Epic should be funny. In the *Dissertation sur Joconde*, if that work is his, he remarks that the *Odyssey* is 'un ouvrage tout comique' (a completely comic work),[5] and he certainly regarded the *Odyssey* as an epic in the grand tradition. Many passages in *Le Lutrin* could grace a serious epic:

> La plaintive Procné de douleur en frémit,
> Et, dans les bois prochains, Philomèle en gémit
> (*Chant III*, ll. 19–20)
> Ils passent de la nef la vaste solitude.   (*ibid.*, l. 58)

The allegory of Chicanery seems as impressive as Virgil's allegories, or Milton's Sin and Death:

> On l'appelle Chicane; et ce monstre odieux
> Jamais pour l'équité n'eut d'oreilles ni d'yeux.
> La Disette au teint blême et la triste Famine,
> Les Chagrins dévorants et l'infâme Ruine,
> Enfants infortunés de ses raffinements,
> Troublent l'air d'alentours de longs gémissements.
> Sans cesse feuilletant les lois et la coutume,
> Pour consumer autrui, le monstre se consume;
> Et, dévorant maisons, palais, châteaux entiers,
> Rend pour des monceaux d'or de vains tas de papiers.
> (*Chant V*, ll. 39–48)

This is sinister rather than amusing, and the rest of the passage hints at one of Boileau's favourite themes:

> En vain, pour le dompter, le plus juste des rois
> Fit régler le chaos des ténébreuses lois.
> (*ibid.*, ll. 55–6)

From a flatterer of Louis XIV, this is a sombre note. As in *L'Art Poétique*, there is a sense of the fragility of civilisation, of the difficult and doubtful struggle by which society keeps at bay chaos and unreason.

The best comment is perhaps by Dryden, who admired Boileau and understood his achievement very well:

He writes in the French heroic verse, and calls it an heroic poem; his subject is trivial, but his verse is noble. I doubt not but he had Virgil in his eye, for we find many admirable imitations of him, and some parodies... we see Boileau pursuing him in the same flights; and scarcely yielding to his master...Here is the majesty of the heroic, finely mixed with the venom of [satire]; and raising the delight which otherwise would be flat and vulgar, by the sublimity of the expression.[6]

To appreciate what Boileau is doing, let us take lines 137–50 of *Chant III*:

> En achevant ces mots, la déesse guerrière
> De son pied trace en l'air un sillon de lumière,
> Rend aux trois champions leur intrépidité,
> Et les laisse tous pleins de sa divinté.
> C'est ainsi, grand Condé, qu'en ce combat célèbre,
> Où ton bras fit trembler le Rhin, l'Escaut et l'Èbre,
> Lorsqu'aux plaines de Lens nos bataillons poussés
> Furent presqu'à tes yeux ouverts et renversés;
> Ta valeur, arrêtant les troupes fugitives,
> Rallia d'un regard leurs cohortes craintives,
> Répandit dans leurs rangs ton esprit belliqueux,
> Et força la victoire à te suivre avec eux.
> La colère à l'instant succédant à la crainte,
> Ils rallument le feu de leur bougie éteinte.

The first two lines have an authentic grandeur, and could belong to a serious epic. The second two lines are less intense, but could also be genuinely heroic; we smile here only because we know that the three intrepid champions are cowards. But the epic simile which follows is no laughing-matter: Condé's heroism was real enough, and his social prestige and patronage of Boileau make it unlikely that the passage was either meant as a sneer or likely to be received as such. The verse, accordingly, is firm and energetic, with no hint of bathos. 'La colère à l'instant succédant à la crainte' is a cunning transition. Like lines 139–40, what it says could seem serious, until we remember the cowardice of the champions. The last line of the quotation completes the switch: the epic preparations lead to the lighting of a candle, and here the use of a 'low' word, *bougie*, perhaps made the point more sharply to a seventeenth-century audience than it does to us.

This gradation of tones does not mean that Boileau is implying disrespect for the serious elements which he introduces. His own precept in *L'Art Poétique* is clear enough:

> Heureux qui, dans ses vers, sait d'une voix légère
> Passer du grave au doux, du plaisant au sévère!
> *(Chant I, ll. 75–6)*

and he follows his own advice. In *Le Lutrin*, as in *Épître IV*, he mixes jokes with seriousness. There is nothing incongruous in his praise of Condé, or his use of Louis XIV in a simile *(Chant IV, ll. 145–52)*. We are perhaps prevented from appreciating this by the tradition that Boileau preaches and practises unity of tone and the distinction of *genres*. So he does, but in a subtler way than the traditional account suggests. The distinction of *genres* really consists in deliberately setting out to achieve a certain effect. *Le Lutrin* does this, but the effect it aims at is a novel one. At least, the particular form it takes is novel: its general tone appears in French neo-classical works more often than might be thought.[7] It is a blend not merely of the grave and the amusing (which many of Boileau's works had achieved), or even of epic nobility and parody. It consists of a complex effect in which the real grandeur of Louis XIV and Condé and the real grandeur of Epic are made to enrich and criticise a tale of pettiness, with the aim of amusing but also of advocating moral and social responsibility.

Chant VI brings in the allegorical figures of Piety and Justice, and the dénouement comes when Piety asks Ariste (the Premier Président de Lamoignon, whom Boileau praises in his *Avis*) to end the dispute. This Canto has been attacked for its incongruous solemnity and sudden ending, but these criticisms underrate Boileau's artistry. Justice praises Ariste/Lamoignon, and the praise is undoubtedly sincere. Piety appears before him, and begs his help in words that are urgent and impressive:

> Que me sert, lui dit-elle, Ariste, qu'en tous lieux
> Tu signales pour moi ton zèle et ton courage,
> Si la Discorde impie à ta porte m'outrage?
> Deux puissants ennemis, par elle envenimés,
> Dans ces murs, autrefois si saints, si renommés,
> A mes sacrés autels font un profane insulte,
> Remplissent tout d'effroi, de trouble et de tumulte.
> De leur crime à leurs yeux va-t'en peindre l'horreur:
> Sauve-moi, sauve-les de leur propre fureur.
> *(Chant VI, ll. 132–40)*

And then, if the resolution comes quickly, the way in which it does so is revealing:

> Elle sort à ces mots. Le héros en prière
> Demeure tout couvert de feux et de lumière.
> De la céleste fille il reconnaît l'éclat,
> Et mande au même instant le chantre et le prélat.
> Muse, c'est à ce coup que mon esprit timide
> Dans sa course élevée a besoin qu'on le guide.
>
> (*ibid.*, ll. 141–6)

Boileau mixes the true sublime with a touch of bathos and a half-serious use of epic machinery. But, if the first three lines are serious, the three following are not simply bathos. Boileau carefully lightens the mood without breaking it: the summons to the contending parties has concision and vigour, and the address to the Muse a note of genuine humility. His concern is to obtain his effect by the blending of the serious and the amusing, the pleasant and the morally instructive. It is our failure to grasp the unity of the apparently different elements that makes us reluctant to accept the seriousness of *Chant VI*, despite the preparation in the rest of the poem. We are so inclined to think that amusement and morality are incompatible that we fail to respond to the passionate artistry by which Boileau contrives to unite them.

The complexity of Boileau's art appears again in *Épître IX*. Addressed to Colbert's son Seignelay, it is clearly intended as flattery to both. Whether or not Colbert appreciated the poem, it appears that Seignelay did not.[8] If, as has sometimes been maintained, Boileau was simply trying to produce an acceptable piece of flattery, he was therefore not very successful.

A traditional alternative view has been that *Épître IX* is an expression of doctrine. It takes up and summarises the essential thesis of *L'Art Poétique*: 'Rien n'est beau que le vrai.' In its most extreme form, this view implies that the occasional nature of the poem is so much gift-wrapping for a serious enunciation of a moral and aesthetic proposition which lies at the heart of French neo-classicism. Indeed, the lines that enunciate it are often extracted for quotation, or even anthologised. We have, rightly, grown sceptical of this approach. Modern scholarship has shown how misleading it is to regard French Classicism as a rigid aesthetic codified by Boileau and founded on any single principle;

recent criticism has shown the value of looking at these apparently didactic utterances in the context, not only of the poems in which they appear, but also of Boileau's attitudes as they appear in his work. This last certainly must be done, since it takes seriously what Boileau actually says. Nonetheless, despite all modern criticism has done to modify the traditional view, my opinion is that *Épître IX* does embody an important statement of Boileau's aesthetic, the aesthetic he set out more fully in *L'Art Poétique*.

Épître IX starts, like many of Boileau's poems, with a slight shock:

> Dangereux ennemi de tout mauvais flatteur,
> Seignelay, c'est en vain qu'un ridicule auteur,
> Prêt à porter ton nom 'de l'Èbre jusqu'au Gange',
> Croit te prendre aux filets d'une sotte louange.
> Aussitôt ton esprit, prompt à se révolter,
> S'échappe, et rompt le piège où l'on veut l'arrêter.
>
> (ll. 1–6)

Seignelay is a 'Dangereux ennemi', which may remind us of the Colbert family's recent enmity for Boileau, and also the real possibility that a Minister's ill-will could be dangerous. The second hemistich of the first line partly repairs the damage by revealing that Seignelay is only the enemy of 'tout mauvais flatteur': but Boileau himself is about to flatter, and the wariness that makes the opening precaution necessary is another sign of Seignelay's dangerousness. Moreover, if Seignelay is the enemy of 'bad' flattery, are we to think he would be taken in by 'good' flattery? And is the badness ethical badness, or merely bad technique? The poem is energised by the tension between a number of opposites, and two of them are already present in the opening line: the ambivalent power of Seignelay (benevolent, but also dangerous) and the dilemma of deciding whether ethical and aesthetic 'goodness' are identical or unconnected.

The ambivalence comes out most strongly in the opening section (ll. 1–36). Seignelay in line 4 is a dangerous animal who cannot be trapped; yet in line 15 he is not a horse who kicks out, however gently handled. The poet who flatters is equally ambivalent: he may intend to please the person flattered, but instead sometimes 'Donne de l'encensoir au travers du visage' (l. 20). There are strongly physical undertones in these lines, with hints of the connection between incense and the smell (l. 17) and

taste (l. 12) of faeces. Some people will swallow the filthiest praise
(l. 12), but Seignelay will not 'feed on' this 'cheap incense' (l. 13);
he prefers the skilful and delicate praise 'Dont la trop forte odeur
n'ébranle point les sens' (l. 17). In Freudian terms, these copro-
philiac overtones fit in with the ambivalence of this section, and
perhaps also with the general neo-classical insistence on rules,
tidiness and morality. Coprophilia and its opposite are common
themes in English neo-classical literature, less prudish than the
French. Swift's obsession is notorious,[9] and Pope's *Dunciad* has
much fun with 'fair Cloacina' and with the 'grateful odours' of
flatus and incense.[10]

The examples of flattery which Boileau gives are also equivocal.
The praise of Colbert in lines 24–32 perhaps has a faint undertone of criticism, if we remember that Boileau was once his
enemy. Whether this is so or not, Boileau brings off one of his
neatest double-takes in line 34. We laugh to think that anyone
could hope Colbert would swallow such flattery as the comparison
'au fils de Pélée ou d'Alcmène' (with the son of Peleus or
Alcmena); then we find that this is applied to the King. Laughing
at Boileau's jokes often turns into uneasiness, as it does here, and
especially in the context. Colbert's eyes and icy manner struck
terror into his contemporaries; and here his eyes (l. 33) freeze
with a glance the Muse and the poet (l. 35).

Having unsettled his audience, Boileau then comes out with a
straightforward passage which closes the first movement of the
poem. First, the *maxime*:

> Un cœur noble est content de ce qu'il trouve en lui
> Et ne s'applaudit point des qualités d'autrui.
>
> (ll. 37–8)

This is followed with a demonstration by analogy: it is no use
being told you are healthy when you feel ill (ll. 39–42), and the
emotional uneasiness engendered by the earlier lines provides the
perfect setting for the example of fever used. After this, Boileau
opens his argument again, with the most famous lines in the
poem:

> Rien n'est beau que le vrai: le vrai seul est aimable;
> Il doit régner partout, et même dans la fable:
> De toute fiction l'adroite fausseté
> Ne tend qu'à faire aux yeux briller la vérité.
>
> (ll. 43–6)

Although these lines mark a stage in the development of the poem's thought, they do not by themselves constitute its whole theme. The provisional nature of their statement is indicated by the issues which they open up but do not follow through to a conclusion. How does truth 'reign' in 'fable'? 'Fable' is usually opposed to 'truth' (cf. *L'Art Poétique, Chant III*, ll. 203–4): but perhaps here it has the connotation of a moral fable which usefully teaches morality, in which case the truth involved here is the truth of morality. But the next two lines propose a different interpretation. As Brody has pointed out, 'fiction' in the seventeenth century retained the connotation of 'feigned', and 'adroit' could mean 'deceptive' rather than 'skilful'.[11] The implication of line 46 is then that fiction shows up the brilliance of truth by contrast.

Having opened up these puzzling questions, the poem begins to explore alternative answers. In lines 47–66, Boileau proposes a triple justification for the success of his own poems. First, they tell the truth, morally; but also there is the implication that aesthetically and socially they 'get things right':

> c'est qu'en eux le vrai, du mensonge vainqueur,
> Partout se montre aux yeux, et va saisir le cœur;
> Que le bien et le mal y sont prisés au juste;
> Que jamais un faquin n'y tint un rang auguste.
> (ll. 53–6)

Secondly, they tell the truth in that Boileau says what he thinks and feels:

> Et que mon cœur, toujours conduisant mon esprit,
> Ne dit rien aux lecteurs qu'à soi-même il n'ait dit.
> (ll. 57–8)

This is misleadingly close to what we often think to be the Romantic justification of poetry: that it is the true voice of feeling. Here, however, there is a clearly neo-classical nuance. Self-revelation is perhaps a good in itself, but there is a hint that what is good about it is really that it brings honesty of thought (not just feeling) into the light of day, and so contributes to the shared honesty of society:

> Ma pensée au grand jour partout s'offre et s'expose.
> (l. 59)

The third justification is different again, and takes up this public theme: Boileau's poems 'say something' (l. 60). The implication is that they have some useful content, and that this is what gives the reader a pleasant shock (l. 61) and distinguishes them from 'tous ces vains amas de frivoles sornettes' (all these futile heaps of frivolous nonsenses) (l. 63).

The poem's thought then turns round in its tracks, and denies that Boileau's explanations of his own worth are right. As usual, it carries along in its change of direction the person to whom it is addressed. In this case, Seignelay is first implicated in the suggestion that Boileau had been 'enivré des vapeurs de ma Muse' (intoxicated with the fumes of my muse) (l. 67) with the reminder of how Seignelay was in danger of being intoxicated by the fumes of incense in lines 5–17. Then with one of his skilful changes of pronoun: 'Cessons de nous flatter' (But let us stop flattering ourselves) (l. 69) Boileau is including them both together. No, says the poem, there is no-one (not even Boileau, not even Seignelay) 'Qui ne soit imposteur et faux par quelque endroit' (l. 70). Everybody takes up the mask, leaves nature behind, and is frightened to show himself as he really is.

The examples that follow (ll. 75–100) propose a clear solution to the problems the poem has opened up. If we follow our natures and reveal ourselves openly, we shall 'please' (in the strong, seventeenth-century sense). The recognition of the true nature of a person gives that immediate, intuitive shock of revelation that Boileau sees as the effect of good poetry:

> Mais la nature est vraie, et d'abord on la sent.
>
> (l. 86)

This seems straightforward enough, but the lines hint that matters are not simple. Is it true that 'Un esprit né chagrin plaît par son chagrin même' (l. 88), or that 'Chacun pris dans son air est agréable en soi' (l. 89)? Doubts are intensified when the poem again turns about. In line 101, we are told that 'L'ignorance vaut mieux qu'un savoir affecté': an obvious paradox redeemed at the last moment by the adjective. Boileau then speaks in his own person, with a rather clumsy insistence that gives emphasis to what he is saying:

Rien n'est beau, je reviens, que par la vérité:
C'est par elle qu'on plaît, et qu'on peut longtemps plaire.
L'esprit lasse aisément, si le cœur n'est sincère.

(ll. 102–4)

The argument has shifted radically, as if because of the falsity
revealed in the preceding examples. Truth is now a necessary, but
not sufficient, precondition of pleasing. The example now given
confirms the change. A clown may be amusing in white-face, but
he is really 'un cœur bas, un coquin ténébreux' (a mean-spirited
fellow, a sinister wretch) (l. 109). Far from being agreeable when
he removes the mask and shows his true nature, 'Son visage
essuyé n'a plus rien que d'affreux' (l. 110). Beauty resides, not in
being true to one's nature, but in being moral:

J'aime un esprit aisé qui se montre, qui s'ouvre,
Et qui plaît d'autant plus, que plus il se découvre.
Mais la seule vertu peut souffrir la clarté:
Le vice, toujours sombre, aime l'obscurité.

(ll. 111–14)

The symbolism of light and darkness, of hiding and self-
exposure, looks back to the earlier 'Ma pensée au grand jour
partout s'offre et s'expose' (l. 59), and furnishes a gloss on it.
There is a great difference between the attitude reached by Boileau
here and the Romantic view that sincere expression of feeling is
in itself good. Boileau thinks in terms of a steady, consistent
revelation of a complete and unvarying truth, and one which has
to be reached by strenuous self-examination. *Épître IX* does not
merely preach this self-scrutiny, but dramatises the process: as we
read it, we are induced to respond to the to-ing and fro-ing of his
hunt for the truth.

Being Boileau, he does not end there. The remainder of the
poem expands his theme until it reaches into the social life of
seventeenth-century France. He brings in another of his fabular
histories. Originally, Man 'ne trompant jamais, n'était jamais
trompé' (never deceiving, was never deceived) (l. 118), another
example in which truth is linked unambiguously with virtue, not
with showing one's true nature. But this is only the introduction
to the satiric assault on Norman chicanery, lying rhetoric, ostentation, the coquetry of women (here the reference is to making-up

the face), and so to the faults of literature. It is after this that Boileau brings in a few lines of praise for Seignelay, sandwiched between warning lines that almost defy him to find their flattery inadequate:

> Mais je tiens, comme toi, qu'il faut qu'elle soit vraie
>
> (l. 151)
>
> Il faudrait peindre en toi des vérités connues
>
> (l. 156)
>
> Tel, qui hait à se voir peint en de faux portraits,
> Sans chagrin voit tracer ses véritables traits.
>
> (ll. 161-2)

The final movement of the poem takes up themes found in the earlier part, and confirms that it is hardly organised to flatter as agreeably as possible:

> Condé même, Condé, ce héros formidable,
> Et, non moins qu'aux Flamands, aux flatteurs redoutable,
> Ne s'offenserait pas si quelque adroit pinceau
> Traçait de ses exploits le fidèle tableau;
> Et dans Seneffe en feu contemplant sa peinture,
> Ne désavoûrait pas Malherbe ni Voiture.
> Mais malheur au poète insipide, odieux,
> Qui viendrait le glacer d'un éloge ennuyeux.
> Il aurait beau crier: 'Premier prince du monde!
> Courage sans pareil! lumière sans seconde!'
> Ses vers, jetés d'abord sans tourner le feuillet,
> Iraient dans l'antichambre amuser Pacolet.
>
> (ll. 163-74)

Condé is certainly praised, but with a trace of ambiguity. In line 21, Boileau had referred to Condé's slightly dubious success in making Monterey raise the siege of Oudenarde. Here, we may recall that the battle of Seneffe (l. 167), though a victory, was narrowly won, and with such great loss of life as to seem a defeat. What is not ambiguous, however, and takes up powerfully a theme prominent in *L'Art Poétique* and in much of Boileau's previous work, is the insistence on the necessary connection of moral, aesthetic and social values. 'Condé même, Condé' approves of good poetry, and has the moral probity and intellectual power needed to judge it. Bad poetry goes into the antechamber to amuse the valets (ll. 173-4). For Boileau, to allow oneself to be duped by bad verse is to be de-graded in the most literal sense. A failure of aesthetic response is intellectual, moral and social degradation. As La Rochefoucauld put it, 'Quand notre mérite baisse, notre goût baisse aussi.'[12]

The three *Épîtres* written in 1677–8 are obviously linked to Boileau's situation at this time, and the circumstances surrounding their composition are known with some precision. *Épître VI* (*A M. de Lamoignon*) and *Épître VII* (*A M. Racine*) both refer to the quarrel about *Phèdre*. *Épître VI* shows Boileau at peace in the country and enjoying the protection of Lamoignon, but finding himself under attack in Paris from a swarm of ridiculous enemies. *Épître VII* attempts to console Racine for the apparent success of the cabal against him. By September 1677, the nomination as historiographer had changed Boileau's social status, and the *Épître VIII* of 1678 (*Au Roi*) expresses his gratitude.

If we look at the poems as poems, they are of unequal value, though no doubt they all, more than most of Boileau's poems, had a direct instrumental purpose for him in the situations in which he found himself. *Épître VI* is a charming representation of his pursuits at the village of Hautisle, which is described with economy and precision:

> C'est un petit village, ou plutôt un hameau,
> Bâti sur le penchant d'un long rang de collines.
>
> (ll. 4–5)

Épître VII is a different matter, and is one of Boileau's best-known poems. It has always been praised for the elegance and personal feeling with which it endeavours to console Racine, including as it does the celebrated tribute to Molière, that other great playwright who was unjustly attacked. Two points, however, are perhaps worth making. First, there is the way in which the poem creates a sense of two worlds: the world to which Racine and Boileau belong and the world of their enemies. Secondly, there is the way in which the first of these worlds is shown as fragile as well as indestructible.

The general tactic is very similar to that of *L'Art Poétique*. The world of the poet of genius is identified with the enduring moral and intellectual qualities: 'your wise works' (l. 7), inspiration by Apollo (l. 9), the obligation of 'growing in virtue' (l. 70). This moral, even religious, element is more important than merely literary talent, the 'poor and useless talent' of Boileau himself (l. 60). Further, this superior world of the poets gains strength from its extension through time, backwards to the great poets of tradition and of the recent past (Sophocles, l. 41; Corneille, ll. 42–52; Molière, ll. 19–39) and forward to the future, which judges rightly (l. 78). As in *L'Art Poétique*, this aristocracy of the spirit is inspired and protected by the social aristocracy of seventeenth-century France (ll. 93–100). Against this superior world is that of 'le vulgaire' (l. 10), 'l'ignorance et l'erreur' (l. 23), 'l'envie' (l. 43), 'un flot de vains auteurs' (a flood of foolish authors) (l. 72), 'un tas grossier de frivoles esprits' (an uncouth heap of frivolous characters) (l. 102).

This is banal enough, but we should note the method Boileau uses to give his simple schema significance. Classical allusions are used not only to lend dignity but also to unify. The direct references to the Classical past (ll. 4–5, 41) are linked with the present by the use of Classical terms: 'La Parque' who killed Molière (l. 34) and the 'Parnasse français' ennobled by Racine (l. 76). The implication that Racine's detractors are the frogs who croak against Apollo (ll. 9–12) links them with the enemies of Louis XIV, who was often symbolised by Apollo: the fountain of Apollo at Versailles was consciously intended to symbolise the triumph of Louis as the Sun King over his enemies turned into frogs. But of more interest, perhaps, is Boileau's majestic treatment of the true poet's enemies. They are not only ignorant and malicious, but they are by implication sub-human: frogs in line 12 and snakes in line 61. In Christianity, the snake is a traditional symbol of evil, and Boileau strongly implies that these enemies of poetry are evil spirits who have taken on the forms of bad critics and poets, but in reality are representations of the darker powers in wait for the human soul: they love darkness and hate the light (ll. 12–13); they are ignorance and error cloaking themselves in the forms of marquises and countesses to persecute Molière (ll. 23–4).

It is this sense of evil that gives a special colouring to this famous *Épître*. The powers of darkness may be vanquished by the power of virtue (ll. 65–70), and in the end they are transient and powerless (l. 74) and serve only to demonstrate the profound wisdom of Providence (ll. 46–7), but in the meantime they are constantly on the watch for Boileau as their prey (l. 64), who must save himself by moral exertion. There is Boileau's character-istically contradictory sense of the world of reason, both, as he confidently asserts, as stretching forwards and backwards in time and protected by the powers of Heaven and Earth, and also nevertheless, as fragile and endangered. Not all the lines in this consolatory Epistle are consoling. Racine is informed that only death can establish the true value of his verse (ll. 15–18). The catalogue of great persons who protect poetry is closed by the reminder that Montausier – one of the grandest and most literarily inclined of the grandees – is on the side of envy and folly (l. 100).

It is in this context that we should interpret the two most famous passages in the poem. Literary historians have, perhaps naturally, taken the references to *Phèdre* and to Molière as inter-esting snippets of literary history. In the structure of the poem, I would see the dubiously accurate reference to 'la douleur vertueuse/De Phèdre malgré soi perfide, incestueuse' (ll. 79–80) as another pointer to the underlying theme of the difficulty and danger of the moral life. And the lines on Molière seem to me to evoke an extremely complex emotion:

> Avant qu'un peu de terre, obtenu par prière,
> Pour jamais sous la tombe eût enfermé Molière,
> Mille de ces beaux traits, aujourd'hui si vantés,
> Furent des sots esprits à nos yeux rebutés.
> L'ignorance et l'erreur à ses naissantes pièces
> En habits de marquis, en robes de comtesses,
> Venaient pour diffamer son chef d'œuvre nouveau,
> Et secouaient la tête à l'endroit le plus beau.
> Le commandeur voulait la scène plus exacte;
> Le vicomte indigné sortait au second acte.
> L'un, défenseur zélé des bigots mis en jeu,
> Pour prix de ses bons mots le condamnait au feu.
> L'autre, fougueux marquis, lui déclarant la guerre,
> Voulait venger la cour immolée au parterre.
> Mais, sitôt que d'un trait de ses fatales mains,
> La Parque l'eut rayé du nombre des humains,
> On reconnut le prix de sa muse éclipsée.
> L'aimable comédie, avec lui terrassée,
> En vain d'un coup si rude espéra revenir,
> Et sur ses brodequins ne put plus se tenir.
>
> (ll. 19–38)

In these lines I would see not simply a sentimental tribute to a departed friend, but something darker. Molière is the natural man surrounded by the hissing spirits of evil. Only prayer gained him a tomb; and there is perhaps even here a hint of ambiguity: if prayer had not closed Molière in his tomb for ever (l. 20) would he perhaps be now one of the walking spirits? Despite this partial and ambiguous salvation, there is something dreadfully final about the fate of Molière, and the fate Boileau attributes to Comedy. From this gloomy point, Boileau moves directly to address Racine (l. 40). The poem moves lightly along its many levels, and its elegance is justly admired, but I do not think this sinister groundswell can be ignored.

Épître VII is much the finest poem of this group, and *Épître VIII* (*Au Roi*) suffers by contrast. It is obviously an obligatory poem, in which the newly appointed historian praises the King and gives thanks for favours received. Although vigorously written, it comes closest of all Boileau's poems to the pattern proposed by some scholars: a piece written for a definite social purpose, and consisting of a simple message tricked out as ingeniously as possible. If Boileau does interpret the neo-classical doctrine of the nature and function of poetry in this way, *Épître VIII* shows that he is not at his best when he does so.

3

The major work which spans the gap which followed *Épître VIII* in Boileau's poetry is *Satire X*, as it apparently contains some material dating from the 1670s. But the *Ode sur la Prise de Namur* (1693) was published before *Satire X*, and deserves some attention for the light it throws on Boileau's conception of poetry and attitude to neo-classical theory.

In part, the poem is meant as an example to Perrault of how a Pindaric ode should be written, full of bold figures and the abrupt transitions of a poet transported by inspiration. But it is also an attack on Perrault for his criticisms of Pindar. Perrault objected that in it Boileau 'in several places used trivial and vulgar expressions', and that in his odes Pindar 'is not sarcastic' (*ne goguenarde point*), whereas Boileau makes satirical points.[18] These criticisms give a clue as to how we should enjoy the poem. The final strophe, which attacks Perrault directly, has been seen as an absurd addendum. Originally, Boileau inserted a strophe after the first which was equally satirical, and which gave early warning of the mixture he was preparing:

> Un torrent dans les prairies
> Roule à flots précipités;
> Malherbe dans ses furies
> Marche à pas trop concertés.
> J'aime mieux, nouvel Icare,
> Dans les airs suivant Pindare,
> Tomber du ciel le plus haut
> Que, loué de Fontenelle,
> Raser, timide hirondelle,
> La terre, comme Perrault.[14]

These satirical passages are not mere asides. The ode as a whole is full of boisterous sarcasm:

> Accourez, Nassau, Bavière,
> De ces murs l'unique espoir:
> A couvert d'une rivière,
> Venez, vous pouvez tout voir
>
> (ll. 101–4)
>
> Courez donc: qui vous retarde?
> Tout l'univers vous regarde:
> N'osez-vous la traverser?
>
> (ll. 128–30)

There is plenty to enjoy in this mixture of grandiloquence, sarcasm and wit, provided we do not ask of it a kind of lyricism which it is not Boileau's purpose to provide. The central feature of his conception of poetry is that it should be an activity which yokes together faculties and qualities which are often thought of as opposites. Poetry is a matter of reason *and* imagination, knowledge *and* intuition, innovation *and* tradition, grandeur *and* satire, public *and* private. In his *Réflexions sur Longin*, Boileau rarely shows interest in the theoretical basis of the Moderns' arguments. He attacks Perrault as lacking taste and knowledge, which in Boileau's world go together. In *Réflexion VIII*, he defends Pindar both because of his poetic audacity *and* because he makes good sense and was up-to-date in the science of his day: 'il faut savoir que Pindare vivait peu de temps après Pythagore, Thalès, et Anaxagore, fameux philosophes naturalistes, et qui avaient

enseigné la physique avec un fort grand succès'.[15] Perhaps he misunderstood Pindar, but if so he did so because of his own striking
conception of how an ode on a public theme should be written.
Within this conception, there is no incompatibility between celebrating Louis XIV and Boileau himself, between scolding William
III and Perrault. The first lines of *Ode sur la Prise de Namur*
give clear enough notice. Inspiration is divine frenzy, but also
connotes learning:

> Quelle docte et sainte ivresse
> Aujourd'hui me fait la loi?

Satire X is also a mixture, but in a rather different sense.
In part, the mixture of tones is no doubt due to the length of time
over which the poem was written and revised. One section which
probably belongs to the earliest stratum is the portrait of the
miser and his wife, which deploys all Boileau's trenchancy and
love of the bizarre, his ability to combine savage humour with a
sense of almost tragic desolation:

> Mais cette soif de l'or qui le brûlait dans l'âme
> Le fit enfin songer à choisir une femme,
> Et l'honneur dans ce choix ne fut point regardé.
> Vers son triste penchant son naturel guidé
> Le fit, dans une avare et sordide famille,
> Chercher un monstre affreux sous l'habit d'une fille
> . . .
> Voilà nos deux époux, sans valets, sans enfants,
> Tout seuls dans leurs logis libres et triomphants
> . . .
>   Mais, pour bien mettre ici leur crasse en tout son lustre,
> Il faut voir du logis sortir ce couple illustre:
> Il faut voir le mari, tout poudreux, tout souillé,
> Couvert d'un vieux chapeau de cordon dépouillé,
> Et de sa robe, en vain de pièces rajeunie,
> A pied dans les ruisseaux traînant l'ignominie.
> Mais qui pourrait compter le nombre de haillons,
> De pièces, de lambeaux, de sales guenillons,
> De chiffons ramassés dans la plus noire ordure,
> Dont la femme, aux bons jours, composait sa parure?
> Décrirai-je ses bas en trente endroits percés,
> Ses souliers grimaçants, vingt fois rapetassés,
> Ses coiffes d'où pendait au bout d'une ficelle
> Un vieux masque pelé presque aussi hideux qu'elle?
>   (ll. 265-70, 299-300, 309-22)

A similar vigour is evident in the portrait of the coquette, who 'dans quatre mouchoirs, de sa beauté salis,/Envoie au blanchisseur ses roses et ses lis' (ll. 199–200). The vigour reappears in a passage which was surely written in the 1690s, as it attacks the new freedom of manners of the woman who 'Fait, même à ses amants, trop faibles d'estomac,/Redouter ses baisers pleins d'ail et de tabac' (ll. 671–2). His raillery of the female scientist is as pointed, and this presumably belongs to the earlier stratum of the poem. Having spent all night on the tiles watching Jupiter (and there is here a hint of the ribald second meaning of 'dans la gouttière', as in the English), she is off to inspect a new microscope or attend the dissection of a pregnant woman and her embryo. As Boileau says, with discreet malice:

> Rien n'échappe aux regards de notre curieuse.   (l. 437)

The portrait of the *précieuse* is hardly less successful:

> Là, du faux bel esprit se tiennent les bureaux:
> Là, tous les vers sont bons, pourvu qu'ils soient nouveaux.
> Au mauvais goût public la belle y fait la guerre;
> Plaint Pradon opprimé des sifflets du parterre.
>   (ll. 447–50)

The portraits that follow, of Madame de Maintenon (ll. 513–20), of the bigot (ll. 537–54), of her confessor (ll. 555–608), and of bigots again (ll. 610–36), are in Boileau's later and less lively manner, but are not lacking in either passion or finesse.

This recital of the virtues of the poem points to the main critical problem: Why, with such merits, has it never been recognised as one of Boileau's masterpieces? The problem is perhaps best approached through a prior question: What is the poem about? This is hard to decide. Some commentators have seen the poem as a manoeuvre by Boileau in his battle against the Moderns: the 1694 version did contain a direct attack on Perrault, which was removed after Boileau's reconciliation with him. Boudhors saw it as an episode in Boileau's struggle against Jesuit casuistry. However, although the longest single section of the poem (136 lines) does attack the bigoted women and their culpable director of conscience, this does not seem a sufficient explanation of the whole theme, unless we regard the rest of the poem as camouflage. It seems to me that the variety of the portraits, and the variety of the styles in which they are written, form the most striking features of the poem. Its main weakness is its lack of unity, and in this it presents a test case for our view of Boileau's poetry.

Satire X is in fact largely a series of satirical portraits. This was perhaps partly an attempt to use a fashionable form, as La Bruyère had done in the first edition of *Les Caractères* in 1688, but Boileau uses it rather mechanically. His emphasis on the device is heavy:

> Je me plais à remplir mes sermons de portraits.
> En voilà déjà trois peints d'assez heureux traits
>
> (ll. 347–8)
>
> Il te faut de ce pas en tracer quelques traits,
> Et par ce grand portrait finir tous mes portraits
>
> (ll. 511–12)

and it is matched by his prominent signposting of what he is doing:

> Mais quoi! je chausse ici le cothurne tragique!
> Reprenons au plus tôt le brodequin comique
>
> (ll. 389–90)
>
> Mais à quels vains discours est-ce que je m'amuse?
>
> (l. 422)
>
> Il est temps de conclure; et, pour tout terminer,
> Je ne dirai qu'un mot.
>
> (ll. 700–1)

Boileau complained, in his correspondence with Racine, of the difficulty of making transitions between the portraits, and the difficulty is revealing. Such unity as the poem possesses does not spring from any central complex of meaning which all the parts combine to express. Its unity is rather that of a sermon, in which, the portraits are inserted merely as illustrations. The method is that of didactic prose rather than poetry. *Satire X* clearly shows a retreat from Boileau's earlier approach, in which his dramatic method permitted the full complexity of poetry.

A similar simplification is evident in *Épître X* and *Épître XI*. These Epistles seem to have been motivated in part by a desire to dispel the impression created by *Satire X* that Boileau was an anti-social being. Both poems are charming, full of carefully tailored self-revelation and verbal felicities. The lines in *Épître*

XI which depict the poet toiling after the Muses are famous for their music, and equally for their delicate blend of humour and a strangely haunting quality:

> Sans cesse poursuivant ces fugitives fées,
> On voit sous les lauriers haleter les Orphées.
>
> (ll. 77–8)

Nevertheless, compared with Boileau's best work, these epistles show a thinning of texture, combined with a simplification of the attitudes behind them. Boileau's half-humorous reference in *Épître X* to the past perhaps reveals more than he intended:

> Le temps n'est plus, mes Vers, où ma muse en sa force,
> Du Parnasse français formant les nourrissons,
> De si riches couleurs habillait ses leçons:
> Quand mon esprit, poussé d'un courroux légitime,
> Vint devant la raison plaider contre la rime,
> A tout le genre humain sut faire le procès,
> Et s'attaqua soi-même avec tant de succès.
>
> (ll. 14–20)

The last line has a flash of the old richness: by attacking himself 'successfully', Boileau had scored a success, and so the attack failed. But the preceding lines show a drastic simplification in his approach to poetry. When, in *Satire VII*, Boileau had said, 'Souvent j'habille en vers une maligne prose' (l. 61), he was confessing a failure, not a strength. Here, in *Épître X*, the metaphor carries overtones of approval. In its most simplistic form, neo-classical theory endorsed the ancient view that poetry should 'dress up lessons' in a decorative form. As we have seen, Boileau's mature poetry, and his interpretation of neo-classical doctrine, had been more complex, and it was from this complexity that his best work had drawn its richness and strength.

4

This brings us to the final group of poems, *Épître XII*, *Satire XI* and *Satire XII*, in which Boileau's continuing slow decline is evident. To the last – especially in *Satire XI* – there are glimpses of the younger Boileau, with his dramatic flair, his ability to knock the reader off balance, his power to suddenly condense his argument into a vigorous *maxime*. There is also, behind the poetry, a sense of the pathos of the old poet, pleading with desperate seriousness for his ideals in a society grown indifferent or hostile to them. But this pathos is extrinsic, and the poems as poems remain inert.

The staple of all three poems is a series of straight statements of moral or religious doctrine. *Épître XII* (*Sur l'Amour de Dieu*) is little more than a theological lecture inappropriately wrapped up in clumsy verse:

> Expliquons-nous pourtant. Part cette ardeur si sainte,
> Que je veux qu'en un cœur amène enfin la crainte,
> Je n'entends pas ici ce doux saisissement,
> Ces transports pleins de joie et de ravissement.
>
> (ll. 75–8)

Satire XI (*Sur l'Honneur*) is livelier. Its first fifty lines contain some trenchant *vers maximes* and some dramatic pictures; for example, of the convict: 'Il plaint, par un arrêt injustement donné,/L'honneur en sa personne à ramer condamné' (ll. 7–8) and the misanthrope who tries to appear good-humoured (ll. 37–42). The middle section (ll. 51–134) is direct harangue, in Boileau's later manner. Then, rarely for Boileau, we can catch him hesitating in his poetic theory. In his translation of Longinus, he had rendered one passage thus:

Aristote et Théophraste, pour excuser l'audace de ces figures, pensent qu'il est bon d'y apporter ces adoucissements: 'Pour ainsi dire. Pour parler ainsi. Si j'ose me servir de ces termes. Pour m'expliquer un peu plus hardiment'. En effet, ajoutent-ils, l'excuse est un remède contre les hardiesses du discours, et je suis bien de leur avis.[16]

In the tenth *Réflexion sur Longin* (written in 1710), he was to make the following comment:

Le conseil de ces deux philosophes est excellent; mais il n'a d'usage que dans la prose; car ces excuses sont rarement souffertes dans la poésie, où elles auraient quelquechose de sec et de languissant; parce que la poésie porte son excuse avec soi.[17]

This is an important example of Boileau's awareness of the independent status of poetry. But in *Satire XI* he goes against his own rule in advance, and his terms are revealing:

> Je doute que le flot des vulgaires humains
> A ce discours pourtant donne aisément les mains;
> Et, pour t'en dire ici la raison historique,
> Souffre que je l'habille en fable allégorique.
>
> (ll. 135–8)

There is the customary flattery of the person to whom the satire is addressed (in this case, Valincour), but the assumption is now that the audience cannot applaud the direct expression of Boileau's message. More or less openly, he is admitting the breakdown of the social relationship with his audience, which in his best poems he had used as the basis for his art. At the same time, he is abandoning poetry for what he himself saw as the method of prose discourse.

In *Satire XII* (*Sur l'Équivoque*), Boileau is more clearly than ever preaching in his own person. The poem contains much of his usual machinery of apostrophe and dramatic dialogue, but this has become tiresome, because irrelevant. The imaginary other persons are left anonymous: 'Mais où tend, dira-t-on, ce projet fantastique?' (l. 25), or are inanimate: 'Halte-là donc, ma plume' (l. 335), or, and this is the major device, are presented as allegorical: 'L'Équivoque' itself, and 'ta fille l'Hérésie' (l. 190). Boileau comments laboriously on his own allegory in his closing address to Equivocation:

> Et toi, sors de ces lieux,
> Monstre à qui, par un trait des plus capricieux,
> Aujourd'hui terminant ma course satirique,
> J'ai prêté dans mes vers une âme allégorique.
>
> (ll. 335–8)

More tiresome still is the poem's repetitive verbosity. It starts with a mild grammatical joke about the gender of the word 'Équivoque', and then takes a line and three-quarters to labour the point:

> Car sans peine aux rimeurs hasardeux,
> L'usage encor, je crois, laisse le choix des deux.
>
> (ll. 3–4)

The staple of the poem is an apparently endless series of couplets weighed down with abstractions and redundant adjectives:

> Ce ne fut plus partout que fous anabaptistes,
> Qu'orgueilleux puritains, qu'exécrables déistes
>
> (ll. 233–4)
>
> l'énorme fondement
> De la plus dangereuse et terrible morale
> Que Lucifer, assis dans la chaire infernale,
> Vomissant contre Dieu ses monstrueux sermons,
> Ait jamais enseignée aux novices démons
>
> (ll. 272–6)
>
> De Pascal, de Wendrock, copiste misérable;
> Et, pour tout dire enfin, janséniste exécrable
>
> (ll. 325–6)
>
> Blâmer de tes docteurs la morale risible:
> C'est selon eux, prêcher un calvinisme horrible.
>
> (ll. 329–30)

There is pathos in the thought of Boileau, old and ill, struggling for so long with this ill-fated poem. Its turgidity and clumsiness are distressing when we think of the agility and verve of his masterpieces. Voltaire found the right word for it: 'la triste *Équivoque*' (sad *Équivoque*).[18]

5

The Preface of the 1701 *édition favorite* is not the latest in date of Boileau's works, but he seems to have intended it as a summing up of his literary credo, so it is fittingly considered last. The themes are what we should expect. Boileau emphasises, in the most literal sense, the importance of social conformity. He says of his public:

> Je ne saurais attribuer un si heureux succès qu'au soin que j'ai pris de me conformer toujours à ses sentiments, et d'attraper, autant qu'il m'a été possible, son goût en toutes choses. C'est effectivement à quoi il me semble que les écrivains ne sauraient trop s'étudier.[19]

Poetry must express truths. These seem to be eternal archetypes: 'L'esprit de l'homme est naturellement plein d'un nombre infini d'idées confuses du vrai, que souvent il n'entrevoit qu'à demi', but they also seem to be identified with the opinions of his seventeenth-century public. One type of truth is that of historical accuracy: Benserade is reproached for confusing Greek and

Christian views on the creation of Man: 'le dieu dont il s'agit à cet endroit, c'est Jupiter, qui n'a jamais passé chez les païens pour avoir fait l'homme à son image: l'homme dans la fable étant, comme tout le monde sait, l'ouvrage de Prométhée'. Boileau does go on to insist on the value of craftsmanship, but it is interesting that the last third of the Preface concentrates not so much on literary technique as on social and moral matters. He praises his distinguished Portuguese translator (no doubt with a touch of irony),[20] and then goes on to stress – with undoubted sincerity – his admiration for Arnauld, and Arnauld's moral endorsement of his work. This emphasis on morality leads naturally to Boileau's defence of himself from the charge of malice, and his acknowledgment of the merits of his former victims: Quinault, Saint-Amant, even Cotin.

The final paragraph revolves around techniques and themes we have found again and again in Boileau. After defending himself from the charge of speaking ill of his enemies, he turns the tables: any reader does just the same when he judges an author. Then comes a snatch of Boileau's use of direct speech: 'N'est-ce pas en quelque sorte dire au public: "Jugez-moi"?' The theme of almost all this last paragraph is the social and dramatic element in poetry: good literature enters into a relationship with its audience; its quality is proved only by the collective verdict of society.

But this is not quite the whole story. Earlier in the Preface, Boileau is simplifying when he condemns word-play: he ignores the subtle double-meanings which so often formed vital cross-connections in his own earlier masterpieces. In this last paragraph, he simplifies again when he describes *Satire IX* as 'putting this reasoning into rhymes'. The method implied may be that of *L'Équivoque*, but his earlier works are more subtle. This Preface is a statement made by the ageing Boileau. Its underlying tendency is to reduce poetry to the unexceptionable expression of commonplaces. It is little more than a parody of the alert and complex attitudes that underlay his earlier and better poetry.

9
Conclusions

In a celebrated essay on Corneille, Dort has remarked on the functions open to the artist under Louis XIV:

> L'art n'a plus de choix qu'entre une fonction décorative: il célèbre, il accorde le monde au grand roi – ce sera Lulli et Bossuet –, et un rôle secrètement négatif: il conteste, il détruit, en opposant au monde un refus intégral – c'est Racine (*Andromaque* est de 1667)...Molière mort en 1673, le dilemme de l'art tient alors en deux noms: Racine – Lulli. D'un côté, le faste, un art purement décoratif qui 'orchestre' les faits et gestes du Roi-Soleil; de l'autre, cet art secret, *tragique*, qui, sans mettre aucune des apparences glorieuses du règne en question, les récuse toutes, les abolit dans la mort du héros seul face à un ciel silencieux.[1]

This seems to me an important point, but I would add two glosses. First, it exaggerates the starkness of the choice, as though tragedy was the only alternative to triviality. I agree that Racine's distinctive achievement is that some of his works are tragic in this special, modern, sense. But most of the great writers of the second half of the century – Racine himself in much of his work, La Rochefoucauld, Madame de la Fayette, La Bruyère, Boileau – in fact occupy a middle ground between Dort's extremes. They are critics of their society, but also exponents of its values.

Second, it seems to me too narrow to see the force that tended to reduce the arts to propaganda or decoration as being solely exerted by the demands of the régime. I would see this force as deriving from something wider and deeper: from the fundamental tendency in European civilisation to seek out and impose a set of values which embraces every aspect of existence, and to which the arts are necessarily subservient. In the seventeenth century this tendency was very strong. In the first half of the century, the dominant set of values of this kind in France was represented by the Counter-Reformation Church, with its effort towards universality and its attempt to restore the mediaeval synthesis.[2] In the latter part of the seventeenth and in the eighteenth century, first in England, then in France, a different world-view became dominant, but one that equally claimed precedence over poetry.

I have argued that these two points give a clue to the importance of neo-classical doctrine. The function of neo-classicism is to defend literature (and especially poetry) from the alternatives which Dort describes, and from some much more general social and intellectual pressures which seek to impose these alternatives. It is in this context that I would set Mairet's advocacy of the neo-classical rules in his Preface to *La Silvanire* (a Preface which starts, not with the rules, but with a defence of 'the excellence of poetry'). The doctrine proclaims that poetry is not trivial, but is founded on truth and has a useful function. At its lowest, the doctrine is a store of technical secrets. At its highest, it gives poetry the support of, in Chapelain's words, 'dogmas of eternal truth'.

This function of neo-classical doctrine as a defence of the value of poetry is what is important, and explains much. It explains the literalness which is perhaps the feature of neo-classical theory which most repels us today. In the works of the theorists, there is little sense of any ideal world beyond what is commonly known and accepted. This seems to me to follow from the nature of the world-view held. The ruling dogma has the answer to everything. Its limits must be accepted as those of the universe; poetry must not claim there are any worlds beyond it. The need to defend poetry by assimilating it to the ideological background also explains why the doctrine aims at completeness, despite the evident difficulty of filling all the gaps. It explains why the doctrine is presented as binding, even where we (and some of its exponents) find it not very relevant. But, above all, it explains why so many great minds over so long a period – from Sidney to Corneille, from Racine, Dryden and Boileau to Pope, Johnson and Voltaire – took the doctrine as something of self-evident importance. The literalness, the gaps, and the occasional absurdity of the doctrine may point to its weaknesses, but they also point to the strength of the need to accept it.

My subject has been the nature of neo-classical doctrine as it emerges from Boileau's poems, and what use Boileau in his poems makes of that doctrine. The basic functions of poetry, as set out in neo-classical theory, are two: 'to please' and 'to teach'. These little words say, by implication, everything about the aim of poetry. The question is how to achieve such a dual aim, and this question is crucial in neo-classicism because of its ideological background, which requires such heavy and literal emphasis on the aim of moral instruction. What is novel in Boileau is the way in which he is able to fulfil the dual aim. In his earliest satires, *Contre les Mœurs de la Ville de Paris* and *Satire I*, it seems intended that the pleasure should come from the malice of his onslaughts on contemporary abuses, and perhaps from a recognition of contemporary allusions; the moral aim seems to be to identify and pillory these crimes and criminals. Both the conception of the function of poetry and the ways of fulfilling it here seem crude and unsatisfying.

In the works of the major part of his career, however, we see some of the scope and richness possible within the neo-classical doctrine. Boileau's method becomes ever more subtle, and so does the implied function. The method is primarily psychological and dramatic. The pleasure comes from the way in which Boileau leads us along, and then doubles back, using every device of ambiguity and double-take. This nimbleness is a source of pleasure, both because we admire his dexterity and because our minds enjoy the exercise. But pleasure here passes into instruction. As we follow his twists and turns, we are made to look at our own responses. Participation in the drama becomes an exercise in moral self-examination. Whether the theme is directly the importance of self-knowledge (as in *Satire IV* or *Épître V*), or literary criticism or the proper praise for the King (in *Satire VII* and *Satire IX*, or *Épître I* and *Épître IV*), the dramatic and psychological centre is this need to examine the roots of morality. But the method is as far as it could be from what we usually regard as didacticism. The drama embodies its own criticism; the best of the poems do not make a plain statement, but explore a complex of different responses.

Boileau's art goes beyond this, and reaches its most serious achievement in the group of works around *L'Art Poétique*, including that poem itself. The basis remains that movement of the mind as it is led to contemplate its own moral activity, but other preoccupations find expression as well. Poetry takes on a more public function. It plays its part in upholding collective values more directly, making attractive and exemplifying the ground-rules which society has worked out in order to build the necessary bulwarks of civilisation. In the case of literature, these are the rules of neo-classicism. In religion, they are Christian doctrine. In the state, they are the social hierarchy, presided over by an élite and regulated by Louis XIV and his laws.

In all this, there is a strong urge to unify: to attempt, in fact, a universal synthesis. Collective and individual morality must be linked. Social, literary and moral excellence must be shown to go together. Poetry, like religion, has achieved a firm doctrine, which defines its usefulness and right to exist. Boileau's work shows a determination to bring these separate elements together, to build an impregnable structure. This comes out clearly in one striking feature of his work which has often been under-emphasised: his desire to bring together seemingly incompatible moods and elements, to blend farce and seriousness, morality and pleasure, the lofty and the undignified.

Despite all this, Boileau is aware of the weaknesses of his structure. He knows that neo-classical prescriptions for Epic do not take us very far (and, indeed, conflict dangerously with the imperatives of both poetry and religion). He sees the moral failures and doctrinal divisions of the Church, as well as the faults of individual Churchmen. In the state, he knows that Montausier's taste is as bad as Pacolet's, that fools and barbarians are there with the Dukes and Princes. He shows, again and again, that he has his doubts about Louis XIV: about the justice of his wars, certainly, but also about his legal reforms.

It is a mistake simply to accuse Boileau of inconsistency or lack of logic. The gaps and failings of the doctrine he upholds are evidence of the needs impelling him to defend it. Literature must be buttressed with rules; the social excellence of Condé and his fellows must join forces with the moral and literary élite; Louis XIV, despite his failings, must function as the leader of civilisation. There is, in much of Boileau's best work, but especially in *L'Art Poétique, Épître VII* and *Épître IX*, a sense of danger and evil. Poetry becomes a rite of protection, preserving society from madness and folly.

For poetry, this strategy had one weakness. To uphold its part in the great synthesis, the doctrine of neo-classicism had to stand firm as the justification and support of poetry. This may seem to us impossible to demonstrate. Even in the seventeenth century, the task must have seemed difficult. Nevertheless, the logic of Boileau's position made it necessary for the task to be attempted. To evade it would have been to abandon his commitment to the value and dignity of poetry. We can perhaps see, therefore, why Boileau was drawn to cast his masterpiece in the form of an *Art Poétique*. We can also see why it received such a rapturous reception from contemporaries, and from Boileau's successors, and why it is such a significant work. It stands at the centre of his art, and shows the achievement of his synthesis. Within *L'Art Poétique*, poetry stands on equal terms with the social, religious and moral order, and the poem celebrates their unity.

In fact, the achievement was impossible, outside the confines of a poem. This is a question not so much of the weakness or otherwise of neo-classicism as a literary theory, as of its relation in the minds of Boileau and his contemporaries to other fixtures of contemporary culture. Just as to their minds the intellectual élite of poetry was not the equal of the social élite, so, in the last analysis, the doctrine of neo-classicism could not stand on an equal footing with religion. The truth of poetry, in any conflict, must give way before the truth of Christianity. Chapelain and Le Bossu had accepted this, and their prescriptions were the death of poetry. Boileau evaded the difficulty in *L'Art Poétique*, but the weakness (and strength) of the section on Epic shows how well he was aware of this crucial difficulty. In his later works, as his dramatic verve declines, his solution to the problem is clear. Didacticism in the most straightforward sense takes over, and the pleasure (such as it is) is meant to come from the poetic devices applied: allegory, fable, apostrophe. The crudity of his last works matches that of his first Satire.

To say this is in large part to repeat what has been said before, but with a change of emphasis which I think is important. I have tried to show that, although modern criticism is certainly right to bring out the inner drama of Boileau's best poetry, with its continual movement and agility in evoking our responses, this view of him is inadequate. If we go back beyond the criticism of the twentieth and nineteenth centuries, we find formulae that present more accurately the nature of Boileau's achievement. In a sense, it can be summed up in that single line of Horace, which also contains the essence of neo-classicism: 'Omnia tulit punctum qui miscuit utile dulci.' Better still, if we give weight to every part of it, is Voltaire's description of Boileau:

> Qui, donnant le précepte et l'exemple à la fois,
> Établit d'Apollon les rigoureuses lois.

Boileau does teach. Simultaneously, he sets an example. This does not mean simply that when recommending correctness he writes correctly, or that when recommending brevity he is brief. He shows how the act of moral perception which forms the basis of good poetry takes place in the fabric of the poem itself. He establishes the doctrine of neo-classicism, not in the sense that he invents it, but in the sense that he gives it definitive form and sets it on a firmer foundation than the inept rationalisations of the theorists. The doctrine he expounds takes the form of strict and binding laws. In the eyes of their upholders, these laws have behind them a quasi-divine sanction: they are not just the pragmatic techniques and customs seen by modern scholarship, but the 'dogmas of eternal truth' of Chapelain.

What Voltaire saw clearly was perhaps obvious while the neo-classical tradition was still vigorous. Later comment, however helpful, has tended to obscure this central insight. When we have said all we usefully can about Boileau's linguistic skill, his moral passion, his dramatic and psychological method, we have illustrated his means without referring to the ends which made them significant. These ends are linked to neo-classical doctrine and its function. For more than two centuries, the doctrine defended the validity of poetry in the face of powerful systems of thought which denied it. Boileau's contribution to this achievement was immense, as his contemporaries and successors recognised. He made the doctrine imaginatively effective, and so enabled it to perform its function. His neo-classicism is an essential part of his significance. His commitment to the defence of poetry fills his best work with its creative urgency. His most vital poems centre round his long struggle to define, uphold and exemplify the doctrine.

NOTES

1 NEO-CLASSICISM AND BOILEAU

1 For a discussion of the development of views on various facets of Boileau's reputation, see Bernard Beugnot and Roger Zuber, *Boileau: Visages Anciens, Visages Nouveaux* (University Press, Montréal, 1973).

2 See especially Antoine Adam, *Histoire de la Littérature Française au XVIIe Siècle* (Domat, Paris, 5 vols, 1949–56). (I have used the 1964 Del Duca reprint.) Boileau is covered in vols III and V. See also Pierre Clarac, *Boileau* (Hatier, Paris, 1964).

3 Jules Brody, *Boileau and Longinus* (Droz, Geneva, 1958). See especially pp. 36–53.

4 John Orr, 'Pour le Commentaire Linguistique de l'Art Poétique', in *Essais d'Étymologie et de Philologie Françaises* (Klincksieck, Paris, 1963), pp. 173–91.

5 Peter France, *Rhetoric and Truth in France: Descartes to Diderot* (Oxford, 1972), pp. 151–72.

6 See, for example, Nathan Edelman, *'L'Art Poétique*: "Longtemps plaire, et jamais ne lasser" ', in *Studies in Seventeenth-Century French Literature Presented to Morris Bishop* (Doubleday Anchor edn, New York, 1966), pp. 229–43.

7 René Bray, *La Formation de la Doctrine Classique en France* (Nizet, Paris, 1963). Bray gives copious references, and in what follows I have not attempted to give chapter and verse for every point, except where it seems to me that the emphasis in Bray or other standard manuals needs correction, or where I am citing a text verbatim.

8 Horace, *Satires, Epistles and Ars Poetica*, with a translation by H. R. Fairclough (Loeb Classical Library, Heinemann, London, 1970), p. 478 (*Ad Pisones*, l. 343).

9 An interesting variant is in the famous anonymous Preface to a *Recueil de Poésies Chrétiennes et Diverses* published in 1671, and printed in La Fontaine, *Œuvres Diverses*, ed. Pierre Clarac (Bibliothèque de la Pléiade, Paris, 1958), p. 779. The attribution to La Fontaine is uncertain. Adam (*Histoire*, vol. III, p. 53) attributes the Preface to Dodart. Its argument is that poetry cannot be banished from society, because it answers to a universal *inclination*, and that people therefore take pleasure in it. The best that can be done is to make poems which are edifying, or at least harmless; but this is a palliative, not an expression of the usual purpose of poetry, which is to give pleasure.

10 Bray, *Doctrine*, pp. 207–8.
11 Jean Chapelain, *Opuscules Critiques*, ed. Alfred C. Hunter (Droz, Paris, 1936), p. 126 (*Lettre sur la Règle des Vingt-Quatre Heures*), and p. 130 (*Discours de la Poésie Représentative*, second version).
12 Bray, *Doctrine*, p. 354.
13 Jean Racine, Preface to *Bérénice*, in *Œuvres Complètes*, ed. R. Groos, E. Pilon, and R. Picard (Bibliothèque de la Pléiade, Paris, 1950), vol. I, p. 467.
14 Chapelain, *Opuscules Critiques*, pp. 296–301.
15 Quoted in Beugnot and Zuber, *Boileau*, p. 41.
16 *Corneille and Racine: Problems of Tragic Form* (Cambridge, 1973), pp. 160–1.

2 LIFE AND EARLY WORKS

1 Adam, *Histoire*, vol. III, p. 57.
2 No precise information survives. An idea of the procedure can be gained from Evelyn's account of the lithotomies he saw in Paris on 3 May 1650 (*The Diary of John Evelyn*, ed. E. S. de Beer, one-volume edition (Oxford, 1959), pp. 284–5).
3 Letter to Brossette, 13 September 1701 (*Boileau: Œuvres Complètes*, ed. Françoise Escal, introduced by Antoine Adam (Bibliothèque de la Pléiade, Paris, 1966) – henceforth referred to as Escal – p. 657).
4 Letters to Brossette, 8 August and 11 August 1701 (Escal, pp. 656 – 7).
5 See the anecdote by Brossette about Félix, Racine and Boileau, noted by Escal in relation to the letter of 28 May 1703 to Brossette (Escal, p. 1147).
6 See, for example, the letters to Racine of 19 May 1687 and 26 May 1687 (Escal, pp. 733–6).
7 Letter to Racine, 13 August 1687 (Escal, pp. 741–3).
8 Letter to Racine, 3 June 1693 (Escal, pp. 756–9).
9 Letters to Racine, 28 August 1687 and 2 September 1687 (Escal, pp. 747–51).
10 René Bray, *Boileau: L'Homme et l'Œuvre* (Nizet, Paris, 1962), p. 125.
11 Letter to Brossette, 15 June 1704 (Escal, p. 688).
12 Letters to Racine, 19 August 1687 and 6 June 1693 (Escal, pp. 743–5 and 763–5).
13 Adam, *Histoire*, vol. V, p. 73.
14 Clarac, *Boileau*, pp. 66–7.
15 Louis I. Bredvold, *The Intellectual Milieu of John Dryden* (Ann Arbor, Michigan, 1956), pp. 76–98.
16 Lucien Goldmann, *Le Dieu Caché* (Gallimard, Paris, 1955); English trans. by Philip Thody, *The Hidden God* (Routledge and Kegan Paul, London, 1964).
17 Adam, *Histoire*, vol. II, p. 215.
18 *Ibid.*, vol. V, p. 77.
19 For modern critical editions of Boileau's works, see the bibliography. His main poems are widely available in standard texts, and I have

quoted them in modern spelling and punctuation, giving the name of the poem and the standard line reference. The Satires and Epistles have numbers, but in most cases Boileau gave them no titles. For ease of identification, I have used on occasion the modern titles often given them (e.g. *Les Embarras de Paris* for *Satire VI*. For variants, the prose works and letters, I give a page reference to Escal.

20 Escal, p. 868.
21 Letter to Racine, 26 September 1696 (Escal, p. 769).
22 Brody, *Boileau and Longinus*, pp. 36–53.
23 *Ibid.*, p. 74.

3 THE HARVEST OF SATIRE

1 Clarac, *Boileau*, p. 168.
2 See the note on him in *Œuvres Complètes de Boileau: Satires*, ed. Charles-H. Boudhors (Belles Lettres, Paris, 1966), pp. 225–7.
3 Frances A. Yates, *Astraea: The Imperial Theme in the Sixteenth Century* (Routledge and Kegan Paul, London, 1975), p. 164.
4 Cotin, *Despréaux, ou La Satire des Satires*, ll. 89–96, in *Anthologie Poétique Française: XVIIe Siècle*, ed. Maurice Allem (Garnier Flammarion, Paris, 1966), vol. 2, pp. 28–33. The attribution to Cotin is uncertain, but Boileau seems to have regarded him as the author.
5 Adam, *Histoire*, vol. III, pp. 110–11.
6 Brody, *Boileau and Longinus*, pp. 54–87.
7 *Ibid.*, p. 84.
8 Adam, *Histoire*, vol. III, p. 89.
9 Escal, p. 893.
10 Brody, *Boileau and Longinus*, p. 92.
11 *Ibid.*, pp. 81–7.
12 Pierre Goubert, *The Ancien Régime: French Society 1600–1750*, trans. Steve Cox (Weidenfeld and Nicolson, London, 1973), pp. 153–67.
13 Adam, *Histoire*, vol. III, p. 55. Clarac (*Boileau*, p. 6) considers that Boileau may not have realised that his claim to nobility was false.
14 Brody, *Boileau and Longinus*, pp. 24–8.
15 Clarac, *Boileau*, pp. 82–4.
16 Brody, *Boileau and Longinus*, p. 59.

4 THE EARLY EPISTLES

1 Escal, p. 781.
2 Clarac, *Boileau*, p. 88.
3 There is a famous anecdote to the effect that Molière announced to the audience: '*L'Imposteur* ne sera pas joué: M. le Premier Président ne veut pas qu'on le joue', but this is of uncertain authenticity, and is in any case ambiguous. (See *Œuvres Complètes de Molière*, ed. Maurice Rat (Bibliothèque de la Pléiade, Paris, 1956), vol. I, pp. 888–9.)
4 Escal, p. 189.
5 Brody, *Boileau and Longinus*, pp. 24–8.

6 Letter of 29 April 1695 (Escal, p. 796).
7 John B. Wolf, *Louis XIV* (Gollancz, London, 1968), p. 214.
8 Escal, p. 327.
9 *Ibid.*, p. 328.
10 *Ibid.*, p. 330.
11 *Ibid.*, p. 329.
12 *Ibid.*, p. 758.
13 *The Poems of Alexander Pope*, ed. John Butt (Methuen, London, 1963), p. 832.
14 Clarac, *Boileau*, p. 100.
15 Adam, *Histoire*, vol. III, p. 121.
16 *Ibid.*, p. 122.
17 Clarac, *Boileau*, p. 98.
18 France, *Rhetoric and Truth*, pp. 167–70.
19 *Ibid.*, p. 169.
20 Escal, p. 719.
21 Wolf, *Louis XIV*, pp. 221–2.
22 Racine, *Œuvres Complètes*, vol. II, pp. 208–9.
23 France, *Rhetoric and Truth*, p. 169.
24 Adam, *Histoire*, vol. III, p. 124.
25 Escal, p. 966.
26 *Réponse du Sieur de la Montagne*, in *Opuscules Critiques*, pp. 318–9.

5 A READING OF *L'ART POÉTIQUE* (I)

1 Orr, 'Commentaire Linguistique'.
2 Famous examples are *Tartuffe*, *Alexandre* and *Pulchérie*.
3 R. C. Knight, *Racine et la Grèce*, revised edn (Nizet, Paris, 1974), p. 42.
4 Direct evidence is lacking. The few verbal resemblances between the two *Arts Poétiques* prove nothing (*L'Art Poétique de Vauquelin de la Fresnaye*, ed. Georges Pellissier (Garnier, Paris, 1885), pp. xcviii–ci). Bray shows that Vauquelin was little remembered in the later seventeenth century, but some scholars knew his work (Bray, *Doctrine*, pp. 26–7). One of these was Huet (Pellissier, *Vauquelin*, p. cvi), who was a friend of Boileau's (Bray, *Doctrine*, pp. 248–9).
5 *Lettre sur la Règle des Vingt-Quatre Heures*, in *Opuscules Critiques*, pp. 125–6.
6 *Opuscules Critiques*, p. 288.
7 Escal, p. 638.
8 Brody, *Boileau and Longinus*, pp. 60, 74.
9 *Ibid.*, p. 67.
10 Orr, 'Commentaire Linguistique', pp. 183–5.
11 Brody, *Boileau and Longinus*, p. 65; Edelman, '*L'Art Poétique*', p. 232.
12 Brody, *Boileau and Longinus*, pp. 73–4.
13 It is not certain that this criticism of Boileau is well founded. No doubt Boileau shared his contemporaries' lack of detailed knowledge of the Middle Ages. But it is arguable that he regarded mediaeval poetry, however strict its formal rules, as governed by 'caprice' because these

rules were arbitrary and produced a pleasure that was not founded on reason: see his comment on 'La ballade, asservie à ses vieilles maximes', which 'Souvent doit tout son lustre au caprice des rimes' (*Chant II*, ll. 141–2).

14 Brody, *Boileau and Longinus*, p. 107.
15 For another example of Boileau's attitude to factual accuracy in poetry, see his insouciance as to whether bees, or wasps, or neither, die when they sting (letter to Brossette of 28 May 1703, Escal, p. 674).
16 Orr, 'Commentaire Linguistique', p. 187.
17 'C'est au français qu'appartient le vaudeville, et c'est dans ce genre-là principalement que notre langue l'emporte sur la grecque et sur la latine' (letter to Brossette of 2 July 1699, Escal, p. 636). There are irony and exaggeration here, but the sentiment fits in well enough with his emphasis on the way in which certain characteristics are pleasing in men, languages and nations because natural to them, and his dislike of attempts to write in dead languages, for which we can have no natural feeling.

6 A READING OF *L'ART POÉTIQUE* (II)

1 Clarac, *Boileau*, p. 109.
2 Jacques Scherer, *La Dramaturgie Classique en France* (Nizet, Paris, n.d. (1950)), App. III, pp. 443–56.
3 *Andromaque*, ll. 14–20, 1613–44.
4 *Œdipe*, ll. 1987–96.
5 *Théâtre Complet de Corneille*, ed. Maurice Rat (Garnier, Paris, n.d.), vol. III, pp. 7–8: it 'ferait soulever la délicatesse de nos dames, qui composent la plus belle partie de notre auditoire'.
6 *Opuscules Critiques*, pp. 129–31.
7 *Épître IX*, ll. 43, 53–4, 86.
8 Gérard Genette, *Figures II* (Éditions du Seuil, Paris, 1969), p. 73.
9 Orr, 'Commentaire Linguistique', p. 188.
10 *De L'Art de la Tragédie*, ed. Frederick West (Manchester, 1939), pp. 25–6.
11 Edelman, '*L'Art Poétique*', p. 230.
12 Brody, *Boileau and Longinus*, p. 67.
13 *The Works of John Dryden*, vol. II, *Poems 1681–1684*, ed. H. T. Swedenberg, Jr (California, 1972), p. 138.
14 *Œuvres Complètes*, vol. I, p. 671.
15 Adam, *Histoire*, vol. II, pp. 60–6.
16 *Opuscules Critiques*, pp. 270–1.
17 *Ibid.*, p. 270.
18 *Ibid.*, p. 271.
19 See Ronsard, *Au Lecteur* before the first four books of *La Franciade*, in *Œuvres Complètes*, ed. Gustave Cohen (Bibliothèque de la Pléiade, Paris, 1950) vol. II, p. 1010.
20 Letter to Brossette, 10 November 1699 (Escal, p. 638).
21 *Œuvres Complètes*, p. 1009.

22 John Lough, *Paris Theatre Audiences in the Seventeenth and Eighteenth Centuries* (Oxford, 1957), p. 42.

23 See the remarks of Bossuet (another member of the Lamoignon circle) on Molière and 'des équivoques les plus grossières dont on ait jamais infecté les oreilles des Chrétiens' (quoted in W. D. Howarth, *Life and Letters in France: The Seventeenth Century* (Nelson, London, 1965), p. 215).

24 Escal, pp. 1000–1.

25 Cf. *Épître V*, ll. 35–8.

7 THE SIGNIFICANCE OF *L'ART POÉTIQUE*

1 E.g., by Brody, *Boileau and Longinus*, p. 79.

2 Adam, *Histoire*, vol. III, p. 154.

3 Escal, p. 856.

4 *Ibid.*, p. 337.

5 *Ibid.*, p. 1071.

6 *Ibid.*, p. 227.

7 *Ibid.*, p. 342.

8 *Ibid.*, pp. 342–3.

9 *Writings on the Theatre*, ed. H. T. Barnwell (Blackwell, Oxford, 1965), p. 1.

10 *Le Temple du Goût*, ed. E. Carcassonne (Droz, Geneva, 1953), p. 141.

11 *Réflexions Critiques*, II, in *La Rochefoucauld: Réflexions and Vauvenargues: Œuvres Choisies* (Garnier, Paris, n.d.), p. 236.

12 *An Essay on Criticism*, ll. 713–14 (*Poems*, p. 167).

13 *Essais*, Book I, ch. xxxvii (*Œuvres Complètes*, ed. Albert Thibaudet and Maurice Rat (Bibliothèque de la Pléiade, Paris, 1962), pp. 227–8).

14 See the discussion in R. A. Sayce, *The Essays of Montaigne: A Critical Exploration* (Weidenfeld and Nicolson, London, 1972), pp. 182–3.

15 *Satire XII*, ll. 239–56.

16 *Essais*, Book III, ch. xiii (*Œuvres Complètes*, p. 1046).

17 *Ibid.*, p. 1049.

18 Brunschvicg fr. 613 (*Pensées et Opuscules*, ed. Leon Brunschvicg (Hachette, Paris, n.d.), pp. 604–5).

19 Brunschvicg fr. 616 (*Pensées*, p. 607).

20 J. S. Spink, *French Free-Thought from Gassendi to Voltaire* (Athlone Press, London, 1959).

21 See, for instance, the essay by the Marxist critic I. Fradkin, 'On the Artistic Originality of Bertolt Brecht's Drama', in *Brecht: a Collection of Critical Essays* (Prentice-Hall, New Jersey, 1962), pp. 97–105.

22 Among other things, Voltaire gives a demonstration of how a simple prose sentence can be turned into poetry (of a sort) by the use of personification and apostrophe. Geoffrey's treatise expounds a similar doctrine in detail. Voltaire's letter is in *Correspondance*, the Besterman edition, with notes translated and adapted by Frédéric Deloffre (Bibliothèque de la Pléiade, Paris, 1977), vol. I, pp. 1041–4. A translation by Jane Baltzell Kopp of the *Poetria Nova* appears in *Three Mediaeval*

Rhetorical Arts, ed. James J. Murphy (California, 1971), pp. 32–108.

23 Russell Fraser, *The War Against Poetry* (Princeton, 1970).

24 See 'An Apology for Poetry', in *English Critical Essays: XVI–XVIII Centuries*, ed. Edmund D. Jones (Oxford, 1922), pp. 1–54.

25 *The Poems of John Milton*, ed. Helen Darbishire (Oxford, 1961), p. 495.

26 *Ibid.*, p. 506.

27 *Théâtre du XVIIe Siècle*, vol. I, ed. Jacques Scherer (Bibliothèque de la Pléiade, Paris, 1975), pp. 479, 481.

28 Frances A. Yates, *Shakespeare's Last Plays: A New Approach* (Routledge and Kegan Paul, London, 1975), p. 130.

29 *Figures II*, pp. 71–99.

30 *Œuvres Complètes*, vol. I, p. 670.

31 Ll. 1345–57, in *Théâtre du XVIIe Siècle*, vol. I, p. 128.

32 *Théodore*, ll. 909–14.

33 Act I, Scene iv, ll. 99–101, in *Five Restoration Tragedies*, ed. Bonamy Dobrée (Oxford, 1928), p. 445.

34 *Figures II*, pp. 150–1.

35 Orr, 'Commentaire Linguistique', p. 174.

36 See the discussion in Michael Black, *The Literature of Fidelity* (Chatto and Windus, London, 1975), especially pp. 43–5. Black brings out the kinship between the seventeenth-century French dramatists and moralists, and emphasises their search for a balance between inner (subjective) and outer (social) values, with a consequent effort at simultaneous self-examination and exploration of society's group ideals. He sees this – rightly, I think – as the distinguishing mark of a classical literature. It is certainly relevant to Boileau's achievement.

37 Adam, *Histoire*, vol. III, p. 138.

38 Will G. Moore, *The Classical Drama of France* (Oxford, 1971), p. 72.

39 *Boileau and Longinus*, p. 84.

40 *Ibid.*, p. 142.

8 COMPLEXITY AND SIMPLIFICATION

1 *Boileau and Longinus*, pp. 24–8.

2 Escal, p. 316.

3 See pp. 121–2 above.

4 Escal, p. 496.

5 *Ibid.*, p. 311.

6 'A Discourse Concerning the Original and Progress of Satire', in *'Of Dramatic Poesy' and Other Critical Essays*, ed. George Watson (Dent, London, 1962), pp. 148–9. See the discussion of this passage in Edward Pechter, *Dryden's Classical Theory of Literature* (Cambridge, 1975), pp. 187–8.

7 Boileau's choice of passages for parody is of interest. He makes reference to *Cinna* (*Chant II*, l. 78 – cf. *Cinna*, l. 1229), as well as to *Andromaque*. Both plays contain elements which strict neo-classical critics regarded as verging on the 'low' and the comic.

8 *Boileau and Longinus*, p. 131.
9 See, for example, *Cassinus and Peter* (*Poetical Works*, ed. Herbert Davies (Oxford, 1967), pp. 528–31).
10 E.g., *The Dunciad Variorum*, Book II, ll. 89–90 (*Poems*, p. 378).
11 *Boileau and Longinus*, p. 133.
12 *Maxime 379*, 1678 text, in *Maximes*, ed. J. Truchet (Garnier, Paris, 1967), p. 90.
13 *Boileau: Odes et Poésies Diverses*, ed. Charles-H. Boudhors (Belles-Lettres, Paris, 1960), p. 121.
14 Escal, p. 1023.
15 *Ibid.*, p. 528.
16 *Ibid.*, p. 383.
17 *Ibid.*, p. 559.
18 *Le Temple du Goût*, p. 141.
19 Escal, p. 1.
20 Letter to Brossette, 10 July 1701: 'je n'entends point le Portuguais...et c'est sur le rapport d'autrui que j'ai loué sa traduction' (Escal, p. 655). In a letter to Brossette of 6 October 1701, he says d'Ericeyra's French verses are not good enough to be made public, and mocks the attempt to write in a foreign language (*Ibid.*, p. 658).

9 CONCLUSIONS

1 *Corneille Dramaturge* (L'Arche, Paris, 1972), pp. 116–17, 128.
2 In the religious sphere, there is the revival of Thomism, the renewal of the monastic orders, and ferocious repression of unorthodox ideas. The structures of mediaeval society in many ways remained intact. A long list of specialist studies could be cited. But, for these phenomena generally, see A. G. Dickens, *The Counter Reformation* (Thames and Hudson, London, 1968), especially pp. 19–28; Orest Ranum, *Paris in the Age of Absolutism* (Wiley, New York, 1968), especially pp. 109–66; Philip Butler, *Classicisme et Baroque dans l'Œuvre de Racine* (Nizet, Paris, 1959), especially pp. 49–56.

SELECT BIBLIOGRAPHY

EDITIONS OF BOILEAU

The most convenient and up-to-date edition is the one-volume *Œuvres Complètes*, edited by Françoise Escal, with an introduction by Antoine Adam (Bibliothèque de la Pléiade, Paris, 1966). This contains all Boileau's writings, with the variants in the printed editions, and full apparatus. The seven-volume edition by Charles-H. Boudhors (Belles-Lettres, Paris, 1932–43, reprinted 1960–7) is also complete, and contains much useful information and discussion. A convenient cheaper collection is the two-volume Garnier Flammarion edition (Paris, 1969: *Satires, Le Lutrin*, introduction by Jerome Vercruysse; *Épîtres, L'Art Poétique, Œuvres Diverses*, introduction by Sylvain Menant). This contains all the poems in a modernised standard text (without variants) and a useful selection of the prose.

GENERAL WORKS

Indispensable is Antoine Adam's *Histoire de la Littérature Française au XVIIᵉ Siècle* (Domat, Paris, five volumes, 1949–56, various reprints). As is perhaps natural in a history, it seems to me to rely too much on the historical context as the main factor in critical evaluation, with unfortunate effects for Boileau. The best and most up-to-date short survey is Pierre Clarac's *Boileau* (Hatier, Paris, 1964), but René Bray's *Boileau: L'Homme et l'Œuvre* (Nizet, Paris, 1962; original edition 1942) is also valuable. The development of Boileau's reputation is surveyed from various angles in Bernard Beugnot and Roger Zuber, *Boileau: Visages Anciens, Visages Nouveaux* (University Press, Montréal, 1973), which also contains a useful short anthology of criticism.

On neo-classicism, the fundamental work remains René Bray's *La Formation de la Doctrine Classique en France* (Hachette, Paris, 1927, several reprints). Jean Chapelain published no systematic treatise. His *Opuscules Critiques* (edited by Alfred C. Hunter, Droz, Paris, 1936) are crabbed and often obscure, but essential for the serious student as a record of the ideas of this influential critic.

CRITICAL STUDIES

Among recent studies the following are outstanding:
Jules Brody, *Boileau and Longinus* (Droz, Geneva, 1958).

Nathan Edelman, '*L'Art Poétique:* "Longtemps plaire, et jamais ne lasser"', in *Studies in Seventeenth-Century French Literature Presented to Morris Bishop* (Cornell, 1962; Doubleday Anchor edition, New York, 1966). The same volume contains a valuable essay by Hugh M. Davidson on 'The Literary Arts of Longinus and Boileau'.

Peter France, *Rhetoric and Truth in France: Descartes to Diderot* (Oxford, 1972).

John Orr, 'Pour le Commentaire Linguistique de l'Art Poétique', in *Essais d'Étymologie et de Philologie Françaises* (Klincksieck, Paris, 1963).

KEY TO TRANSLATED PASSAGES

page/line

16/10–22   It is not a flexible rule, like that of Lesbos, but a rigid rule, which serves equally to recognise what is right and what is not. It is the result and quintessence of a thousand different observations, which have produced unchanging precepts, dogmas of eternal truth, which convince the mind, which spare it the need for doubtful searchings, and which in one moment allow it to know what one man could only have found out for himself in several hundreds of years...I am convinced that, guided by this torch, they [poets and critics] will feel the pleasure there is in building soundly, without fear of having to demolish, give judgment on what is good and bad in poems without fearing that anyone will appeal against their sentence as invalid; already I seem to see born from this precious seed a thousand new works which, by no means inferior to those of former times, will render our century equal in that respect also to past centuries.

16/29–31   a perfect set of laws, the application of which is found to be just in every case, a perpetually valid code of which the decisions will serve for ever to recognise what ought to be condemned and what ought to be applauded.

23/16–26   But I, myself, live in Paris? Who would want to do that At my age, I do not know how to lie, and if I could I would not. I cannot place in the sphere of perfection beyond the moon a man whose effrontery has enabled him to prosper; nor dissemble and praise a bad book, eagerly asking to be allowed to read it; nor waste a whole day with a scoundrel. I am a country fellow, proud, with an unsophisticated heart: I can only call a thing by its proper name. I call a cat a cat and Rollet a villain.

24/3–4   The road to riches is the road to Tyburn [literally, to la Grève – the square where criminals were executed].

24/31   I am a country fellow, proud, with an unsophisticated heart.

25/5–7   So you see, sir, that if I am not a good poet, I must be good at recitation.

25/16–17   Proud Vice...a mitre on its head and a cross in its hand.

26/1–10   Good Lord, what smites the heavens with these dismal

shrieks? In Paris, then, do you go to bed to stay awake?
And what interfering sprite, for whole nights at a time, brings
together here the cats from all the tiles? In vain do I leap
out of bed, all disturbed and anxious. I think all hell is
around me, not just the cats. One of them miaows and roars
like a raging tiger, another squalls like a screaming child.
That is not yet all, the mice and rats seem in league with the
cats to keep me awake.

26/20–3   For the fire, advancing in a sea of flame, makes our district
into a second Troy, in which many a famished Greek, many
a greedy Argive, crosses the cinders to pillage the Trojan.

26/26–7   The twenty coaches which soon arrive one after the other
are in less than a moment followed by more than a thousand.

26/33–4   There, the gloomy ceremonial of a funeral paces slowly and
mournfully towards the church.

26/39   In vain do I leap out of bed, all disturbed and anxious.

27/1–2   One bangs me with a plank and I'm shaken all over; with
another blow I see my hat knocked sideways.

27/4–5   I vault over twenty gutters, I dodge, I push forward;
Guénaud goes by on horseback and spatters me with mud.

27/7–8   I stagger along; despite the difficulty, fear of the night
hastens my steps.

27/10–13   But I've hardly put out the light in my bedroom than I'm no
longer allowed to close my eyelids. Bold robbers shatter my
window with a pistol shot and smash through my shutter.

28/17   Rich man, beggar, sad or happy, I want to write poetry.

28/21   Then, most certainly, then, I know I am a poet.

28/26–7   Merit, however, is always dear to me; but every blockhead
pains me, and offends my eyes.

29/10–17   Muse, let us change our style, and abandon satire. Speaking
ill of people is a dreadful trade. It always brings bad luck to
the author who takes it up. The evil you speak of others only
begets evil. Many a poet, blinded by this mania, tries to get a
reputation but achieves ignominy. And a saying which has
given the reader pleasure has very often cost the author tears.

29/28   Makes enemies of the very people who laugh.

29/32–3   And this man, who admires each stroke as he reads you, in
the bottom of his heart both fears and hates you.

30/1–4   It is in vain that, in the middle of my furious passion, I
sometimes read myself a lesson; in vain do I try at least to
let someone off: my pen would be sorry to spare any one of
them.

30/9–12   Poor Wit, one will say, how I pity your madness! Moderate
these gloomy outbursts of yours; and be careful that one of

those whom you have taken it into your head to attack does not quench in your blood this passion for rhyming.

30/15–26 Nobody knows my name or talent: my poems don't emulate Montreuil's, you don't see them swelling a collection with impunity. I barely force myself, occasionally, to give readings of them, to please a friend whom satire delights – who perhaps is flattering me, and with a deceitful air laughs out loud at the work, but is secretly laughing at the author. Anyway, it pleases me; I must give myself this satisfaction. I cannot speak well, and would not know how to keep quiet; and, as soon as a good joke comes gleaming into my mind, I cannot rest until it is down in writing: I do not resist the torrent which carries me along.

30/36 Let us stop. But, Muse, to start again tomorrow.

32/12–14 How learnedly you jest!; The man who was able [literally, knew how] to conquer Numantia…was he able [literally, did he know how] to jest better than you?; If you could [literally, knew how to] please less…

32/35–7 Here the author grants his friend a facility in turning a verse and finding rhymes that his friend did not have, but it is a question of praising him and giving him pleasure.

33/19–21 this man, whose wit is everywhere praised, would rather, for his own peace, never have written at all.

33/23–6 You, then, who sees the troubles in which my muse is over-whelmed, please teach me the art of finding rhymes: or, since in the end your efforts would be superfluous, teach me, Molière, the art to rhyme no more.

34/10 For whom Apollo holds all his treasures open.

34/11 Sometimes with rage, being unable to find it.

34/13–14 But I, whom (for my sins, I think) a vain whim, a strange temperament, made a rhymer.

34/16–19 But since the moment when this madness disturbed my imagination with its dark fumes, and when a sprite hostile to my happiness inspired in me the plan of writing correctly.

40/8–12 Young and valiant hero, whose sublime wisdom is not the tardy fruit of slow age, and who alone, without a minister, emulating the gods, by yourself sustain everything, and see everything with your own eyes, GREAT KING.

40/27 But I do not know very well how to praise…

40/31–2 who every day, with importunate voices, keep boring you with the tale of your own achievements.

41/1–2 their rejected talent was always the joke and laughing-stock of the muses.

41/31–2 the too heavy responsibility of such a great burden.

41/34–5   There is no hope of rewards, no reason, no conventional wisdom which could drag out of me a verse in your favour.

42/11–12   But when I see you, with such noble zeal, apply yourself unremittingly to the cares of your greatness...

42/34–5   Love Reason, then: let your writings always borrow from her alone both their brilliance and their value.

43/16–17   pure, constant, clear, certain and ever-present light.

44/19–23   to versify my opinion here in two words, despite those fools called the wise men of Greece, there is no perfect wisdom in this world: all men are mad, and, in spite of all their efforts, the only difference between them is their degree of madness.

45/9–11   Enjoy the delights your age demands, and do not complain about those innocent pleasures which money can provide in abundance for your desires every day.

45/21–33   Chapelain wants to be a poet, that is where his madness lies. But, although his harsh verses, swollen with epithets, are mocked by the merest scribblers in Ménage's salon, he himself applauds himself, and complacently claims precedence on Parnassus over Virgil. Alas, what would he do if some bold person unhappily for him opened his eyes, making him see those feeble and graceless lines stuck up on two grand words like two stilts, those terms unnecessarily forced apart from each other, and those frigid decorations planted in straight lines? How he would curse the day when his senseless soul lost the pleasing error that held his mind entranced!

47/3–7   You need to be more circumspect with important people. All right, I will tone it down. Your family is well known. Since when? Answer. For all of a thousand years, and you can show twice sixteen quarterings: that is a lot.

47/22–5   Two dishes followed, one of which was adorned with a stewed tongue, crowned with parsley, the other with forcemeat all burned on the outside, swimming with sticky butter all round it.

47/31–3   Two rustic nobles, great readers of novels, who quoted the whole of *Cyrus* in their lengthy greetings. I got angry.

48/1–2   And immediately the gathering stopped warbling, and in a tone of grave madness began to talk seriously.

48/6–12   one of the rustics, raising his moustache, and his bushy felt hat shaded with a plume, imposes silence on everyone, and in a preacher's tone of voice says, 'Heavens! La Serre is a delightful writer! His poems are beautifully written, and his prose flows nicely. *The Maid of Orleans* is still a very elegant work, and I do not know why I yawn while reading it.'

49/21–4   But I confess that I have been a little surprised at the strange annoyance of certain readers, who, instead of being amused at a quarrel among authors, of which they could have been disinterested onlookers, preferred to take sides, and to get themselves upset along with the fools, rather than to enjoy themselves with the people of good sense.

49/32–3   To fit in with their private taste, do we have to renounce common sense?

49/34–7   It annoys them to have seriously admired works which my satires expose to everyone's mockery, and to see themselves condemned to forget in their old age the very verses which they formerly learned by heart as masterpieces of literature.

50/4–11   Satire, prolific in lessons and novelties, alone is able to make appetising what is pleasant and useful, and, with a poem purified in the light of good sense, disabuse people's minds of the errors of their time. It alone, defying pride and injustice, goes even into high places to make vice go pale, and often, with the help of a witticism, fearlessly gives reason its revenge for the attacks of a fool.

51/30–1   It is in this way that Lucilius, supported by Laelius, in his time did justice to the Cotins of Italy.

52/7–8   That it was which, opening up the path I had to follow, fifteen years ago inspired in me hatred of a foolish book.

52/12–14   Since you wish it, I am going to change my style. So I say it out loud: Quinault is a Virgil; Pradon has appeared like a sun in our epoch.

52/22–3   But do you not see that their furious mob is going to take even these lines as a satire?

52/27–8   A man who scorns Cotin does not respect his king, and, according to Cotin, knows no God, no faith, no law.

52/33   Belgium in terror fleeing on her ramparts.

52/34–5   Cotin and I, who take rhyming as it comes.

53/1–6   Allow a fool to die in obscurity. Cannot an author rot away in peace? *Jonas* withers in the dust, unknown; *David* has been printed, but has not seen the light of day; *Moses* is beginning to go mouldy at the edges. What harm does that do? Those who are dead are dead.

53/17–20   In an eclogue, surrounded by flocks, shall I take to puffing my pipes in the middle of Paris, and, sitting at the foot of the beech-trees in my study, make the echoes ring with pastoral nonsenses?

54/6–9   An author, on his knees, in a humble preface, vainly begs the pardon of the reader whom he bores; he will get nothing from this angry judge, who has full power to proceed against him.

54/13–16   In vain does a minister form a cabal against *Le Cid*: all Paris sees Chimène in the way Rodrigue does; it is no use for the Academy in a body to censure it; the disobedient public obstinately admires it.

54/23–4   It is you, my wit, to whom I wish to talk. You have some failings which I cannot hide.

54/32–5   No, to praise a king whom all the universe praises, my tongue does not wait for money to loosen it, and, without hoping for anything from my feeble writings, the honour of praising him is too worthy a reward for me.

55/3–6   What have they done to you – Perrin, Bardin, Pradon, Hainaut, Colletet, Pelletier, Titreville, Quinault – whose names in a hundred places, ranged as if in their niches, fill the hemistiches of your spiteful verses?

55/8–11   Do I need to depict the madness of a frigid poet? My lines flow on to the paper like a torrent: I find at the same time Perrin and Pelletier, Bonnecorse, Pradon, Colletet, Titreville.

56/10   Who can. . . – What? – I know. – But what, then? – Be quiet.

57/16–19   Ruled by its advice [he] does everything at the wrong time, and is unreasonable and senseless in everything he does. Everything pleases him and displeases him in so far as it thwarts him or attracts him; he is happy without a reason, he is sad without a reason.

59/17–20   Are you still the same great lord who came to sup with a poor poet, and would you carry your new laurels to the fourth floor without being ashamed?

60/5–7   the gracious access that he gave me into his illustrious house helped me by acting as my defence against those who wanted to accuse me of free-thinking and immorality.

61/20–1   nobly and with that beauty which is the true mark of poetry.

61/23–4   our neighbours deprived of those servile tributes which the luxury of our towns paid to their ingenuity.

61/30–6   Who does not feel the effect of your noble efforts? Under your reign, does the universe have any unfortunates? Is there any virtue, in the snows of the Great Bear or in those torrid lands where the day originates, which sad poverty still dares to come near, and which your multitudinous gifts do not first seek out? . . . An Augustus can easily create Virgils.

63/1–4   Oh, how I like to see them, alarmed by your glory, foolishly deprive themselves of the help of our grain, while our ships, everywhere masters of the waves, carry off for us the riches of the two worlds.

63/7–8   But what! Already I hear some austere critic who finds the fable rather comical [i.e. low and undignified] in this context.

63/21-6   Great king, it is in vain that, forswearing satire, I had
            vowed to write for you alone from now on. As soon as I take
            up my pen, Apollo is alarmed, and seems to say to me: Stop,
            silly man; what are you doing? Do you not know what
            dangers you are letting yourself in for? This sea on which
            you sail is famous for shipwrecks.

64/18   It is annoying, great king, to find oneself without readers.

64/22-3   I leave to bolder men the honour of the struggle, and watch
            the field of conflict, seated on the fence.

65/15   Peace presents him to my eyes, calmer and more serene.

65/19   Yes, great king, let us leave there sieges and battles.

65/22-3   Let someone else go overturning walls in his poetry.

65/29   What is the use, with a muse geared up for slaughter.

66/1-2   Let us enjoy at leisure the fruits of what you have done for
            us, and not get tired of the pleasures of peace.

66/7-32   Why these elephants, these weapons, this baggage-train, and
            these ships all ready to leave the shore? said a wise intimate
            to King Pyrrhus – a very sensible counsellor of a very rash
            king. Said the prince to him, I am going to Rome, where I
            am summoned. – What to do? – To besiege it. – The under-
            taking is very fine, and worthy only of Alexander or of you.
            But, my lord, when Rome is at last taken, where do we go
            then? – Conquering the rest of the Latins is easy. – No doubt
            we can conquer them: is that all? – From there, Sicily
            beckons us; and soon, effortlessly, Syracuse will receive our
            vessels in its harbour. – Will you stop your progress there? –
            As soon as we have taken it, we only need a favourable wind,
            and Carthage will be conquered. The ways are open: who
            can stop us? – I understand, my lord, we are going to
            conquer everything: we are going to cross the sands of Libya,
            impose our yoke as we go on Egypt and Arabia, hurry
            beyond the Ganges into undiscovered countries, make the
            Scythian tremble on the banks of the Tanais, and range
            under our laws all this vast hemisphere; But, back at last,
            what do you intend to do? – Then, dear Cineas, victorious
            and happy, we can laugh, at ease, and enjoy ourselves. – Ah,
            my lord, this very day, without leaving Epirus, what stops
            you laughing from morning till night?

67/7-10   The advice was wise and easy to appreciate. Pyrrhus would
            have lived happily if he could have listened to it. But to
            oppose prudence to ambition is to preach to courtier-bishops
            they should stay in their dioceses.

67/28   Such a benevolent reign did not last long.

67/35-7   And it is from that angle, great king, that I want to praise
            you. Enough other people, without me, in a less timid style,
            will follow your swift courage to the fields of Mars.

68/10	An Augustus can easily create Virgils.
68/12	But, without a Maecenas, what use is an Augustus?
68/16	Can avoid the outrage of the hurtful years. [*Athalie*: To repair the irreparable outrage of the years]
69/3–4	Great king, I see it is time to finish. That is enough: it is sufficient.
70/7–13	No doubt of it, Arnauld, the most frightful hindrance for proud mortals is to be ashamed of what is good. This skilful enemy of the most noble virtues depicts honour in our eyes with the features of infamy, subjects our minds beneath a rigorous yoke, and makes us miserable slaves of each other. Because of this, virtue becomes cowardly and timid.
70/16–19	The intrusive thistle pushed up its prickles in the fields, the venomous serpent slithered through the forests, the fiery dog-star laid waste the countryside, the angry North wind roared on the mountains.
70/22–6	The miser, among the first to be prey to his desires, making goodness consist of sordid gain, accounted poverty the only shame: honour and virtue no longer dared show themselves; piety sought the deserts and the cloister.
70/36–8	No doubt of it, Arnauld, the most frightful hindrance for proud mortals is to be ashamed of what is good...That is the fatal foundation of all our ills.
71/6	I myself, Arnauld, who am preaching to you here in these rhymes...
71/14–16	Yes, Arnauld, in the face of Claude's sophistries, you uncover without difficulty the fraud of the innovators, and break the deceitful nets of their errors.
72/9–14	banish from the Schools of Philosophy the formalities, materialities, entities, virtualities, ecceities, Petreities, Policarpeities, and other imaginary beings, all children of and proceeding from the late Master John Scotus their father. The which would notably prejudice, and cause the total subversion of, the Scholastic Philosophy, of which they compose the whole mystery, and which derives from them its whole existence.
72/29–37	Forbids the blood to rove around any longer, to wander or circulate in the body, on pain of being entirely given over and rendered up to the Faculty of Medicine...And in any case of a cure against the rules by such drugs, allows the doctors of the said Faculty, following their usual method, to give the sick persons their fever back, with cassia, senna, syrups, juleps and other medicines proper for the purpose; and to put the said sick people back in such and the same state as they were beforehand; to be then given treatment

according to the rules, and if they do not recover, at least to
be led into the other world sufficiently purged and emptied.

73/3–6 M. l'Abbé Dongois came into my room with the little note
which you wrote to Madame Racine, and in which you send
word of the happy, surprising, incredible, prodigious, delightful, wonderful, astounding, entrancing outcome of your
negotiations.

73/30–1 often I dress spiteful prose in verse.

73/36–8 Obliged to remove his fable from the epistle to the king, he
composes, to receive it, at the beginning of 1673, the in-
significant epistle II.

73/38 ff. But because he was attached to his fable, he had the idea of
writing, soon after 1674, an epistle which is number II in the
collected works, and in which he introduced, by means of an
uninspired transition, the lines he could not bring himself to
suppress.

74/10 Punish the innocent paper for my faults.

74/15 In the Law Courts, we live on other people's follies.

75/35–6 the story of the angry river, which I learned from one of his
naiads, who has taken refuge in the Seine.

76/21–2 is more a matter of the thoughts than the words.

76/27 He has the build and face of Jupiter.

76/32 The Rhine at ease, and proud of the progress of his streams.

76/34 Under the spirited steeds the stream foams and murmurs.

76/36 A rumour spreads that Enghien and Condé have crossed.

77/6 You know the sad disasters of grand verses.

77/12–21 The striking defeat of the river overcome in this way carries
fear to Wurts right into his camp. Wurts, the hope of his
country and the support of its bulwarks; Wurts...Ah, great
king, what a name, what a Hector, this Wurts! But for this
terrible name, born unfortunately for the ears, what marvels
I was going to set before your eyes! Soon you would have
seen Skink carried away in my verses, and give the lie to the
pride of its famous ramparts; soon...But Wurts stands in
the way of the zeal which inspires me. Let us stop, it is time.

78/1–2 scythe in hand, among your fens, go and cut your rushes and
press your dairy produce.

79/18–21 Muses, to depict it, seek out all your pencils: for, since
everything in this achievement seems incredible, and in it the
pure truth looks like a fable, you can enliven it with all your
embellishments.

80/14–16 At these words, wiping his muddy beard, he takes on the
dusty face of an old warrior. His scarred brow gives him a
furious aspect.

80/22	Shame achieves in them the same effect as courage.
81/31	I am concerned to know myself, and myself seek myself.
81/34–5	I have a better feeling for the balance of right reason.
82/1–3	if, in the fine flame of the zeal which sets me on fire, I can satisfy my heart by a work on this subject which at last conquers the critics...
82/7–8	Let someone else, astrolabe in hand, go and seek whether the sun is fixed or turns on its axis.
82/20–2	anyway, there would be only an error in falconry, not in poetry...Aristotle has already absolved poets who sin in a matter outside poetry.
85/22–5	Sire, I set out here the fine teachings of the art of poetry, and how poems began; what authors and what paths it is necessary to follow for those who want to climb Parnassus.
85/36–7	In vain does a rash author think he can achieve the heights of the art of verse on Parnassus.
86/13–17	as for the verses and the language, these are instruments of such small consideration in epic, that they do not deserve that such serious judges spend time on them...purity of diction, rhythm of verse, and richness of rhyme, make up no more than the dress of the poetic body, which has sentiments and actions for its limbs, and, for its soul, invention and the arrangement of its parts.
86/30–1	O you, therefore, who, burning with a dangerous ardour...
87/8–19	Whatever subject you treat, whether light or sublime, let good sense and rhyme always agree; it is no use if they seem to hate each other; rhyme is a slave and should only obey. When you try from the beginning to look for it properly, your mind easily becomes accustomed to finding it; it bends without trouble to the yoke of reason, and, far from torturing it, serves and enriches it. But, when you neglect it, it becomes rebellious, and the sense runs after it to catch it. Love reason, then: let your writings always borrow from it alone both their brilliance and their value.
89/13	A man who cannot contain himself was never a writer.
89/30–1	The fullest verse, the noblest thought, cannot please the mind if the ear is wounded.
89/36–9	Everything must tend towards good sense; but the road for getting there is slippery and difficult to keep to; leave it just a little, and immediately you drown. Often reason has only one path on which to walk.
90/3–4	Happy the man who in his verses can pass with a light voice from the solemn to the sweet, from the pleasant to the severe.
90/9–12	Everything must be set in its place; the beginning and the

end must accord with the middle; let the elements, matched with subtle art, form only a single whole from the various parts.

90/17–20   A line was too weak, and you make it harsh; I avoid being prolix, and I become obscure; one author is not too bedizened, but his Muse is too naked; another is afraid to be crawling on the ground, and he loses himself in the clouds.

91/15–22   Above all, let the language be held in respect and always sacred to you when you are most greatly daring. In vain do you impress me with melodious sound if the word is wrong and the construction faulty: my mind will not accept a grand barbarism, nor the arrogant solecism of a turgid line. In one word, without correctness of language, the most godlike author is always, whatever he does, a bad writer.

91/29–30   But often a mind which flatters itself and suffers from self-love misunderstands its talent and lacks self-knowledge.

91/35   What is clearly thought finds clear expression.

92/14–15   the least noble style still has its nobility.

92/21–2   Whim alone made all the laws.

93/21–2   Taught the power of a word set in its right place.

94/1–2   A fool always finds a bigger fool to admire him.

94/22   Do you fear the public's condemnation of your verses?

94/34 ff.   You may say, The expression of this line is flat, – Ah, sir, he will reply at once, I ask you to look kindly on that line. – That word seems to me frigid; I would cut it out. – That is the best part! – This expression does not please me. – Everybody admires it. So, always consistent in not taking anything back, if a word in his work seems to have offended you, that in his eyes is a reason for not removing it. Nevertheless, to hear him, he loves criticism; you have absolute power over his poetry. But all these fine words with which he flatters you are no more than a clever trap to allow him to recite his lines to you. He leaves you immediately; and, happy with his muse, goes off to look elsewhere for some fool to impose on. And often he finds some: our age is fertile in foolish admirers as well as foolish authors; and, not counting those which the city and the provinces provide, they exist in the palace of the duke, they exist in the palace of the king. The dullest work has always found zealous supporters among the courtiers; and, to end with a stroke of satire, a fool always finds a bigger fool to admire him.

96/36–7   The road between the two extremes is difficult.

96/37   A faultless sonnet is in itself worth a long poem.

97/1–2   this lucky phoenix has not yet been found.

97/28–9   Zeal to display itself, not love of slander, armed Truth with the verse of Satire.

98/14–15   Even in songs, you need good sense, and art.

100/1–8   There is no serpent or hateful monster which cannot please the eyes when imitated by art: the pleasurable artifice of a subtle brush makes a delightful object of the most hideous object. Thus, to enchant us, weeping Tragedy made vocal the grief of Oedipus, covered with blood; expressed the terrors of Orestes the parricide; and, to give us pleasure, drew tears from us.

101/9–10   Where all of Paris crowds to vote in favour.

101/35–9   Dramatic or representative poetry has for its object the imitation of human actions, for its necessary precondition verisimilitude, and, for its perfection, what arouses our wonder...
             The excellence of works of this kind arises from the judicious mixture of verisimilitude and what arouses wonder...

102/1–14   [Poets] are particularly concerned to make each person speak in accordance with his rank, age and sex; and they call 'conformity', not what conforms to good behaviour, but what is suitable to the characters, whether good or bad, and how they are presented in the play...
             All this [the unities and other rules] founded on the precondition of verisimilitude, without which the mind is neither moved nor persuaded...
             The noblest and most pleasing outcome of plays is when by their skilful construction the spectator is kept in suspense in such a way that he is concerned about the ending and cannot work out how the story will end...
             In the first [act] the foundations of the action are laid; in the second the difficulties begin; in the third the agitation increases; in the fourth, things reach an almost desperate pitch; in the fifth the knot is untangled in a probable and lifelike way, by unforeseen means, from which arises our wonder.

103/3–4   I prefer Bergerac and his bold burlesque to those lines in which Motin chills himself and makes us freeze.

103/28–9   Let love, often opposed by remorse, appear a weakness and not a virtue.

103/32–6   with their foolish and simple-minded zeal, acted the saints, the Virgin and God, out of piety. Knowledge, dissipating ignorance at last, made people realise the attempt was religiously unwise. These unauthorised preachers were dismissed.

104/19–21   finds mouths always ready to hiss him. Anyone can treat him as a fool and ignoramus: it is a right you buy at the door as you come in.

104/28-9   He must be fertile throughout in noble sentiments; he must be elegant, solid, pleasant, profound.

104/34   With surprising strokes of art he must continuously keep us alert.

104/37-8   He must move rapidly in his verses from wonder to wonder.

105/1-2   And everything he says must stay easily in our minds, and leave in us a lasting remembrance of his work.

105/15-18   But we, whom Reason obliges to obey its rules, we want the action to be managed artistically; that the stage should be occupied to the end with a single action completed in a single place, in one day.

106/1-4   The other side of the Pyrenees, a rhymer can cram years into a day on the stage with impunity. There, the hero of an unsophisticated show is often a child in the first act and a greybeard in the last.

107/12-13   The mind is not moved by what it does not believe. What should not be seen, let a narration represent to us.

107/19-24   In all your speeches, let passion be aroused, and go to seek the heart, to warm and move it. If the pleasing passion of a fine emotion does not often fill us with a sweet terror, or does not arouse in our soul a magical pity, you display a knowledgeable scene in vain.

108/3-5   have been moved by the same things which have formerly brought tears to the eyes of the wisest nation in Greece.

109/20-1   Is nourished by mythology and lives on fiction. In it, everything is made use of to bewitch us.

109/28-9   The poet enjoys himself by inventing a thousand things. . . and finds ready to hand flowers always blossoming.

109/31   That is what astonishes us, strikes us, seizes our imaginations, captivates us.

109/33-4   That is getting foolishly worried by an empty scruple, and wanting to please readers without using what is pleasant.

109/36   Do you want to give lasting pleasure, and never boredom?

110/1   Enliven your work with innumerable figures of speech.

110/3   Throughout, he [Homer] gives pleasure, and never bores.

110/10-13   The awesome mysteries of a Christian's faith do not lend themselves to frivolous ornaments. On every side, the Gospel offers to our minds nothing but the need for repentance and the torments we have deserved.

110/25   But in a profane and smiling picture.

110/26   Let everything in it present a smiling picture to the eye.

110/27–30   I would rather have Ariosto and his comic tales than those authors who are always frigid and miserable, who, being temperamentally gloomy, would think it an insult to themselves if the Graces ever unwrinkled their foreheads.

110/33–6   It is no longer a vapour which produces thunder, it is Jupiter armed to bring terror to the Earth...In this way, in this mass of noble fictions, the poet enjoys himself, inventing a thousand things.

111/8–13   I will add that poetry, and above all that which celebrates heroes, being full of images and hyperbole...departs from that exact verisimilitude which some would want to require of the poet, according to the doctrine of Aristotle as wrongly interpreted...What obliged these great geniuses [Homer and Virgil] to use incidents in this way, contrary to ordinary verisimilitude, was the need to give their poems a more majestic air.

111/20–3   tries to life our hearts to the level of extraordinary deeds, by giving vivid impressions of those it depicts, so that, if we cannot reach such heights, at least we follow them as closely as our abilities can manage.

111/24–6   the better to stimulate men to do what they can, by showing them actions that may even be impossible.

111/30–1   in short, this book is a novel, like the *Iliad* and the *Aeneid*.

111/33–4   Everything is easily excused in a frivolous novel; it is enough that the made-up story diverts us as it goes along.

112/1   To be able to enjoy it is to have profited by it.

112/10   Those are examples of the absurd delusions of your Christians.

112/11   O transient illusion! O dangerous error!

113/22–3   That is keeping your eyes on objects that are too worthless. Give your work a proper scale.

114/1–2   So let us allow them to struggle among themselves in peace, and pursue our theme without wandering from the way.

114/23–4   born to mock, distilled the venom of his malicious sallies through a thousand playful jests.

115/6   with low and dirty jokes to enchant the mob.

116/32–3   His example is an excellent prescription for us. Better be a stonemason, if that is your talent.

117/1–4   Poetry does not tolerate a middling author: his writings terrify the reader everywhere: the shops in the Law Courts complain of them, and Billaine's shelves are reluctant to bear them.

117/18   I have already told you, enjoy being criticised.

117/35 ff.   Authors, give ear to my instructions. Do you wish to make
               your lavish inventions loved? Let your Muse, fertile in wise
               lessons, in every part link to what is pleasing what is solid
               and useful. A wise reader shuns a futile diversion, and wants
               to profit from his entertainment.

118/9–11   Love virtue, then, nourish your soul with it. It is no use if
               the mind is full of noble energy, poetry always partakes of
               the baseness of the heart.

118/23–6   But in the end, poverty brought in baseness, and Parnassus
               forgot its original nobility; a sordid love of profit, infecting
               people's minds, soiled all writings with gross lies.

118/39   Everywhere ensures that merit does not know what it is to be
               poor.

119/10–21   Nevertheless, you will see me, in this glorious field of
               endeavour, at least encourage you with my voice and eyes;
               offer you the lessons which my muse, while still young,
               brought back from Parnassus from its acquaintance with
               Horace; support your zeal, arouse your minds, and show you
               from afar the crown and the prize. But also forgive me if,
               full of this admirable zeal, a faithful observer of your
               illustrious progress, I sometimes separate the good gold from
               the false, and attack the failings of unsophisticated authors;
               a rather tiresome critic, but often necessary, more inclined
               to find fault than knowing how to do well himself.

121/3–4   Whatever subject you treat, whether light or sublime, let
               good sense and rhyme always agree.

121/6–7   Love reason, then: let your writings always borrow from it
               alone both their brilliance and their value.

121/9   Whatever you write, avoid baseness.

121/11   Never let this style sully your work.

121/13   Authors, give ear to my instructions.

121/30–2   But I thought the reader would not be displeased to see it
               here, following *L'Art Poétique*, to which this treatise bears
               some relation, and in which I have even inserted several
               precepts which are drawn from it.

121/34–5   I thought that it was here not simply a matter of translating
               Longinus; but of giving to the public a Treatise on the
               Sublime which could be useful.

121/37 ff.   It is an extremely useful work, and for my own part I frankly
               confess that reading it has benefited me more than all that
               I have ever read in my life.

122/5–8   By all appearances, this critic is not very convinced by the
               precept that I put forward in my *Art Poétique*, on the subject
               of the Ode...This precept, which in effect gives as a rule

that sometimes the rules should not be obeyed, is a mystery of the art.

122/11–12   The Sublime. . .is born in us, and is not learned.

122/12–13   it is a mistake to try and reduce it to a technique, and to give rules for it.

122/16–24   although Nature never shows herself more unconstrained than in sublime and emotional writings, it is nevertheless easy to see that she does not let herself range at random, and that she is not entirely the enemy of technique and rules. I confess that in all our works it is necessary to take her as the basis, principle and prime foundation. But it is also certain that our minds need a method to teach them how to say only what is necessary, and to say it in its right place; and that this method can help us greatly to acquire the accomplished habit of the Sublime.

122/26–7   It is agreed that there are precepts, because there is a technique.

122/30–1   this master of Parnassus, who, giving the precept and the example at the same time, established the rigorous laws of Apollo.

122/33–4   Boileau was not satisfied by putting truth and poetry into his works, he taught his technique to others.

123/30–4   To a small extent, it can be judged by precepts and by technique. But the good, the excessive, the divine is above rules and reason. Whoever sees its beauty by looking at it steadily and calmly does not see it, any more than the the splendour of a flash of lightning. It does not attract our understanding; it overpowers and ravishes it.

125/8–15   In China, a kingdom whose government and arts, without contact with and knowledge of ours, surpass our example in many parts of excellence, and whose history teaches me how much bigger and more various the world is than either the Ancients or ourselves realise, the officials deputed by the Ruler to survey the condition of his provinces, just as they punish those who are guilty of malpractices in their positions, they also, out of pure generosity, reward those who have behaved well in them, beyond the usual measure and beyond the call of duty.

125/23–5   This religion. . .has always existed on Earth. The Messiah has always been believed in. The tradition of Adam was still fresh in Noah and Moses.

132/34–9   Properly speaking, a poet is he who, endowed with excellence of mind and impelled by a divine frenzy, expresses in beautiful verses thoughts which it seems could not have been produced by the human mind alone...I move on to the praises of poetry, which cannot be denied to be the worthiest of all the arts, whether on account of the nobility of its origin, in that this comes directly from Heaven, or on account of the excellence of the beautiful effects it produces.

135/22-7   What likelihood is there that I should have sullied the stage with the horrible murder of a person as virtuous and lovable as Iphigenia ought to be presented as being? And what likelihood, either, of resolving the plot of my tragedy with the help of a goddess and a machine, and with a change of shape, which could well gain some credence in the age of Euripides, but would be too ridiculous and incredible among us?

147/35-7   Beauties of this sort are of the kind that must be felt, and cannot be proved...But, after all, it is something indefinable; and if your friend is blind, I do not undertake to make him see clearly.

148/9-10   Our minds, even in the Sublime, need a method to teach them how to say only what is necessary, and to say it in its right place.

148/28-40   Wife, said he, in a soft and proud voice, I in no way wish to deny the solid benefits with which your generous love has fulfilled my desires; and the Rhine will increase the Loire with its waters before your favours leave my memory. But do not presume that in giving you my troth, marriage has subjected me for ever to your commands. If Heaven had put my fate into my hands, we would both have evaded the yoke of matrimony, and, without saddling ourselves with these alleged duties, we would still be tasting forbidden pleasures. So cease to display an empty title before my eyes: do not take from me the honour of setting up a lectern.

149/15-16   Sad Procne shudders with grief at it, and, in the neighbouring woods, Philomel complains.

149/18   They pass through the vast solitude of the nave.

149/21-30   They call it Chicanery; and this hateful monster never had eyes or ears for justice. Pale Want and sad Famine, devouring Sorrows and disgraceful Ruin, the unfortunate children of its sophistications, disturb the air all around with long moanings. Always leafing through the laws and records of customary practice, the monster consumes itself, in order to consume others; and, devouring houses, palaces, whole castles, gives useless piles of paper in exchange for heaps of gold.

149/34-5   In vain, to tame it, the most just of kings had the chaos of the shadowy laws methodised.

150/12-25   Finishing this speech, the warlike goddess traces with her foot a furrow of light in the air, gives back to the three champions their fearlessness, and leaves them full of her godhead. It is thus, great Condé, that in that famous battle, in which your arm made the Rhine, the Scheldt and the Ebro tremble, when our harassed armies on the plain of Lens were almost dispersed and overthrown before your eyes; your courage, stopping the flying troops, rallied their frightened cohorts with a glance, spread your martial spirit through their ranks, and forced victory to follow you, as well as them. Anger immediately replacing fear, they relight their candle, which had gone out.

151/3–4   Happy the man who in his verses can pass with a light voice from the solemn to the sweet, from the pleasant to the severe!

151/31–9   What use is it to me, Ariste, she said, that everywhere you display your zeal for me, and your courage, if impious Discord insults me at your door? Within these walls, formerly so holy and famous, two powerful enemies, made venomous by her, profanely insult my sacred altars, fill everywhere with alarm, tumult and uproar. Go and make them see the horror of their crime: save me, save them from their own fury.

152/3–8   With these words, she leaves. The praying hero remains all covered with fire and light. He recognises the splendour of the heavenly maid, and sends at the same time for the cantor and the prelate. Muse, it is at this juncture that my timid mind needs someone to guide it in its lofty course.

152/31   Nothing is beautiful but what is true.

153/11–16 Seignelay, dangerous enemy of every bad flatterer, it is in vain that an absurd author, ready to make your name known 'from the Ebro to the Ganges', thinks he can take you in the nets of his foolish praise. Immediately, your mind, quick to rebel, escapes, and breaks the trap in which he tries to hold you.

153/38   Swings the censer across his face.

154/3–4   Which does not stagger the senses with too strong an odour.

154/27–8   A noble heart is content with what it finds in itself, and does not congratulate itself on possessing other people's good qualities.

154/36–9   Nothing is beautiful but what is true: only what is true is lovable; it should rule everywhere, and even in fiction: the skilful artifice of what is invented only aims to make the truth shine before our eyes.

155/19–22 it is because in them truth, victorious over lies, everywhere shows itself to our eyes and takes us by the heart; because in them good and evil are given their right value; because in them a rogue is never given an exalted place.

155/26–7   And that my heart, always guiding my mind, says nothing to its readers that it has not said to itself.

155/36	My thought everywhere offers and exposes itself to broad daylight.
156/18–19	Who is not an impostor and a fake in some part.
156/28	But Nature is true, and you feel it immediately.
156/31–2	A character born melancholy gives pleasure by his very melancholy.
156/32–3	Each man, taken according to his nature, is agreeable in himself.
156/34–5	Ignorance is better than an affected knowledge.
157/1–3	Nothing is beautiful, I repeat, except by being true: it is by truth that one pleases, and can give lasting pleasure. The wit soon becomes tedious if the heart is not sincere.
157/11–12	His face, wiped clean, is no longer anything but horrible.
157/14–17	I love a mind at ease with itself, which shows itself, which reveals itself, and which pleases even more, the more it displays itself. But only virtue can bear the light; vice, always gloomy, loves the darkness.
158/5	But I believe, like you, that it has to be true.
158/7	It would be necessary to depict in you what is known to be **true.**
158/9–10	Such a man, who hates seeing himself painted in lying portraits, without displeasure sees his true features depicted.
158/15–26	Condé, that formidable hero, not less terrifying to flaterers than to the Flemings, even Condé would not be offended if some skilful brush drew a faithful picture of his exploits; and contemplating his portrait in the flames of Seneff, would not disavow Malherbe or Voiture. But woe betide the insipid, hateful poet who comes to chill him with a boring eulogy. In vain would he declaim: 'Leading Prince of the world! Matchless courage! Unrivalled intelligence!' Thrown away at once, without a page turned, his verses would go into the antechamber to amuse Pacolet.
159/2–3	When our merit declines, so does our taste.
159/21–2	It is a little village, or rather a hamlet, built on the slope of a long line of hills.
161/17–18	the virtuous agony of Phaedra, perfidious and incestuous in spite of herself.
161/22–41	Before a little earth, obtained by supplication, had closed Molière for ever beneath the tomb, a thousand of those fine strokes, so much praised today, were rejected before our eyes by foolish spirits. At his plays as they were born, ignorance and error, in the costumes of marquises, in the dresses of countesses, came to cast aspersions at his new masterpiece, and shook their heads at the most beautiful part. The com-

mander wanted the piece more exactly in accord with the rules; the viscount was outraged and left during the second act. One, the eager defender of the bigots who were made fun of, condemned him to the stake for his jokes. Another, a fiery marquis, declaring war on him, wanted to avenge the Court for being sacrificed to the pit. But, as soon as Fate, with a stroke of her fatal hands, had struck him from the number of mankind, the value of his vanished muse was recognised. Lovable comedy, struck down with him, in vain hoped to recover after such a heavy blow, and could no longer keep on her feet [literally, on her socks – i.e. the footwear of the ancient comic actors].

163/5–14   A torrent in the fields flows with rapid waters; Malherbe in his raptures proceeds with too regular steps. A new Icarus, following Pindar in the skies, I prefer to fall from the highest Heaven, rather than – praised by Fontenelle – be a timid swallow skimming along the earth, like Perrault.

163/17–20   Come running, Nassau, Bavaria, the only hope of these walls: protected by a river, come, you can see everything.

163/22–4   Run, then: who is holding you up? The whole universe is looking at you: do you not dare to cross it?

163/38 ff. It needs to be known that Pindar lived a short time after Pythagoras, Thales and Anaxagoras, the famous natural philosophers, who taught physical science with very great success.

164/9–10   What learned and holy rapture imposes its law on me today?

164/18–39   But that thirst for gold which burned in his soul at last made him think of choosing a wife, and in this choice honour was completely disregarded. His natural inclination was guided towards his sad weakness, and made him seek, in an avaricious and vile family, a frightful monster in the costume of a girl... There, then, are our married couple, with no servants and no children, alone in their house, free and triumphant... But, in order to display their squalor properly here, in all its glory, it is necessary to see this illustrious pair leaving the house. It is necessary to see the husband, all dusty and dirty, wearing an old hat with its worn band, and as he walks dragging his shame in the gutters, with his robe vainly repaired with patches. But who could count the number of bits, patches, shreds, filthy tatters, rags picked out from the vilest dirt, from which his wife made up her costume on her good days? Shall I describe her stockings, with holes in thirty places, her gaping shoes, twenty times cobbled together, her cap from which there hung down, on the end of a piece of string, an old worn mask nearly as hideous as she was?

165/2–3   in four handkerchiefs, soiled with her beauty, sends her roses and lilies to the laundry.

165/5–7   makes even her lovers – too weak in the stomach – dread her garlic- and tobacco-laden kisses.

165/14   Nothing escapes the eyes of our curious woman.

165/16–19   There, swap-shops of false taste in art do business: there, all verses are good, provided they are new. The fair lady wages war on the bad taste of the public; pities Pradon persecuted by the bulk of the audience.

166/9–10   I amuse myself by filling my sermons with portraits. That is already three of them painted with quite happy strokes.

166/12–13   Now it is necessary to trace for you several of their features, and finish all my portraits by this great portrait.

166/17–18   But what! here I am donning the tragic buskin! Let us put back on as soon as possible the comic sock.

166/20   But what empty speeches am I passing my time with?

166/22–3   It is time to finish; and, to bring it all to a close, I will only say one word.

167/4–5   We see these Orpheuses out of breath beneath their laurels, endlessly pursuing these fugitive sprites.

167/11–17   My verses, the time is no more when my muse in her vigour, educating the nurslings of French poetry, dressed her lessons in such rich colours: when my mind, impelled by legitimate anger, came in front of reason to plead against rhyme, was able to criticise the whole human race, and attacked itself so successfully.

168/11–14   Let us explain ourselves, however. By that holy zeal, which I maintain that in the end fear instils into the heart, I do not here mean that sweet rapture, those transports full of joy and ecstasy.

168/18–19   He bewails honour, by a sentence unjustly given, condemned in his person to row in the galleys.

168/25–9   Aristotle and Theophrastus, to excuse the boldness of these rhetorical devices, think it is good to introduce these pallia-tives: 'So to say. To speak thus. If I dare use these terms. To express myself a little more boldly'. In effect, they add, the excuse is a remedy against the audacities of the language, and I am quite of their opinion.

168/32–5   The advice of these two philosophers is excellent; but it is to be used only in prose; for these excuses are rarely tolerated in poetry, in which they would seem dry and feeble; because poetry carries its own excuse in itself.

169/1–4   I doubt, however, if the crowd of ordinary people will easily give their approval to this discourse; and, to tell you the historical reason for it, allow me to dress it up in an allegorical fable.

169/18–19   But where, someone will say, is this fantastic plan leading you?

169/19   Then stop there, my pen.

169/24–7   And you, get out of here, Monster, to whom as I end my career as satirist today I have, by a very bizarre stroke, lent an allegorical soul.

169/33–4   For usage, I think, without difficulty still leaves the choice between the two open for daring rhymers.

170/1–2   Everywhere there were no longer anything but anabaptist madmen, arrogant puritans, detestable Deists.

170/4–8   the huge foundation of the most dangerous and dreadful morality that Lucifer, seated in his infernal preaching-chair, vomiting against God his monstrous sermons, has ever taught to his apprentice demons.

170/10–11   Pitiful copyist of Pascal and Wendrock, and, to sum it all up, a detestable Jansenist.

170/13–14   According to them, to find fault with the laughable morality of your teachers is to teach a horrible Calvinism.

170/28–31   I could only attribute such a happy outcome to the care I have taken to adapt myself always to its feelings, and, as far as was possible for me, to catch its taste in everything. In fact, this is what, it seems to me, writers could not study too much.

170/33–5   the human mind is by nature full of an infinite number of confused ideas of the truth, which it often only half glimpses.

171/1–4   the god in question at this point is Jupiter, who was never regarded by the pagans as having created Man in his own image: in mythology, as everyone knows, Man being the creation of Prometheus.

171/19–20   Is it not in a way to say to the public: 'Judge me'?

177/6–7   Who, giving the precept and the example at the same time, established the rigorous laws of Apollo.

180/n.3   *The Impostor* will not be acted today; M. le Premier Président does not want it acted (or, does not want to be laughed at).

182/n.13   The ballad, subjected to its old maxims.

182/n.13   Often owes its brilliance to the caprice of its rhymes.

182/n.17   the vaudeville belongs to the French language, and it is mainly in that *genre* that our tongue has the advantage over Greek and Latin.

183/n.23   the most indecent puns with which the ears of Christians have ever been infected.

185/n.20   I don't understand Portuguese. . .and it is on the basis of the opinion of others that I praised his translation.

INDEX

Adam, Antoine, 20, 22, 33, 44, 73–4,
    75, 81, 121, 123, 140, 143, 178,
    179, 181, 182, 183, 184, 186
Addison, Joseph
    Cato, 136
Aeschylus, 142
Alexander, 57, 62, 113
Ancients and Moderns, Quarrel of,
    19, 146, 165
Aristophanes, 114
Aristotle, 6, 8, 10, 100, 101, 107
    Poetics, 85, 133–4
    Rhetoric, 121–2
Arnauld, Antoine, 70–1, 171
Arnauld d'Andilly, Robert, 34

Bacon, Francis, 128
Beckett, Samuel
    En Attendant Godot, 55
Benserade, Isaac, 170–1
Bergerac, Cyrano de, 103
Beugnot, Bernard, 178, 179, 186
bienséances, les, 7, 8, 10, 120, 134,
    135–6
Black, Michael, 184
Boileau, Gilles, 147
    Avis à Ménage, 33
Boileau, Nicolas Despréaux
    GENERAL: achievement, 176–7;
    character, 19–22, 38; life and
    career, 18–19, 38–9, 58, 59–60,
    146, 159, 170; reputation, 1–3,
    38, 47, 144–5, 176–7
    IDEAS AND ATTITUDES: Boileau
    and allegory, 110, 169, 176; and
    the ballade, 182; bombast in,
    22, 61, 162–3; changes in his
    conception of poetry, 25, 31,
    35–7, 59–60, 144–5, 147, 168–9,
    171, 173–6; and Christianity,
    20, 21, 24–5, 38–9, 59–60,
    103–4, 112, 138, 175, 176; and
    comedy, 99, 114–15; and
    didacticism, 89, 90–3, 104–5,

111–12, 116–18, 120–3, 138–9,
140, 152–3, 156–7, 166, 168–9,
171, 174, 176, 177; and the
didactic poem, 98, 118, 138–9,
142; dramatic nature of his
poems, 24–5, 31, 35–6, 55–6,
84–5, 93–6, 139–40, 157, 167–8,
171, 174, 176, 177; and the
epic, 79, 81, 99, 109–14, 120,
138–9, 149–52, 175, 176, 177;
evolution of his poetry, 144–5,
147, 171, 174–6; and the fable,
73, 98, 138–9; and free-thought,
21, 38–9, 43, 59–60, 71, 98,
141–2; grandiloquence in, 22,
53, 62, 76, 79–81; and intuition,
2, 123, 147–8, 156, 163; and
Jansenism, 21, 35, 140–2, 146–
7; and joining together of
opposites, 163–4, 175; and
knowledge, 2, 31–2, 81–2, 163;
and Louis XIV, 20, 27–8, 53,
57, 60–9, 74, 75, 78–9, 80, 84,
113, 118–19, 138, 149, 151, 162,
164, 175; and *le merveilleux
chrétien*, 99, 110, 138; and
minor *genres*, 5, 98; mixture of
high and low styles in, 25–6,
39–42, 53, 76–8, 80–1, 148–52;
mixture of seriousness and
humour in, 53, 62–6, 77, 78, 90,
148–52, 162–4, 175; and
money, 20, 115, 118–19; and
moral self-examination, 54, 81,
94–6, 137, 138, 155–7, 160–1,
174–5; and morality, 23–4, 25,
28, 36, 54, 56, 69, 71, 90–2, 94,
97, 103, 118, 120, 136–8, 153,
155, 158–9, 171, 174, 175; and
neo-classicism, 1, 2, 3, 12, 16–
17, 33–6, 51, 56, 71, 83, 96,
101–8, 142–5, 162, 167, 173–7;
and noble rank, 20–1, 46; and
novateurs, 71, 72; and the novel,

For EU product safety concerns, contact us at Calle de José Abascal, 56–1°,
28003 Madrid, Spain or eugpsr@cambridge.org.

www.ingramcontent.com/pod-product-compliance
Ingram Content Group UK Ltd.
Pitfield, Milton Keynes, MK11 3LW, UK
UKHW010335140625
459647UK00010B/616